The Prisoner at the Bar
Sidelights on the Administration of Criminal Justice

Arthur Cheney Train

Alpha Editions

This edition published in 2024

ISBN 9789362516312

Design and Setting By
Alpha Editions
www.alphaedis.com
Email - info@alphaedis.com

Contents

PREFACE TO THE SECOND EDITION

The favorable reception accorded to the "Prisoner at the Bar," not only in the United States but in England, and the fact that it has won a place in several colleges and law schools as a reference book, and in some instances as a sort of elementary text-book upon criminal procedure, have resulted in a demand for a new edition. When the book was written the author's sole intention was to present in readable form a popular account of the administration of criminal justice. Upon its publication he discovered to his surprise that it was the only book of its exact character in the English language or perhaps in any other. Reviewers pointed out that whereas there were annotated text-books of criminal procedure and isolated articles on special topics, most of them relating to the jury system, there was in existence no other sketch of criminal justice as a whole, from arrest to conviction, based upon either actual experience or hearsay.

This new edition has been indexed and is supplied with cross-references to other works on allied subjects. A chapter has been added upon "Insanity and the Law," and such statistics as the book contains have been brought down to date. It is satisfactory to add that these show a greatly increased efficiency in the jury system in criminal cases in New York County, and that the tabulations of an eight years' experience as a prosecutor only serve to confirm the conclusions set forth in the first edition.

The author desires to express his thanks to Prof. John H. Wigmore, of the Northwestern University Law School, for his many kind suggestions and flattering references to this book in his masterly work upon the law of evidence; to Augustin Derby, Esq., of the New York bar, who most unselfishly gave much time to the examination of references, and voluntarily undertook the ungrateful task of compiling the index; and to those many others who, by comment or appreciation, have made a second edition necessary.

Bar Harbor, Me.,
Sept. 1, 1908.

PREFACE TO THE FIRST EDITION

The prisoner at the bar is a figure little known to most of us. The newspapers keep us steadily informed as to the doings of all sorts of criminals up to the time of their capture, and prison literature is abundant, but just how the criminal becomes a convict is not a matter of common knowledge. This, however, does not prevent the ordinary citizen from expressing pronounced and, frequently, vociferous opinions upon our methods of administering criminal justice, in the same way that he stands ready at any time to criticise the Darwinian theory, free trade or foreign missions. Full knowledge of any subject is inevitably an impediment to forcible asseveration. Generalities are easy to formulate and difficult to disprove. The man who sits with his feet up and his chair tilted back in the "drummer's" hotel will inform you that there is no such thing as criminal justice and that the whole judiciary, state and federal, is "owned" or can be bought; you yourself doubtless believe that the jury system is a failure and successfully evade service upon it; while your neighbor is firmly convinced that prosecutors secure their positions by reason of their similarity to bloodhounds and retain them by virtue of the same token.

The only information available to most people on this exceedingly important subject is that offered by the press, and the press (save in the case of sensational murder trials) usually confines itself to dramatic accounts of the arrest of the more picturesque sort of criminals, with lurid descriptions of their offences. The report or "story" concludes with the statement that "Detective-Sergeant Smith immediately arraigned his prisoner (Robinson) before Magistrate Jones, who committed the latter to jail and adjourned the hearing until the following Tuesday." This ends the matter, and the grewsome or ingenious details of the crime having been served up to satisfy the public appetite, and the offender having been locked up, there is nothing, from the reporters' point of view, any longer in the story. We never hear of Robinson again unless he happens to be the president of a bank or a degenerate millionaire. He is "disposed of," as they say in the criminal reports, without exciting anybody's interest, and his conviction or acquittal is not attended by newspaper comment.

If on the other hand the case be one of sensational interest we are treated daily to long histories of the defendant and his family, illustrated by grotesque reproductions from the ancestral photograph album. We become familiar with what he eats and drinks, the number of cigars he smokes and his favorite actor and author. The case consumes months in preparation and its trial occupies weeks. A battalion of "special" talesmen marches to the court house,—"the standing army of the gibbet," as one of my professional brethren (on the other side of the bar) calls them. As each of the twelve is chosen his physiognomy appears on the front page of an evening edition, a tear dropping from his eye or his jaws locked in grim determination, in accordance with the sentiments of the editor or the policy of the owner. Then follows a pictorial procession of witnesses. The prosecutor makes a full-page address to the public in the centre of which appears his portrait, heroic size, arm sawing the air.

"I am innocent!" cries a purple defendant, in green letters.

"Murderer!" hisses a magenta prosecutor, in characters of vermilion.

Finally the whole performance comes to an end without anybody having much of an idea of what has actually taken place, and leaving on the public mind an entirely false and distorted conception of what a criminal trial is like.

The object of this book is to correct the very general erroneous impression as to certain phases of criminal justice, and to give a concrete idea of its actual administration in large cities in ordinary cases,—cases quite as important to the defendants and to the public as those which attract widespread attention.

The millionaire embezzler and the pickpocket are tried before the same judge and the same jury, and the same system suffices to determine the guilt or innocence of the boy who has broken into a cigar store and the actress who has murdered her lover. It is in crowded cities, like New York, containing an excessive foreign-born population, that the system meets with its severest test, and if tried and not found wanting under these conditions it can fairly be said to have demonstrated its practical efficiency and stability. Has the jury system broken down? Are prosecutors habitually vindictive and over-zealous? It is the hope of the writer that the chapters which follow may afford some data to assist the reader in formulating an intelligent opinion upon these and kindred subjects. It is needless to say that no attempt is made to discuss police corruption, the increase or decrease of crime, or penology in general, and the writer has confined himself strictly to that period of the criminals' history described in the title as "AT THE BAR."

To my official chief, William Travers Jerome, and to my associates, Charles Cooper Nott, Charles Albert Perkins, and Nathan A. Smyth, I desire to acknowledge my gratitude for their advice and assistance; to my friend, Leonard E. Opdycke, who suggested the collection and correlating of these chapters, I wish to express my thanks for his constant interest and encouragement; but my debt to these is naught compared to that which I owe to her to whom this book is dedicated, who, with unsparing pains, has read, re-read and revised these chapters in manuscript, galley and page and who has united the functions of critic, censor and collaborator with a patience, good humor, and discretion which make writing a joy and proof-reading a vacation.

ARTHUR TRAIN.

Bar Harbor, Me.,
Sept. 1, 1906.

INTRODUCTION

BY PROF. JOHN H. WIGMORE,
Dean of the Law School of Northwestern University.

Mr. Train's book, "The Prisoner at the Bar," as an entertaining and vivid picture of the criminal procedure of to-day, and a repertory of practical experience and serious discussion of present-day problems in the administration of justice, is, in my opinion, both unique and invaluable. I know of no other book which so satisfyingly fills an important but empty place in a modern field. At one extreme stand the scientific psycho-criminologists, usefully investigating and reflecting, but commonly severed from the practical treatment of any branch of the subject until the prison doors are reached. At another extreme are the professional lawyers, skilled in the technique of present procedure, but too much tied by precedent to take anything but a narrow, backward-looking view. Off in a third corner are the economists, sociologists, physicians, and serious citizens in general, who notice that some things are going wrong, but have no accurate conception of what is actually seen and done every day in courts of justice; these good people run the risk of favoring impracticable fads or impossible theories.

Now comes Mr. Train's book, casting in the centre of the field an illumination useful to all parties. It enlightens the serious citizen as to the actual experiences of our criminal justice, and shows him the inexorable facts that must be reckoned with in any new proposals. The professional lawyer is stimulated to think over the large tendencies involved in his daily work, to realize that all is *not* necessarily for the best, and to join and help with his skill. The scientific criminologist is warned against trusting too much to the cobwebs of his ideal theories, or adhering too implicitly to the Lombrosan school or other foreign propaganda, and is forced to keep in mind a living picture of the practical needs of American justice.

I do not hesitate to say that every thoughtful American citizen ought to know all the things that are told in this book; and if he did, and as soon as he did, we might then begin to work with encouragement to accomplish in a fashion truly practical as well as scientific the needed improvements in our criminal justice. Such effort is likely to be hopeless until people come to realize *what the facts are.* Judging by my own case, I feel that most people will never really know and appreciate the facts unless they read Mr. Train's book.

CHAPTER I

WHAT IS CRIME?

A crime is any act or omission to act punishable as such by law. It is difficult, if not impossible, to devise any closer definition. Speaking broadly, crimes are certain acts, usually wrongful, which are regarded as sufficiently dangerous or harmful to society to be forbidden under pain of punishment. The general relation of crimes to wrongs as a whole is sometimes illustrated by a circle having two much smaller circles within it. The outer circle represents wrongful acts in the aggregate; the second, wrongful acts held by law to be *torts*, that is to say, infractions of private rights for which redress may be sought in the civil courts, and the smallest or inner circle, acts held to be so injurious to the public as to be punishable as crimes.

This does well enough for the purpose of illustrating the relative proportion of crimes to torts or wrongful acts in general, and, if a tiny dot be placed in the centre of the bull's-eye to represent those crimes which are actually punished, one gets an excellent idea of how infinitely small a number of these serve to keep the whole social fabric in order and sustain the majesty of the law. But the inference might naturally be drawn that whatever was a crime must also be a tort or at least a wrong, which, while true in the majority of instances, is not necessarily the case in all. In a certain sense crimes are always wrongs or, at least, wrong, but only in the sense of being infractions of law are they *always* wrongs or wrong.

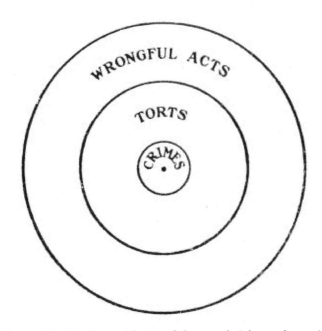

The word wrong being the antithesis of the word right, and carrying with it generally some ethical or moral significance, will vary in its meaning according to the ideas of the individual who makes use of it. Indeed, it is conceivable that the only really right thing to do under certain circumstances would be to commit an act designated by law as a crime. So, conversely, while a wrong viewed as an infraction of the laws of God is a sin, that which is universally held sinful is by no means always a crime. Speaking less broadly, a wrong is an infraction of a right belonging to another, which he derives from the law governing the society of which he is a member. Many wrongs are such that he may sue and obtain redress therefor in the courts. But it by no means follows that every crime involves the infraction of a private right or the commission of a tort. Thus "perjury" and most crimes against the State are not torts at all. It will thus be seen that no accurate definition of a crime can be given save that it is an act or omission which the State punishes as such, and that technically the word carries with it no imputation or implication of sin, vice, iniquity, or in a broad sense even of wrong. The act may or may not be repugnant to our ideas of right. Numerically considered, only a minority of crimes have any ethical significance whatever, the majority being designated by the law itself as *mala prohibita*, rather than *mala in se*.

It is the duty of a prosecutor to see that infractions of the criminal law are punished and to represent the public in all proceedings had for that purpose, but, in view of what has just been said, it will be observed that his duties do not necessarily involve familiarity with vice, violence or even sin.

The crimes he is called upon to prosecute may be disgusting, depraved and wicked, or they may be, and frequently are, interesting, ingenious, amusing or, possibly (though not probably), commendable. For example, a man who chastises the foul slanderer of a young woman's character may have technically committed an assault of high degree, yet if he does so in the proper spirit, in a suitable place, and makes the offender smart sufficiently, he deserves the thanks and congratulations of all decent men and honest women. Yet, indubitably, he has committed a crime, although, thanks to our still lingering spirit of chivalry, he would never be stamped by any jury as a criminal.

A prosecutor is frequently asked if he does not find that his experience has a "hardening" effect.

"Why should it?" he might fairly reply. "I have to do with criminals, it is true, but the criminals as a rule are little or no worse than the classes of people outside from which they have been drawn. Their arrest and conviction are largely due to accidental causes, such as weak heads, warm hearts, quick temper, ignorance, foolishness or drunkenness. We see all of these characteristics in our immediate associates. A great many convicted persons have done acts which are not wrong at all, but are merely forbidden. Even where their acts are really wrong it is generally the stupid, the unfortunate, or the less skilful who are caught. For every rogue in jail there are at least ten thousand at large. The ones who escape are wiser and very likely meaner. Last, but not least, a very great number of the most despicable, wicked, and harmful deeds that can be committed are not crimes at all. The fact that a man is a criminal argues nothing at all against his general decency, and when I meet a convict I assume, and generally assume correctly, that to most intents and purposes he is a gentleman. The code which puts one man in stripes and allows another to ride in an automobile is purely artificial, and strictly speaking proves not a whit which is the better man."

Now while such an answer might seem frivolous enough to the lay reader, it would nevertheless be substantially true. Your criminal, that is to say, strictly, the law-breaker who is brought to book for his offence, is very likely a pretty good sort of fellow as fellows go. If he has been guilty merely of an act which is prohibited, not because of its inherent wrong, but simply on grounds of public policy—*malum prohibitum*—he is probably as good as anybody. His offence may be due to ignorance or accident. Assuming that his crime be one which would seem to involve moral turpitude—*malum in se*—there are very likely mitigating circumstances which render his offence, if not excusable, at least less reprehensible than would appear at first glance.

Crimes bear no absolute relation to one another. A murderer may or may not be worse than a thief,—and either may be better than his accuser. The actual danger of any particular offender to the community lies not so much in the kind or degree of crime which he may have committed as in the state of his mind. Even the criminals who are really criminal, in the sense that they have a systematic intention of defying the law and preying upon society, are generally not criminal in all directions, but usually only in one, so that taken upon their unprofessional side they present the same characteristics as ordinary and, roughly speaking, law-abiding citizens. The bank robber usually is a bank robber and nothing more. He specializes in that one pursuit. It is his vocation and his joy. He prides himself on the artistic manner in which he does his work. He would scorn to steal your watch and is a man of honor outside of bank-breaking hours,—"Honor among thieves." Often enough he is a model husband and father. So, too, may be your forger, gambler, swindler, burglar, highwayman, or thief,—any in fact except the real moral pervert; and of course murder is entirely compatible on occasion with a noble, dignified and generous character. "There is nothing essentially incongruous between crime and culture." The prosecutor who begins by loathing and despising the man sitting at the bar may end by having a sincere admiration for his intellect, character or capabilities. This by way of defence to crime in general.

Our forefathers contented themselves with a rough distinction between crimes as *mala prohibita* and *mala in se*. When they sought to classify criminal acts under this arrangement they divided them accordingly as the offence carried or did not carry with it a suggestion of moral turpitude. Broadly speaking, all felonies were and are regarded as *mala in se*. Murder, arson, burglary, theft, etc., in general indubitably imply a depraved mind, while infractions of Sunday observance laws or of statutes governing the trade in liquor do not. Yet it must be perfectly clear that any such distinction is inconclusive.

There can be no general rule based merely on the name or kind of crime committed which is going to tell us which offender is really the worst. A misdemeanor may be very much more heinous than a felony. The adulterator of drugs or the employer of illegal child labor may well be regarded as vastly more reprehensible than the tramp who steals part of the family wash. So far as that goes there are an alarming multitude of acts and omissions not forbidden by statute or classed as crimes which are to all intents and purposes fully as criminal as those designated as such by law. This is the inevitable result of the fact that crimes are not crimes merely because they are wrong, but because the State has enjoined them. For example, to push a blind man over the edge of a cliff so that he is killed upon the rocks below is murder, but to permit him to walk over it, although by stretching out your hand you might prevent him, is no crime at all. It is a crime to defame a woman's character if you write your accusation upon a slip of paper and pass it to another, but it is no crime in New York State to arise in a crowded lecture hall and ruin her forever by word of mouth. It is a crime to steal a banana off a fruit-stand, but it is no crime to borrow ten thousand dollars from a man whose entire fortune it is, although you have no expectation of returning it. You can be a swindler all your life—the meanest sort of a mean swindler, but there is no crime of being a swindler or of being a mean man. It is a crime to ruin a girl of seventeen years and eleven months, but not to ruin a girl of eighteen. The "age of consent" varies in the different States. It is a crime to obtain a dollar by means of a false statement as to a past or existing fact, but it is no crime to obtain as much money as you can by any other sort of a lie. Lying is not a crime, but lying under oath is a crime,—provided it be done in a legal proceeding and relates to a *material* matter. The most learned jurists habitually disagree as to what is material and what is not.

Even when the acts to be contrasted are all crimes there is no way of actually discriminating between them except by carefully scrutinizing the circumstances of each. The so-called "degrees" mean little or nothing. If you steal four hundred and ninety-nine dollars out of a man's safe in the daytime it is grand larceny in the second degree. If you pick the same man's pocket of a subway ticket after sunset it is grand larceny in the first degree. You may get five years in the first instance and ten in the second. If you steal twenty-five dollars out of a bureau drawer you commit petty larceny and may be sent to prison for only one year.

If the degree of any particular crime of which a defendant is found guilty is no index to his real criminality or of his danger to society, still less is the name of the crime he has committed an index to his moral character, save in the case of certain offences which it is not necessary to enumerate. Most men charged with homicide are indicted for murder in the first degree. This may be a wise course for the grand jury to pursue in view of the additional evidence which often comes to light during a trial. But it frequently is discovered before the case goes to the jury that in point of fact the killing was in hot blood and under circumstances which evince no great moral turpitude in the slayer. For example, two drunken men become involved in an altercation and one strikes the other, who loses his equilibrium and falls, hitting his head against a curbstone and fracturing his skull. The striker is indicted and tried for murder. Now he is doubtless guilty of manslaughter, but he is less dangerous to the community than a professional thief who preys upon the public by impersonating a gasman or telephone repairer and by thus gaining access to private dwellings steals the owner's property. One is an accidental, the other an intentional criminal. One is hostile to society as a whole and the other is probably not really hostile to anybody. Yet the less guilty is denominated a murderer, and the other is rarely held guilty of more than petty larceny. A fellow who bumps into you on the street, if he be accompanied by another, and grabs your cane, is guilty of robbery in the first degree,—"highway" robbery,—and may get twenty years for it, but the same man may publish a malicious libel about you, and by accusing you of the foulest practices rob you of your good name and be only guilty of a misdemeanor. Yet the reader should not infer that definitions and grades of crime capable of corresponding punishments are not proper, desirable, and necessary. Of course they are. The practical use of such statutes is to fix a maximum sentence of punishment. As a rule the minimum is anything the judge sees fit. Hence you may deduce a general principle to the effect that the charge against the prisoner, even assuming his guilt, indicates nothing definite as to his moral turpitude, danger to the community, or general undesirability.

But we may honestly go much further. Not only are the names and degrees of the crimes which a defendant may have committed of very little assistance in determining his real criminality, but the fact that he has committed them by no means signifies that he is morally any worse than some man who has committed no so-called crime at all. Many criminals, even those guilty of homicide, are as white as snow compared with others who have never transgressed the literal wording of a penal statute.

"We used to have So and So for our lawyer," remarked the president of a large street railway corporation. "He was always telling us what we *couldn't* do. Now we have Blank, and pay him one hundred thousand dollars a year to tell us how we *can* do the same things." The thief who can have the advice of able counsel "how to do it" need never go to jail.

Many of the things most abhorrent to our sense of right do not come within the scope of the criminal law. *Omissions*, no matter how reprehensible, are usually not regarded as criminal, because in most cases there is no technical legal duty to perform the act omitted. Thus, not to remove your neighbor's baby from the railroad track in front of an on-rushing train, although it would cause you very little trouble to do so, is no crime, even if the child's life be lost as a result of your neglect. You can let your mother-in-law choke to death without sending for a doctor, or permit a ruffian half your size to kill an old and helpless man, or allow your neighbor's house to burn down, he and his family peacefully sleeping inside it, while you play on the pianola and refuse to ring up the fire department, and never have to suffer for it—in this world.

Passing from felonies—*mala in se*—to misdemeanors—generally only *mala prohibita*—almost anything becomes a crime, depending upon the arbitrary act of the legislature.

It is a crime in New York State to run a horse race within a mile of where a court is sitting; to advertise as a divorce lawyer; to go fishing or "play" on the first day of the week; to set off fire-works or make a "disbursing noise"[1] at a military funeral in a city on Sunday; to arrest or attach a corpse for payment of debt; to keep a "slot machine"; to do business under any name not actually your own full name without filing a certificate with the county clerk (as, for example, if, being a tailor, you call your shop "The P.D.Q. Tailoring Establishment"); to ride in a long-distance bicycle race more than twelve hours out of twenty-four; to shoe horses without complying with certain articles of the Labor Law; to fail to supply seats for female employés in a mercantile establishment; to steal a ride in a freight car, or to board such a car or train while in motion; to set fire negligently to one's own woods, by means of which the property of another is endangered; to run a ferry without authority, or, having contracted to run one, to fail to do so; to neglect to post ferry rates (under certain conditions) in English; to induce the employé of a railroad company to leave its service because it requires him to wear a uniform; to wear a railroad uniform without authority; to fish with a net in any part of the Hudson River (except where permitted by statute); to secretly loiter about a building with intent to overhear discourse therein, and to repeat the same to vex others (eavesdropping); to sell skimmed milk without a label; to plant oysters (if you are a non-resident) inside the State without the consent of the owner of the water; to maintain an insane asylum without a license; to enter an agricultural fair without paying the entrance fee; to assemble with two or more other persons "disguised by having their faces painted, discolored, colored or concealed," save at a fancy-dress ball for which permission has been duly obtained from the police; or to wear the badge of the "Patrons of Husbandry," or of certain other orders without authority. These illustrations are selected at random from the New York Penal Code.

Where every business, profession, and sport is hedged around by such *chevaux-de-frise* of criminal statutes, he must be an extraordinarily careful as well as an exceptionally well-informed citizen who avoids sooner or later crossing the dead-line. It is to be deprecated that our law-makers can devise no other way of regulating our existences save by threatening us with the shaved head and striped shirt.

The actual effect of such a multitude of statutes making anything and everything crimes, punishable by imprisonment, instead of increasing our respect for law, decreases it, unless they are intended to be and actually are enforced. Acts *mala in se* are lost in the shuffle among the acts *mala prohibita*, and we have to become students to avoid becoming criminals.

Year by year the legislature goes calmly on *creating* all sorts of new crimes, while failing to amplify or give effect to the various statutes governing existing offences which to a far greater degree are a menace to the community. For example, it is not a crime in New York State to procure money by false pretences provided the person defrauded parts with his money for an illegal purpose.[2]

In the McCord[3] case, in which the Court of Appeals established this extraordinary doctrine, the defendant had falsely pretended to the complainant, a man named Miller, that he was a police officer and held a warrant for his arrest. By these means he had induced Miller to give him a gold watch and a diamond ring as the price of his liberty. The conviction in this case was reversed on the ground that Miller parted with his property for an unlawful purpose; but there was a very strong dissenting opinion from Mr. Justice Peckham, now a member of the bench of the Supreme Court of the United States.

In a second case, that of Livingston,[4] the complainant had been defrauded out of five hundred dollars by means of the "green-goods" game; but this conviction was reversed by the Appellate Division of the Second Department on the authority of the McCord case. The opinion was written by Mr. Justice Cullen, now Chief Judge of the New York Court of Appeals, who says in conclusion:

"We very much regret being compelled to reverse this conviction. Even if the prosecutor intended to deal in counterfeit money, it is no reason why the appellant should go unwhipped of justice. *We venture to suggest that it might be well for the legislature to alter the rule laid down in McCord vs. People.*"

Well might the judges regret being compelled to set a rogue at liberty simply because he had been ingenious enough to invent a fraud which involved the additional turpitude of seducing another into a criminal conspiracy. Livingston was turned loose upon the community, in spite of the fact that he had swindled a man out of five hundred dollars, because he had incidentally led the latter to believe that in return he was to receive counterfeit money or "green goods" which might be put into circulation. Yet, because, some years before, the judges of the Court of Appeals had, in the McCord matter, adopted the rule followed in civil cases, to wit, that as the complaining witness was himself in fault and did not come into court with clean hands he could have no standing before them, the Appellate Division in the next case felt obliged to follow them and to rule tantamount to saying that two wrongs could make a right and two knaves one honest man. It may seem a trifle unfair to put it in just this way, but when one realizes the iniquity of such a rule as applied to criminal cases, it is hard to speak softly. Thus the broad and general doctrine seemed to be established that so long as a thief could induce his victim to believe that it was to his advantage to enter into a dishonest transaction, he might defraud him to any extent in his power. Immediately there sprang into being hordes of swindlers, who, aided by adroit shyster lawyers, invented all sorts of schemes which involved some sort of dishonesty upon the part of the person to be defrauded. The "wire-tappers," of whom "Larry" Summerfield was the Napoleon, the "gold-brick" and "green-goods" men, and the "sick engineers" flocked to New York, which, under the unwitting protection of the Court of Appeals, became a veritable Mecca for persons of their ilk.

The "wire-tapping" game consisted in inducing the victim to put up money for the purpose of betting upon a "sure thing," knowledge of which the thief pretended to have secured by "tapping" a Western Union wire of advance news of the races. He usually had a "lay out" which included telegraph instruments connected with a dry battery in an adjoining closet, and would merrily steal the supposed news off an imaginary wire and then send his dupe to play his money upon the "winner" in a pretended pool-room which in reality was nothing but a den of thieves, who instantly absconded with the money.

In this way one John Felix was defrauded out of fifty thousand dollars on a single occasion.[5] Now the simplest legislation could instantly remedy this evil and put all the "wire-tappers" and similar swindlers out of business, yet a bill framed and introduced in accordance with the suggestion of the highest court in the State was defeated. Instead the legislature passes scores of entirely innocuous and respectable acts like the following, which became a law in 1890:

AN ACT FOR THE PREVENTION OF BLINDNESS

Section 1. Should ... *nurse having charge of an infant* ... *notice* that one or both eyes of such infant are inflamed or reddened at any time within two weeks after its birth it shall be the duty of such nurse ... to report the fact in writing within six hours to the health officer or some legally qualified practitioner of medicine ...

Section 2. Any failure to comply with the provisions of this act shall be punished by a fine not to exceed one hundred dollars, *or imprisonment not to exceed six months, or both.*

The criminal law which had its origin when violence was rife is admirably adapted to the prevention, prosecuting and punishment of crude crimes, such as arson, rape, robbery, burglary, mayhem, assault, homicide, and "common-law" larceny,—theft accompanied by a trespass. In old times everything was against the man charged with crime—at least that was the attitude of the court and jury. "Aha!" exclaims the judge as the evidence goes in. "You thought you were stealing only a horse! But you stole a *halter as well!*" And the spectators are convulsed with merriment.

We take honest pride in the protection which our law affords to the indicted prisoner. It is the natural expression of our disapproval of a system which at the time of our severance from England ignored the rights of the individual for those of the community. We touched the lips of the defendant and gave him the right to speak in his own behalf. We gave him an unlimited right of appeal on any imaginable technicality.[6] But while we have been making it harder and harder to convict our common criminals, we have to a very great extent failed to recognize the fact that all sorts of new and ingenious crimes have come into existence with which the law in its present state is utterly unable to cope. The evolution of the modern corporation has made possible larcenies to the punishment of which the law is entirely inadequate. "Acts for the prevention of blindness" are perhaps desirable, but how about a few statutes to prevent the officers of insurance companies from arbitrarily diverting the funds of that vague host commonly alluded to as "widows and orphans"? The careless nurse is a criminal and may be confined in a penitentiary; while perhaps a man who may be guilty of a great iniquity and known to be so drives nonchalantly off in his coach and four.

What is crime? We may well ask the question, only eventually to be confronted by that illuminating definition with which begins the Penal Code—"A crime is an act or omission forbidden by law and punishable upon conviction by ... penal discipline." Let us put on our glasses and find out what these acts or omissions are. When we have done that we may begin to look around for the criminals. But it will be of comparatively little assistance in finding the *sinners*.

So-called criminologists delight in measuring the width of the skulls between the eyes, the height of the foreheads, the length of the ears, and the angle of the noses of persons convicted of certain kinds of crimes, and prepare for the edification of the simple-minded public tables demonstrating that the burglar has this kind of a head, the pickpocket that sort of an ear, and the swindler such and such a variety of visage. Exhaustive treatises upon crime and criminals lay down general principles supposed to assist in determining the kind of crime for which any particular unfortunate may have a predilection. One variety of criminal looks this way and another looks that way. One has blue eyes, the other brown eyes.[7] Some look up, others look down. My friend, if you examine into the question, you will probably discover that the clerk who sells you your glass of soda water at the corner drug store will qualify for some one of these classes, so will your host at dinner this evening, so, very likely, will the family doctor or the pastor of your church.

The writer is informed that there has recently been produced an elaborate work on political criminals in which an attempt is made to set forth the telltale characteristics of such. It is explained that the tendency to commit such crimes may be inherited. You are about as likely to inherit an inclination to commit a political crime as you are to derive from a maiden aunt a tendency to violate a speed ordinance or make a "disbursing" noise.

Let some one codify all the sins and meannesses of mankind, let the legislatures make them crimes and affix appropriate penalties, then those of us who still remain outside the bars may with more propriety indulge ourselves in reflections at the expense of those who are not.

FOOTNOTES:

[1] New York Penal Code, Section 276.

[2] No longer the law of New York. After this book was published the Court of Appeals reversed the conviction of Tracy for his $50,000 fraud upon Felix by means of the "wire-tapping" game and affirmed as law the doctrine of People *vs.* McCord. The author takes satisfaction in recording that the Legislature thereupon awoke to its duties and amended the penal code in such a fashion as to render such offences criminal.

[3] 46 New York 470.

[4] 47 App. Div. 283.

[5] The operations of these swindlers recently became so notorious that the District Attorney of New York County determined to prosecute the perpetrators of the Felix swindle, in spite of the fact that the offence appeared to come within the language of the Court of Appeals in the McCord and Livingston cases. Accordingly Christopher Tracy, alias Charles Tompkins, alias Topping, etc., etc., was indicted (on the theory of "trick and device") for the "common-law" larceny of Felix's fifty thousand dollars.

The trial came on before Judge Warren W. Foster in Part III of the General Sessions on February 27, 1906. A special panel quickly supplied a jury, which, after hearing the evidence, returned a verdict of guilty in short order.

It now remains for the judges of the Court of Appeals to decide whether they will extend the doctrine of the McCord and Livingston cases to a fraud of this character, whether they will limit the doctrine strictly to cases of precisely similar facts, or whether they will frankly refuse to be bound by any such absurd and iniquitous theory and consign the McCord case to the dust-heap of discarded and mistaken doctrines, where it rightfully belongs. Their action will determine whether the perpetrators of the most ingenious, elaborate and successful bunco game in the history of New York County shall be punished for their offence or instead be turned loose to prey at will upon the community at large. (See "The Last of the Wire-Tappers" in the *American Magazine* for June, 1906; also incorporated in the author's "True Stories of Crime," pp. 103-121, published by Charles Scribner's Sons, 1908.)

[6] Cf. in general, references given *infra*, p. 339.

[7] The following appeared in the New York *Globe* for April 25, 1905: "Criminal eyes—It is well known," says Dr. Beddoe, F.R.S., "that brown eyes and dark hair are particularly common among the criminal classes. An American observer calls the brown the criminal eye, etc., etc."

CHAPTER II

WHO ARE THE REAL CRIMINALS?

Some reader of the preceding chapter may perhaps remark, "This is all very well so far as it goes. It doubtless is entirely true from a purely technical point of view. But that is only one side of the matter. How about the *real* criminals?" This is neither an unexpected nor an uninvited criticism. Who *are* the "*real*" criminals? Charles Dudley Warner says: "Speaking technically, we put in that [the criminal] class those whose sole occupation is crime, who live upon it as a profession and who have no other permanent industry. They prey upon society. They are by their acts at war upon it and are outlaws." Now the class of professional criminals to which Mr. Warner refers as contrasted with the great mass of criminal defendants as a whole is, in point of fact, relatively so small, and so easily recognized and handled, that it plays but an inconspicuous part in the administration of criminal justice.

The criminals who conform accurately to childhood's tradition are comparatively few in number. The masked highwayman, the safe-cracker and even the armed house burglar have, with a few exceptions, long since withdrawn from the actual pursuit of their romantic professions and exist practically only in the eagerly devoured pages of Sherlock Holmes and the "memoirs of great detectives." New and almost more picturesque figures have taken their places,—the polite and elegant swindler, the out-at-the-elbows but confidence-inspiring promoter of assetless corporations, the dealer in worthless securities, and the forger who drives in his own carriage to the bank he intends to defraud. In some cases the individuals are the same, the safe-cracker merely having doffed his mask in favor of the silk hat of Nassau Street. Of yore he stole valuable securities which he was compelled to dispose of at a tremendous discount; now he sells you worthless stocks and bonds at a slight premium. Mr. J. Holt Schorling, writing in *The Contemporary Review* for June, 1902, points out that while all crimes other than fraud decreased materially in England from 1885 to 1899, the crime of fraud itself materially increased during the same period.[8]

The subject is a tempting one, but it is not essential to our thesis. The devil is not dead; he has merely changed his clothes. Criminal activity has not subsided; it has instead sought new ways to meet modern conditions, and so favorable are these that while polite crime may be said still to be in its infancy, it is nevertheless thriving lustily.

While the degenerate criminal class is the subject of much elaborate and minute analysis by our continental neighbors, its extent is constantly exaggerated and its relation to the other criminal classes not fully appreciated. To read some supposedly scientific works one would imagine that every court of criminal justice was or should be nothing but a sort of clinic. To these learned authors, civilization, it is true, owes a debt for their demonstration that some crime is due to insanity and should be prevented, and, where possible, cured in much the same manner. But they have created an impression that practically all crime is the result of abnormality.

Every great truth brings in its train a few falsehoods,—every great reform a few abuses. The first penological movement was in the direction of prison reform. While perhaps the psychological problem was not entirely overlooked, it was completely subordinated to the physical. It is a noble thing that the convict should have a warm cell in winter and a cool one in summer, with electric light and running water, wholesome and nutritious food, books, bathrooms, hospitals, chapels, concerts, ball games and chaplains. "But it must be noted that along with this movement has grown up a sickly sentimentality about criminals which has gone altogether too far, and which, under the guise of humanity and philanthropy, confounds all moral distinctions." To a large number of well-meaning people every convict is a person to whom the State has done an injury.

Then came the study of degeneracy, with the cranium of every criminal as a subject of investigation. In 1881 or thereabouts Professor Benedickt published his conclusion that "the brains of criminals exhibit a deviation from the anthropological variety of their species, at least among the cultured races." It was a commendable thing to point out the relation of insanity to crime. It is an undeniable truth that there are insane people who are predisposed to crime just as there are those who are predisposed to dance.

The vicious criminal class contains many who are actually or incipiently insane, and it numbers a great many more who are physically and mentally normal, who yet by reason of their education and environment are not much to be blamed for doing wrong. But it is far from true that a majority of the "real" criminals are mentally defective. Crime and insanity are no more closely related than sin and insanity. Certain criminals are also perverts. But they would be criminals even if they were not perverts. The fact that a man who takes drugs is also a criminal does not prove that he is a criminal because he takes drugs. We know many drug-takers who are otherwise highly respectable. Go to the General Sessions and watch the various defendants who are brought into court and you will discover little more degeneracy or abnormality than you would find on the corner of

Twenty-third Street and Fifth Avenue among the same number of unaccused citizens.

The point which the writer desires to make is that, leaving out the accidental and experimental criminals, there is a much closer relation between all law-breakers than the public and our legislators seem to suppose. The man who adulterates his milk to make a little extra money is in the same class with the financial swindler. One waters his milk, the other his stock. The same underhanded desire to better one's self at the expense of one's neighbor is the moving cause in each case. The forger belongs to the class whose heads the criminologists delight to measure, but they would not measure your milkman's. The man who steals your purse is a felon and a subject of scientific investigation and discussion; the man who forges a trade-mark commits only a misdemeanor and excites no psychological interest. But they are criminals of exactly the same type.

The "crime-is-a-disease" theory has been worked entirely too hard. It is a penologic generality which does not need any truckling to popular sentimentality to demonstrate its truth. But there are as many sorts of this "disease" as there are kinds of crime, and some varieties would be better described by other and less euphemistic names. Crime is no more a disease than sin, and the sinners deserve a good share of the sympathy that is at present wasted on the criminals. The poor fellow who has merely done wrong gets but scant courtesy, but once jerk him behind the bars and the women send him flowers. If crime is a disease, sin is also a disease, and we have all got a case of it. It is strange that there is not more "straight talk" on this subject. Every one of us has criminal propensities,—that is to say, in every one of us lurks the elemental and unlawful passions of sex and of acquirement. It is but a play on words to say that the man who yields to his inclinations to the extent of transgressing the criminal statutes is "diseased." Up to a certain point it is his own business, beyond it becomes ours, and he transgresses at his peril.

The ordinary criminal usually is such because he "wants the money"; he either does not like to work or wants more money than he can earn honestly. He has no "irresistible impulse" to steal,—he steals because he thinks he can "get away with it."

The so-called professional thief is usually one who has succeeded in so doing or who, having been convicted of larceny, finds he cannot live agreeably other than by thieving; but the man is no less a professional thief who systematically puts money in his pocket by dishonest and illegal methods in business. The fact that it is not, in the ordinary sense, his "sole occupation" does not affect the question at all. Indeed, it would be difficult for one whose business life was permeated by graft to refute the general allegation that his "sole occupation" was criminal. Granting this, your dishonest business man fulfils every requirement of Mr. Warner's definition, for he "preys upon society and is [secretly] at war upon it." He may not be an "outlaw," but he should be one under any enlightened code of criminal laws.[9]

There is no practical distinction between a man who gets all of a poor living dishonestly and one who gets part of an exceedingly good living dishonestly. The thieving of the latter may be many times more profitable than that of the former. So long as both keep at it systematically there is little to choose between the thief who earns his livelihood by picking pockets and the grocer or the financier who swindles those who rely upon his representations. The man who steals a trade-mark, counterfeits a label, or adulterates food or drugs, who makes a fraudulent assignment of his property, who as a director of a corporation declares an unearned dividend for the purpose of selling the stock of himself and his associates at an inflated value, who publishes false statements and reports, makes illegal loans, or who is guilty of any of the thousand and one dishonest practices which are being uncovered every day in the management of life insurance, banking, trust, and railroad companies, is precisely as "real" a criminal as one who lurks in an alley and steals from a passing wagon. *Each is guilty of a deliberate violation of law implying conscious wrong*, and each commits it for essentially the same reason.

Yet at the present time the law itself recognizes a fictitious distinction between these crimes and those of a more elementary sort. The adulteration of foods, the theft of trade-marks, stock-jobbing, corporation frauds, and fraudulent assignments are as a rule only misdemeanors. The trouble is that we have not yet adjusted ourselves to the idea that the criminal who wears a clean collar is as dangerous as one who does not. Of course, in point of fact he is a great deal worse, for he has not the excuse of having a gnawing at his vitals.

If a rascally merchant makes a fraudulent conveyance of his property and then "fails," although he may have secreted goods worth fifty thousand dollars, the punishment of himself and his confederate is limited to a year in the penitentiary and a thousand dollars fine, while if a bank cashier should steal an equivalent amount and turn it over to an accomplice for safe keeping he could receive ten years in State's prison. Even in this last case the receiver's punishment could not exceed *five* years. Thus Robert A. Ammon, who was the sole person to profit by the notorious "Franklyn Syndicate,"[10] when convicted of receiving the proceeds of the fraud, could be sentenced to only five years in Sing Sing, while his dupe, Miller, who sat at the desk and received the money, although he acted throughout by the other's advice and counsel, in fact did receive a sentence of ten years for practically the same offence. However inequitable this may seem, what inducements are offered in the field of fraudulent commercial activity when a similar kind of theft is punishable by only a year in the penitentiary?

One can hardly blame such picturesque swindlers as "Larry" Summerfield, who saw gigantic financial and commercial frauds being perpetrated on every side, while the thieves who had enriched themselves at the expense of a gullible public went scot-free, for wanting to participate in the feast. Almost every day sees some new corporation brought into being, the only object of which is to enable its organizers to foist its worthless stock among poorly paid clerks, stenographers, trained nurses, elevator men and hard-working mechanics. The stock is disposed of and the "corporation" (usually a copper or gold mining enterprise) is never heard of again. Apparently if you do the thing correctly there can be no "come back." Accordingly Summerfield and his gang of "sick engineers" hawked through the town nearly eighty thousand dollars' worth of the securities of the Horse Shoe Copper Mining Company, which owned a hole in the ground in Arizona. It was all done under legal advice and was undoubtedly believed to be within the letter of the law. But there were a few unnecessary falsehoods, a few slips in the schedule, a few complainants who would not be placated, and "Larry" found himself in the toils. He was convicted of grand larceny in the first degree, secured a certificate of reasonable doubt and gave bail in a very large amount. Within a short time he was re-arrested for working the same game upon an unsuspecting southerner. This time his bail was increased to thirty thousand dollars. It was not long after the investigations into the Ship-Building Trust scandal and New York had been edified by seeing the inside workings of some very high finance. After his temporary release Summerfield strolled over to Pontin's restaurant for lunch, where he sat down at a table adjoining one occupied by the assistant district attorney who had prosecuted and convicted him.

"How are you, Mr. ——?" inquired "Larry" with his usual urbanity. "How are things?"

"So so," replied the prosecutor, amused at the nonchalance of a man who might reasonably expect to be in Sing Sing within three months. "How's business?"

"Oh, pretty good," returned Larry. "You know there is a sucker born every minute."

"I should think after your conviction you would have had sense enough to keep out of swindling for a while," continued the assistant.

"Swindling!" exclaimed Summerfield. "Swindling nothin'! My lawyer says I didn't commit any crime. Didn't the Supreme Court say there was a reasonable doubt in my case? Well, I'm just giving myself the benefit of it,—that's all. I'm entitled to it. How about those Ship-Building fellers?"

The "Ship-Building fellers" have never been convicted of any wrong-doing. Perhaps they committed no crime. Summerfield has three years more to serve in Sing Sing.[11]

In this connection the reader will recall the attitude of the inhabitants of Lilliput as chronicled by Gulliver.—"They look upon fraud as a greater crime than theft, and therefore seldom fail to punish it with death; for they allege that care and vigilance, with a very common understanding, may preserve a man's goods from theft, but honesty has no *defence* against superior cunning; ... the honest dealer is always undone, and the knave gets the advantage. I remember when I was once interceding with the king for a criminal who had wronged his master for a great sum of money, which he had received by order, and ran away with; and happening to tell his Majesty by way of extenuation that it was only a breach of trust, the Emperor thought it monstrous in me to offer as a defence the greatest aggravation of the crime; and truly I had little to say in return, further than the common answer, that different nations had different customs; for, I confess, I was heartily ashamed."

Any definition of the criminal class which limits it to those who "make their living" by crime is inadequate and begs the question entirely. There is no choice between the grafter and the "professional" thief, the boodler and the bank robber. They are all "real" criminals. One is as "diseased" and "degenerate" as the other. Every reversed conviction of a "grafter" lowers a peg the popular respect for law. The clerk in the corner grocery in Dakota feels the wireless influence of the boodler in St. Louis, and the "successful" failure in New York sets some fellow thinking in San Francisco.

The so-called degenerate and professional criminals constitute a very small fraction of the law-breakers and it is not from either class that we have most to fear. Our real danger lies in those classes of the population who have no regard for law, if not an actual contempt for it, and who may become criminals, or at least criminal, whenever any satisfactory reason, coupled with adequate opportunity, presents itself. From this class spring the experimental criminals of every sort, who in time become "professionals," and from it the embezzler, the stock jobber, the forger and business thief. From it as well are largely recruited those who commit the crimes of violence which, however undeservedly, give the United States such an unenviable place upon the tables of the statisticians. From it spring the "fellow who does not care" or who "will take a chance," the dynamiter, the man who is willing to "turn a trick" at a price, and all those who need the strong arm of the law to restrain them from yielding to their entirely normal evil inclinations.

The man who deliberately violates the law by doing that which he knows to be wrong is a real criminal, whether he be a house-breaker, an adulterator of drugs, the receiver of a fraudulent assignment or a trade-mark thief, an insurance "grafter," a bribe giver, or a butcher who charges the cook's commission against next Sunday's delivery. The writer fails to see the slightest valid distinction between them and believes it should be made possible to punish them all with equal severity. There is no reason why one should be a felon, another guilty of only a misdemeanor, while still another is guilty of nothing at all. The cause of crime is our general and widespread lack of respect for law, and this in turn is largely due to the unpunished, and often unpunishable, dishonesty which seems to permeate many phases of commercial activity. Diogenes's job is still vacant.

FOOTNOTES:

[8] Including under the general term "fraud," obtaining money by false pretenses, thefts by solicitors, bankers, agents, directors, trustees, etc. ("generally recorded under the euphony 'misappropriation'"), falsifying accounts, etc., Mr. Schorling found that taking the number of these two divisions of crime between 1885-1889 as 100% there had been the following relative decrease and increase between them:

All Crimes Except Fraud		*Frauds*	
1885-1889	100%	1885-1889	100%
1890-1894	96.2%	1890-1894	110.1%
1895-1899	90.4%	1895-1899	138.3%

A similar table constructed for the United States during the last fifteen years would be instructive but perhaps unduly depressing. Recent financial and other disclosures would probably send up the mercury of the "fraud" thermometer until it burst.

[9] Cf. "Unpunished Commercial Crime" in "Moral Overstrain," by G.W. Alger. Houghton, Mifflin & Co., 1906.

[10] See "True Stories of Crime," referred to *supra*, p. 15.

[11] Since the publication of this book Summerfield has been discharged from prison, having earned his parole by exemplary conduct. He has gone West to lead a new and better life, and there is reason to believe that he will succeed in doing so.

CHAPTER III

THE ARREST

To most of us modest folk a police officer looks not an inch less than eight feet in height,—and his blue coat and brass buttons typify the majesty and inflexibility of the law. At his most trivial gesture the coachmen rein in their curvetting steeds upon the crowded thoroughfare, and at his lightest word the gaping pedestrian obediently "moves on." When necessity compels we address him deprecatingly and, as it were, with hat in hand, and if he deign to listen to us, and still more if he condescend to reply, we thrill with pride. We experience a certain surprise that he has seen fit to give heed to us at all and has not, instead, ordered us roughly about our business with threatening mien and uplifted club. That he has rendered us assistance fills us with humble gratitude. One feels like Dr. Holmes,

"How kind it was of him
To mind a slender man like me!
He of the mighty limb!"

It rarely occurs to us that these stomachic Titans are in fact our servants and that they have no authority save that which they have received from ourselves,—that, horrible thought! they wear our livery as assuredly as does Jeames or Wilkins. Why do these big men patrol the streets and order us about? Simply because in these busy days the ordinary citizen has neither time nor inclination to attend to his own criminal business, and because it is better upon the whole for the State to attend to it for him.

Eight hundred years ago the punishment of crime was a matter of private vengeance gradually evolving itself into the criminal procedure of modern English law. The injured citizen took his appeal "to the county" and fought it out with his wrong-doer either personally or by proxy. The idea was, originally, that the man who had been injured ought to have his revenge, and criminal justice in England even to-day savors for this reason somewhat of private litigation. Of course, nowadays, crime is punished on the theory that the public has been injured; and that not only does the safety of the community require that a repetition of the same crime by the same offender should be prevented, but also that an example should be made of the evil-doer as a lesson to others. Be this as it may, vengeance and not public spirit is still the moving cause of ninety per cent of all prosecutions for crime.

Just as the right to apprehend a wrong-door was an inherent right at the common law of every free-born English subject, it is our inherent right to-day, modified or extended by the statute law of the several States, and, save where a court of justice has issued its warrant and commands its agents to apprehend the party named therein, one person has substantially the same right as another to arrest a criminal, even if that other be an officer of the law.

The policeman has no greater rights in the matter of preventing crime or arresting evil-doers than the citizen. He is merely hired by the citizen to do it for him. The only difference is that it is the *duty* of the officer by virtue of his position to make arrests, just as it is that of the fireman to extinguish fires. Yet it is undoubtedly the fact that nine-tenths of us really believe that the policeman's blue coat, helmet, and club invest him with some sacred and peculiar authority of his own. If every citizen recognized the fallacy of this idea, and if some elementary instruction in such matters were given in the public schools, even at the sacrifice of clay modelling and decorative art, it might add much to the spirit of independence and to the practical efficiency of the coming generation. We are slaves to the magic of the word "police." We imagine that without a representative of the law we can do nothing.

Of course we know in general that we may defend the persons and protect the property of ourselves and others by the exercise of reasonable force. Beyond this rather vague principle we are not prepared to go. Where the situation offers no particular inconvenience we are ready to do our part, but if anything disagreeable is going on we prefer to be excused. We are out of the habit of doing the simplest police duty. Most of us would have enough public spirit to summon an officer if a felony were being committed before our very eyes, provided we could do so without making ourselves ridiculous, but few of us, the writer fancies, would join the hue and cry after a pickpocket unless ours happened to be the pocket he had picked. We leave that to those whose natural bellicosity is greater and who do not object to being undignified. It is nevertheless true, however unpleasant the thought may be, that at any moment we may find ourselves in the centre of a whirlpool of events where individual action on our part will be necessary unless we are willing to allow some vicious and cruel violation of the law to go unpunished. Such exigencies may run all the way from the malicious beating of an overloaded horse to the garrotting of a feeble old man. Our efficiency on such occasions might be represented by a fraction, of which our physical capacity would be the numerator and our disinclination the denominator, but obviously, to make the formula complete, this would have to be multiplied by another representing our knowledge of our rights.

Suppose for example that Mr. Ordinary Citizen on a nocturnal ramble should, at about three o'clock in the morning, observe some ill-favored person with a heavy bag in his hand, furtively making his exit from the area door of a stylish mansion in the residential district. What should he do? What would *you* do? Without discussing this embarrassing question, does the reader know what he would have a right to do? The chances are largely in favor of his being obliged to answer this question in the negative. Indeed, our indifference to the unexpected is so great that we are generally mute and helpless in the face of any unusual situation where anybody's rights are concerned. We hesitate to act without the advice of counsel, and in the meantime the burglar has made his escape!

In the State of New York and generally in this country, any person, whether he be an officer of the law or not, may make an arrest, without a warrant, for any crime, of any grade, actually committed in his presence. It makes no difference whether the offence be that of spitting in a street-car or murder in the first degree, the offender may be haled before a magistrate by any one who has seen him commit it.

But the statutes governing the right of arrest, while extensive enough to safeguard the public interest, are carefully limited to prevent arbitrary interference with the liberty of innocent persons. The law, therefore, makes it a positive condition that before any one, whether he be citizen or officer, may arrest another for a felony *not* committed in his presence the felony must *in fact have been committed.* Thus the right to apprehend a suspected wrong-doer is invoked at the peril of him who seeks to exercise it. If no felony has been committed the arrest is illegal.

In one respect only does the law recognize any difference between the private citizen and the public officer paid to keep the peace,—if a felony has in fact been committed, the officer may arrest any one who he has *reasonable ground to believe* is the guilty party, while a citizen may arrest only the person who is actually guilty. Thus the citizen must guarantee not only the commission of the crime but the identity of the criminal, while the officer, so long as the law has actually been violated, may take a chance as to the identity of the perpetrator of the offence.

Now, the police invariably interpret the law to mean that they may arrest anybody who they *have reasonable cause for believing has committed a felony,*—but of course the statute gives them no such power.[12] The *felony must have been committed*; the "reasonable cause" refers only to the *identity* of the criminal. This, however, does not worry the average policeman at all.

He sees "Mr. O.C.'s" burglar coming out of the area with his bag, promptly pounces upon him and hales him off to the precinct house in spite of the burglar's protests and expletives. If the burglar prove refractory he is clubbed into submission, or if he attempt to run he may be shot in the leg. Now suppose that on reaching the police station the burglar turns out not to be a burglar at all but the family doctor? Or a late caller upon the cook? Or a gentleman who has mistaken some one's else area for his own? Of course no felony has been committed. The policeman had no right to make the arrest. Assuming that the house *had* been burglarized, the officer beyond a doubt had reasonable cause for a hastily formed opinion that the man in the area was the guilty party and had a right to make the arrest, but in law he makes this assumption at his peril. If he is wrong the victim has a good cause of action against the policeman for false arrest. But the execution following his civil judgment against the latter will probably be returned *nulla bona* by the sheriff, and he will have to pay for his own medical treatment and legal advice.

Now let us see in what position is O.C., who is not a peace officer, when he discovers the suspicious figure in the area. He may lawfully make an arrest, although he has not seen the crime committed, "when the person arrested has committed a felony." In other words, if it turns out that no crime has occurred, or that if one has in fact been perpetrated he has got hold of the wrong man, he will have to patch up the matter and very likely his own head as best he can.

We will assume O.C. to be a public-spirited citizen and that he forthwith lays hands on his burglar and reduces him to subjection. Having done so he rings the front door bell and rouses the owner of the house, who in turn discovers that the mansion *has* been burglarized. They then investigate the prisoner and find that he is a commercial traveller in an advanced state of intoxication who has rambled into that particular area by accident. O.C. has been guilty of an illegal arrest. Even should it prove that the intruder was in fact a burglar, but not the *right* burglar, the arrest would still have been without authority.[13]

To carry the illustration a little further let us assume that in each case a burglary has been committed and that the prisoner is the guilty party. What can the officer do, and what can "O.C." do, if his quarry attempt to escape?

Roughly speaking, a person lawfully engaged in arresting another for a felony or in preventing the escape of such an one lawfully arrested, may use all the force necessary for the purpose, even to taking the life of the prisoner.[14]

It is by virtue of this salutary provision of law that the unscrupulous policeman gets "square" with his enemies of the under world. When the officer clubs the "drunk" on the corner, it is on the pretext that the latter is "resisting" arrest. It is practically an impossibility to prove that it was not justifiable unless there be eye-witnesses to what has occurred, and an officer may safely be guilty of a good deal of physical brutality so long as he brings his victim to the station house under actual arrest for some alleged offence. It is only when the victim of such an assault is not arrested that the officer finds himself in an awkward situation. He must then explain why he clubbed the citizen unless the latter had committed some offence and was trying to resist arrest, and, if so, why he did not then conduct him to the station house.

There is a story told of an old veteran upon the force who was heard to remark to a companion as they left court together after the acquittal of an ex-convict on the charge of assaulting the officer:

"Begorra, Tom, 'twon't be long before I'll be afther arrestin' the cuss agin, and whin I do, *pray God that he resists arrest!*"

It is said that in some of the southwestern states the personal right to make an arrest at times resulted, practically, in the privilege of shooting cattle thieves upon sight. The foreman would send out Jack to "look for" cattle thieves. Jack would lie all day in a gully and when Sonora Slim hove in sight, perhaps on an entirely lawful errand, would "let him have it." Then he would ride leisurely over, abstract Sonora's "gun," discharge it a couple of times and throw it carelessly upon the ground. Half an hour later he would appear at the ranch.

"Sorry, Bill," he would report, "but I caught Sonora Slim driving off three of our two-year-olds. I headed him off and says,

"'Look here, Sonora, you've got some of our heifers there.'

"'Go to——!' says Sonora and pulls his gun.

"'That's all right,' says I. 'You're under arrest!'

"We swapped a few shots and I had to drop him to prevent his escape."

"All right, Jack," the foreman would reply, "we'll ride over and tell the sheriff about it."

"See here, sheriff," he would announce on their arrival, "Jack here arrested Sonora Slim stealin' our cattle, and the feller resisted arrest and Jack had to shoot him. Jack's here if you want him."

"Yes, sheriff, here I am," Jack would say.

The sheriff would rub his forehead and reply:

"No, I don't want you. Sorry you had to kill him, but I'll have to have some evidence that what you say ain't true."

It may be well to suggest that, while a thorough knowledge of our rights is always desirable, it by no means follows that it is wise to invoke them upon every occasion when we observe a technical violation of the law. Regrettable as it may seem, no police force, however large, could arrest all the violators of every law, and no system of courts could dispose of the multitude of offenders. We do the best we can and make an example of a few, hoping thus to persuade the others to be good. If every citizen undertook to exercise his right of arresting every individual whom he saw committing petty crime, the business of the community would come to a standstill and the magistrates' courts would be hopelessly congested with great hordes of prisoners, irate witnesses, and gratuitous policemen. The prisons would overflow and the magistrates would resign. Moreover, the enforcement of such a disused and unexpected technical right would lead to immense disorder and violence. The ignorant infractor of an obscure section of the Penal Code would rise in his wrath and in resisting arrest become guilty of assault in the second degree or of manslaughter. It is probably very much better that trivial offences should go unpunished than that public conveyances and thoroughfares should be made the scenes of violent altercations and obstructive volunteer police work. Having hired a certain class of persons to attend to this business for us, it is better to leave it to them when possible. We need the best police force that we can get, and this naturally depends upon the efficiency of the higher police officials who hold their offices by appointment. An active interest on the part of our citizens in the betterment of municipal conditions through the purification of politics is probably more to be desired than any general attempt to participate in the ordinary duties of "the man on the beat."

FOOTNOTES:

[12] An attempt has apparently been made by the legislature of New York State to enlarge the powers of the police during the night-time by giving them authority to arrest "on reasonable suspicion of felony." The statute (Penal Code) reads as follows: "Section 179. *May arrest at night, on reasonable suspicion of felony.*

"He may also, at night, without a warrant, arrest any person whom he has reasonable cause for believing to have committed a felony, and is justified in making the arrest, *though it afterwards appear that a felony had been committed,* but that the person arrested did not commit it."

This statute clearly stultifies itself. The writer is not aware of any judicial interpretation of its meaning up to the present time.

[13] In People v. Hochstim (36 Misc., 562, 571) it is said that "in the matter of arresting without a warrant, whether for a misdemeanor or for a felony, a private citizen and a peace officer have the very same right and power

under the law, namely: (1) Either may without a warrant arrest a person who commits any crime, whether misdemeanor or felony, in his view, and (2) either may without a warrant arrest any person who has in fact committed a felony although not in his view, but (3) neither may arrest any one without a warrant in the case of a felony unless the alleged felony has in fact been committed. If no felony has in fact been committed, then the arrest without a warrant is in every case unlawful and may be lawfully resisted. The law does not justify either an officer or a private citizen in arresting for a felony without a warrant on mere suspicion or information that a felony has been committed. If either act without a warrant on groundless suspicion or information on the question of whether a felony has in fact been committed, he acts at his peril. Nothing but the absolute fact that the felony has actually been committed will suffice to justify and protect the person making such an arrest, whether an officer or a private citizen. But if a felony has in fact been committed, the law does justify an officer, but not a private citizen, in arresting a person therefor without a warrant 'on reasonable cause for believing' (to quote the words of the statute) that such person is the one who committed it. In a word, an officer, the same as a private citizen, is not permitted to act on mere grounds of belief on the question of whether a felony has in fact been committed; nothing but the absolute fact that it has been committed will suffice; but an officer is permitted to act on reasonable cause for belief on the question of whether the person arrested is the person who committed it. All of this is plain statute law (Code of Criminal Procedure, secs. 177, 183)."

[14] A distinction exists in this respect between misdemeanors and felonies. In the case of the former it is not lawful to kill a prisoner even if his escape cannot otherwise be prevented, and although there be a warrant for his apprehension. In the case of a felony the offender's life may be taken provided there is *absolute necessity* for so doing to prevent his escape. Conraddy v. People, 5 Park 234.

CHAPTER IV

THE POLICE COURT

The procedure by which a law-breaker is convicted for his offence begins with his arrest and ends with the formal pronouncement of sentence against him after he has been declared guilty. Prior to his arrest he has been merely a criminal; after sentence (or, to be strictly technical, after the verdict against him) he becomes a convict; during the proceedings he is a "prisoner at the bar."

Whatever has been the manner of his arrest he is in most instances taken at once before the nearest magistrate in order that the latter may inquire into the charge against him and determine whether upon the evidence there is reasonable cause to believe him guilty.[15] If the arrest takes place after four o'clock in the afternoon, or no magistrate happens to be holding court, the prisoner is locked up until the following morning.[16] If he be charged with a felony he must remain in confinement until the magistrate admits him to bail, for no police official can fix or receive bail in such cases: if, however, he has been arrested for the commission of a misdemeanor only, the sergeant on duty at "the desk" must fix the bail and give him a reasonable opportunity to procure it.

If arrested while a police court is in session he is entitled to an immediate hearing, and to the services of counsel, for whom the magistrate must send, free of charge, through an officer. After the arrival of counsel or after waiting a reasonable time for his appearance, the magistrate may then proceed to examine into the case, and can only adjourn the hearing for forty-eight hours at a time for "good cause," unless at the request of the defendant himself.

The subjects of the rights of apprehended persons is too extensive to be adequately treated in a few pages. The power which the magistrate may arbitrarily exercise of holding persons merely "suspected" of crime for further examination is very great. Where a prisoner is brought in under arrest as a fugitive from another State he is frequently "held" (without any formal charge being made against him) for several days at the mere telegraphic request of some police official in a distant city. The writ of habeas corpus may secure his release, but persons unjustly arrested on "suspicion" have little redress in ordinary cases, whether they are discharged immediately or held for long periods. While no technical authority exists for such detentions (the right of arrest being strictly limited as set forth in the last chapter) they are practically necessary to prevent the escape of dangerous criminals. "Arrest on suspicion" is a euphemistic description of a technically illegal proceeding, which is universally recognized as necessary for the protection of society.[17]

The police court is the great clearing house of crime. Inasmuch as all persons arrested, whether innocent or guilty, are brought there together, they should naturally, so far as possible, be accorded the benefit of the doubt as to their guilt in the treatment which they receive. They are presumed to be innocent, and indeed many of them are, until a jury has declared to the contrary. However, the attitude generally taken towards a prisoner in a police court is that he is guilty and that it is useless for him to deny it, and he feels the discomfort and ignominy of his position far more at this state of the proceedings than he does later, when he is accorded more individual importance. As a rule he is brought into a crowded, stuffy court where a vociferous pair of shyster lawyers are shouting at each other's witnesses and the magistrate is with difficulty trying to preserve order. A great throng of complainants, defendants, witnesses, policemen, lawyers and idlers fill the room, and the prisoner instantly becomes the centre of vision for all eyes as the officer leads him up to the clerk's desk and makes his formal accusation. The altercation in front of the magistrate is suspended long enough for the latter to "commit" the defendant, who instantly finds himself locked in a narrow cell where he must remain until some friend or relation has had an opportunity to reach a lawyer, secure a bondsman, and compass his release.

What he must naturally feel most is his own insignificance. He is merely one of a huge multitude of miserable people who are all in the same box. The hours until his lawyer arrives are very dark indeed,—particularly as he probably has no idea of what is going to happen to him in the meantime. If he be a poor man accused of drunkenness or disorderly conduct he may be, and frequently is, sent to the island before he has any adequate opportunity to notify his family, who may suffer an agony of anxiety before they discover what has become of him. The punishment of the minor offender for trifling breaches of the peace is not only swift, but is characterized by a certainty unknown to that which the law attaches to crimes of a higher order.

The police court has sometimes been termed "The Poor Man's Court of Appeals." So far as this implies that five out of every seven defendants arraigned there are summarily disposed of and accept the decision or sentence of the presiding judge as final, and that the same number of aggrieved persons who seek justice there do the same, it is a correct description. No court has a more direct influence for good or evil, or for the creation of a respect or a disregard for law. For an overwhelming majority of our citizens, particularly those of foreign birth or extraction, it is the only court of justice in existence.[18]

There may be higher courts or higher laws but they know them not. To them the magistrate is an autocrat. They are avenged or punished by virtue of his will alone, and as he is just or unjust, honest or corrupt, so do they come to regard American institutions as a whole. The officers of the precinct are his minions, only a little lower in majesty, and even more terrible and implacable.

When it is considered that the magistrates in the first division of the City of New York (namely, the Boroughs of Manhattan and the Bronx) alone disposed of 138,047 cases in the year 1907, and that in 104,622 of these they exercised a summary jurisdiction over the liberty of the prisoner, with power in many instances to inflict severe punishment, it will be seen that the importance of these courts cannot be easily overrated. Including the defendants arraigned in the "Children's Court" and before certain judges of the Special Sessions sitting as magistrates, there were 149,494 persons arrested during 1907 in New York County alone.

The summary jurisdiction of the police judge embraces all offences classed as "disorderly conduct," violations of so-called "corporation ordinances" (such as peddling without a license, etc.), infractions of the "Sabbath law," the disposition of persons alleged to be insane, vagrancy, and the offence (not recognized by any statute) of being a "suspicious person." Any person whom the magistrate finds guilty of any of these charges (except the last) he may fine or imprison. It is quite true that the defendant may, if convicted, take an appeal to the Court of General Sessions or test the jurisdiction of the magistrate by a writ of habeas corpus, but the grounds of appeal are few, and the victim rarely is aware or advised of his rights in this respect. Even were he fully informed, his purse would not usually permit of further proceedings, unless taken for him from charity by some outside party or organization. The fact that there were, out of this multitude of cases, but one hundred and fifty-nine appeals taken (of which only seventy-seven were successful) speaks for itself.

Besides those charged with the offences over which the magistrate has final jurisdiction, before him come all persons arrested for crimes which are triable in higher courts.[19] These persons he must "hold for trial" (either for the court which tries misdemeanors or for the grand jury) or discharge. Should he have reasonable ground to believe that the accused has committed the crime alleged he is obliged by law to "hold" him, but if the judge sees fit to discharge the prisoner, the aggrieved person has no appeal and his only alternative is to try to persuade the district attorney in spite of the decision of the magistrate to take personal action either by laying the matter before the grand jury, or in cases of misdemeanors by filing an information in the Court of Special Sessions. He is usually unaware of this possibility and at all events it is a difficult proceeding, so that even in the case of crimes in which the magistrate has not a final jurisdiction, his action, so far as setting free the prisoner is concerned, is generally a conclusion of the matter. When a police judge unwarrantably discharges a prisoner accused of a felony the complainant rarely takes any further steps to get justice.

The enormous power wielded by what people are accustomed to call "mere police judges" is obvious when we realize that one of them may send a woman to a reformatory for *three years*, and boys to similar institutions for the same period. Their jurisdiction is, however, strictly confined to certain classes of offences; and if, for example, the crime charged be "larceny" in any form they are compelled to hold the defendant for the action of a higher court even if he admit his guilt. Thus a vagrant who is caught begging can be sent away for six months, but if the same man steal an old rug from a door-step or a gunny-sack from a wagon he must willy nilly be sent to the Tombs to await a trial in Special Sessions. Now, in any case where he is going to plead guilty he would probably vastly prefer to have his case disposed of by the magistrate and have done with it.

There would seem to be good reason for believing that coincident with other reforms in the magistrates' courts their original jurisdiction might well be extended to cases of petit larceny where the defendant admits the commission of the offence. A deal of time, money, and inconvenience to the prisoner might be saved. The present situation results in a tendency on the part of the judge to construe as many cases as he can of "petit larceny" into "disorderly conduct." Very often a trivial theft is accompanied by acts which make it perfectly proper for the magistrate to overlook the larceny for the disorder. Certainly it is better for the offender, where possible, to be classed as a "disorderly" rather than as a thief. In the latter case he may, with the stigma thus fastened upon him, go forth to a life of crime; in the first he would never be regarded as a criminal. This jurisdiction to punish any act or omission tending to create a breach of the peace offers a boundless opportunity for an arbitrary judge to arrogate to himself powers which an ignorant or helpless offender can hardly be expected successfully to defy. If illegally "committed" his only redress is a writ of habeas corpus, which probably is a phrase entirely unintelligible to him and which will cost more money to procure than he has ever had at any one time in his existence.

The magistrates might also be given jurisdiction to impose punishment in all cases of "simple assault," and in certain cases even of assaults with weapons. There is no particular reason why, if the magistrate can send an old woman away for begging, or for being drunk of a Saturday night, he cannot be trusted to punish her properly for hitting her husband over the head with a hot-water kettle. Moreover, the magistrate before whom the damaged party hales the offender is able to see with his own eyes the actual extent of the injuries which have been inflicted, whereas, by the time the case is tried before the judge of the Sessions, Dame Nature has usually restored the victim's battered physiognomy to its pristine condition of refined elegance.

No one could fail to profit by a day spent upon the police-court bench watching the judge exercise his many diverse yet not inconsistent duties, which variously include those of magistrate, lawyer, clergyman, almoner, arbitrator of domestic difficulties, and general adviser. He will begin his day's work, which, before it be concluded, will have required him to pass upon anywhere from fifty to eighty cases, by disposing of a long line of drunks and disorderlies of both sexes. Justice is plentifully tempered with mercy, however, and the unpleasant business is soon over. Next comes the disposition of unfinished business, which includes the continuance of trials not concluded on the preceding court day. These, of course, embrace every possible offence known to the law. The extraordinary number of petty burglaries is sure to attract the attention of the spectator.[20] Boy after boy is brought to the bar charged with breaking into a tobacco shop, or a small grocery, or a room used for the storage of merchandise, push-carts or fruit. At the very outside the value of the plunder cannot exceed a few dollars.

One defendant, his head heavily bandaged, is half carried to the bar by a husky officer and charged with attempting to burglarize the shed adjoining Isadore Aselovitch's junk store. He is clearly much the worse for a severe clubbing. "Izzy," the complainant, exhibiting an iron bar several feet in length and weighing upwards of twenty pounds, proudly claims to have effected the arrest of the defendant by merely giving him "a little poke mit it." In response to the interrogatories of the magistrate, Izzy explains that he and another kept their junk in a certain rear room and from time to time noticed that various odd pieces of iron seemed to be missing. They thereupon concealed themselves behind a pile of old push-cart wheels and waited for the thief. After several hours of inactivity they finally heard a rattling among the iron and discovered the defendant apparently in the very act of stealing a crowbar. Being upon his hands and knees he was unable to offer any effectual resistance to their combined onslaught and barely succeeded in escaping with his life. His cries had brought an officer who had arrested him, upon Izzy's complaint, for attempted burglary. The defendant in turn had charged the two with felonious assault, alleging that he had a right to be in the store-room, inasmuch as he was accustomed to leave junk there himself. He further tearfully asserts that he is a rival of

Izzy's in the push-cart business, which accounts for the extreme animosity of the latter.

"It vas a lie, your honor, chuge," urges Izzy. "Dot man vas a purglar. He ain't got no push-cart. Gif him ten years, chuge!"

The judge, who is wise in his generation, fines "the burglar" three dollars for disorderly conduct, to the intense disgust of Izzy.

"Tree dollars!" he cries with fine scorn. "Tree dollars for a purglar! *I* vould be a purglar *myself* for *tree dollars!*"

Very likely the next case will be that of a small merchant charged with obstructing the sidewalk with his boxes. He is let off with a warning or, if it be a second offence, with a small fine. Then a couple of boys will be brought in charged with "shooting craps," and on their heels a half-drunken driver who is accused by a little girl (having on an S.P.C.A. badge) of driving an overloaded horse. The crap boys are let go, but as the "cop" agrees with the little girl that the driver was abusing his horse the latter is "held" for Special Sessions.

While these matters are being attended to a great uproar is heard and a large crowd forces its way into the court-room. Above the clamor the wails of a young Jewess make themselves distinctly audible. The judge has just ordered the drunken driver locked up and is all ready to take up the new case. The defendant, a slick, pale-faced young Hebrew, loudly proclaims his innocence and demands an immediate hearing. No time is lost, for the parents of the girl have procured a lawyer who at once causes a charge of robbery to be entered. The girl, hysterically weeping, tells her story. Up to a certain point it is lucid enough. She had been walking along the street when a nice-looking young "feller" had accosted her and inquired the way to the nearest pawnbroker's. While they were conversing pleasantly upon this subject a second young gentleman had joined them and asked the first to purchase a pair of beautiful diamond earrings which he exhibited. This the other regretfully had explained he could not do, since he had no money (being even then on the way to the pawnbroker's). The diamonds had glistened and sparkled in the sunlight. The girl had asked to look at them and while she was doing so the owner had suggested that perhaps she might like to purchase them herself, giving as part of the consideration her own modest little baubles. This tempting offer she says she refused, on the ground that she did not know the young gentleman. She then rapidly states that the two set upon her, struck her, and that she "knew no more," until on recovering her senses she found that her own earrings had disappeared and that those of the stranger were in her ears.

"Hm!" says the magistrate; "and do you say that the defendant struck you?"

"Shure, your honor," replies the young lady.

"And that you fainted?"

"Shure, your honor."

"Did you fall?" inquires the judge sharply.

"N—n—no," admits the complainant.

"Defendant discharged," announces the magistrate.

"Get out of here, all of you," orders the officer at the bridge. "Get along, now!"

The explanation, as the reader already guesses, is simply that by a time-honored trick the girl has been persuaded by an oily-tongued trickster to exchange her own earrings for his worthless ones. This she has done quite voluntarily. She has then hurried home only to find that her newly acquired gems are paste. The family goes into a paroxysm of anger and lamentation. The nearest lawyer is consulted, who, of course, agrees to secure the return of the earrings. They pay him a five-dollar fee, the defendant is sought for and arrested, and in her eagerness to see him punished and to obtain her property the victim swears away her own case. Probably had she told the truth the defendant could have been "held" for grand larceny by false pretenses.

These proceedings may no sooner be concluded than perchance a giant negro is brought in charged with assault. A dozen officers bring him manacled to the bar, while a crowd of reporters follow and gather on each side, notebook in hand. It appears that the prisoner suddenly ran out of a saloon, drew a revolver and began an indiscriminate shooting. The "reserves" were called out and three policemen now lie dangerously wounded in the hospital. He is held for examination, pending a possible inquest by the coroner.

Meantime a lank youth from New Jersey listens vacantly while an officer accuses him of abandoning a horse which has suddenly expired while harnessed to the defendant's truck wagon. He pays a fine and vanishes. Two young Irish-Americans, mutually damaged, are arraigned for "disorderly conduct." They, too, are fined, being already substantially punished—by each other. A man accused of "Sunday selling" follows a woman who tells a pitiful tale of how her husband has abandoned her and her five little ones. Later in the day the husband is found and ordered to pay her ten dollars per week. Two retail milk dealers charged with adulteration or "keeping a cow in an unhealthy place," a band of pickpockets who have been caught "working" a horse-car, a woman accused of "soliciting," and a bartender who has allowed a "slot machine" to be left upon the premises, give place to a vociferous store-keeper who has caused the arrest of a very stout man for the larceny of four pairs of trousers. He explains loudly that the defendant (who weighs at least 325 pounds) came into the store, asked to see some "pants," and while the clerk was not looking stuffed four pairs of these articles inside his waistband and made his escape. The complainant not only identifies the defendant with absolute certainty but goes so far as to state with equal positiveness that the accused now has on the very trousers into which he stuffed the stolen property. Four pairs identical in size and material with those alleged to have been purloined are produced and marked in evidence. The fat man indignantly denies having been in the store at all. The reporters are interested.

"Gentlemen," says the judge, "I appoint you a committee to conduct the defendant to my private room for the purpose of determining whether or not you can stuff these articles of apparel inside his waistband."

The reporters, followed more slowly by the perspiring defendant, make their way to a back room, from which they presently emerge to announce through their spokesman that it would be impossible to thrust any object, much less four pairs of trousers, inside the band of the defendant's trousers.

In the interim the judge has been settling matrimonial difficulties, giving all sorts of gratuitous legal advice, acting as arbitrator over the question of the mutual use of the "landings" on the stairs in tenement houses, issuing warrants, and endeavoring to find an opportunity to continue the hearing in a complicated "false label" case. In this last several rather well-known attorneys are retained, who stand about disgustedly while the more immediate business of the court is being attended to. In most cases, however, the lawyers are hardly likely to add to the general reputation of the profession for ability.

The inordinate number of cases which the magistrates have to dispose of results oftentimes in an inconclusive method of hearing charges of misdemeanors or of felonies, which, if the defendant be held at all, must of necessity be tried in a higher court or, as the magistrates say, "go downtown." If the defendant be a man of some influence, with enough money to retain a boisterous and bully-ragging lawyer, the line of least resistance may lead the judge almost unconsciously to regard the case as having "nothing in it." If, on the other hand, the complainant be a man of independence and insistence, with perhaps a bit of a pull, it is much easier to "hold" a defendant than to assume the responsibility of "turning him out." In point of fact some magistrates are prone to shift the responsibility off their own shoulders and to "hold" anyway. Thus there can be "no kick coming" so far as they are concerned. There are also cases where, rather than take the time for a careful examination of the case, the magistrate will "hold," when, if he had really examined into it with the necessary care, he would find that there was no *reasonable* ground for his action. Now the grand jury is apt to find an indictment almost as a matter of course, and the defendant must then be placed on trial before a petit jury. In large measure this is the reason why the calendars of the criminal courts are crowded with cases which should never have gone beyond the police court, and why prisoners charged with homicide often lie for months in the Tombs before the petty business of the General Sessions can be cleaned up sufficiently to allow time for their trial. In this way much of the work which should be done by the police judge is cast upon the already over-burdened petit jury. The evil, however, does not stop there. When a petit jury finds that a majority of the cases brought before it have little or no merit it frequently gets the idea that all criminal business is of the same character and that it is empanelled for the purpose of a general jail delivery. After a jury has "turned out" twenty men in succession it can hardly be blamed for thinking that the twenty-first, who may be a real sinner, ought likewise to be sent home with the others to join his family. Respect for law cannot be maintained unless each part of the machine of justice does its full duty and assumes its own burdens and responsibilities.

It goes without saying that no official comes into closer contact with the police than the magistrate. He gets to know them collectively and individually as no other person can. In determining what should be done in any given case he takes largely into consideration the personal equation of the officer making the arrest. He is able to detect exaggerated or manufactured evidence, which might easily pass as truth and perhaps convince a jury in a higher court. Hence one of the arguments for giving him a wider original jurisdiction. Petit juries are ordinarily disinclined to convict and send a man to State's prison in what seems to them trivial cases. If the magistrate had a wider scope in the disposal of such cases one of the principal reasons for our lack of respect for law (the sentimental and arbitrary action of juries) would be largely done away with.

The magistrate, if he be the right kind of a man, can do more real good, right more real wrongs, and exert a more wholesome and salutary influence upon the working people of large cities than any benevolent or charitable association. He can do much to break up the alliance of the police with crime and to prevent arbitrary acts of violence and lawlessness upon their part committed either to compel the payment of blackmail or cover derelictions of duty.

The police judge also soon learns the character of the practitioners who appear so constantly before him. Many a case which on its face seems founded on justice may be shown by a little questioning on the part of the magistrate to be nothing but an attempt to "hold up" or injure the defendant. The quasi-criminal classes know well the power of the criminal law and frequently invite it to secure private vengeance. When two rogues fall out there is often a race to see who can get to the police court first. In other cases the dense ignorance of complainant or defendant renders justice almost impossible. The shyster plays upon this to his profit. There is a story told of a practitioner with a large Italian following who was accustomed to display prominently upon a table in his office a small Testament and a huge Webster's Dictionary. After his clients had stated their case he would turn to them and ask:

"Do you wish the law from the big book or the little book?"

The clients would inquire the relative cost.

"The law from the little book is ten dollars—the law from the big book is twenty-five dollars."

The clients would consult together and on the assumption that the bigger the book the better the law, would almost invariably pay their twenty-five dollars and procure the best advice which Noah Webster could give.

The fact that most police magistrates are appointed for purely political reasons is much to be deprecated. The days of bribery are over, but occasionally the public has some excuse for believing that the desire to do "a favor" for a political friend may have influenced the action of one of them. This would have less color were they usually appointed for some other and better reason than mere party fealty. Ordinarily the appointment goes to some faithful worker, who has won distinction in ward politics. Like enough he may make an excellent judge. At any rate he has a direct personal knowledge of the people with whom he is called to deal. He has equally first-hand information of local conditions and the *personnel* of the police attached to the neighboring precincts. His judgment is apt to have a practical wisdom that a mere student of law could never achieve. He knows a crooked officer, a crooked lawyer, and a crooked complainant when he sees one. Whatever the verbal testimony happens to be he may very well "know different." He is, as the slang phrase accurately puts it, "wise to his job." And when all is said and done the "influence" exerted upon him will probably be only a request to "Do the best you can for So and So,—he's a friend of mine," which will not affect his action in the least. A college-bred lawyer with no actual knowledge of existing conditions might have the wool pulled over his eyes at every turn, and, while theoretically enforcing the law as it is printed on the statute books, fail utterly to achieve the rough-and-ready justice which the situation demands and which his less educated brethren can dispense by virtue of instinct acquired from long experience. It must be admitted, however, that the system of political appointments is just as bad, if not worse, when applied to police magistracies as when exercised in higher places. The appointees may or may not turn out successfully, and in New York we have had some extraordinary surprises in both directions.

Did space permit a judicious selection of the historic rulings of traditional magistrates would make entertaining reading. One of the most famous was that of a certain learned member of this bench who is said to have discharged a defendant accused of killing a robin in Central Park in the following words:

"You are charged with breaking a park ordinance forbidding the public to kill the robins. Of course you ought *not* to kill the robins for they are harmless birds, but I have looked this thing up a little, and I find that from time immemorial it has been held that there can be no right of property in wild beasts. Now, a robin is clearly *ferræ naturæ*—of a wild nature—and so the city has no property in it. The ordinance is therefore unconstitutional, and I am constrained to discharge you. You may go."

Nowhere than on the magistrate's bench is better illustrated the proverb that a little learning is a dangerous thing, but only a little learning, even such as classifies an innocent park robin as a wild beast, is preferable to an openly expressed intention of enforcing only those laws which appeal to the judge's individual sense of propriety. The writer recalls endeavoring some six years ago to induce a certain magistrate to hold a defendant for the grand jury for a certain statutory offence. The learned magistrate positively refused to do so on the ground that there was "no *sense* in the law."

"But it *is the law*!" returned the writer.

"Well, I don't care if it is," replied the judge tartly. "I didn't make it. It's no law of mine, and I don't propose to follow it. Go and get the grand jury to indict if you can, but I won't hold this man for doing what I might want to do myself some day."[21]

Taken as a body our magistrates, with a few obvious exceptions, are men of wide experience and practical common sense, who handle the enormous stream of business which comes before them with efficiency and dispatch. A forbidding exterior and, occasionally, a diction which might startle a Friday evening prayer meeting may co-exist with a fair mind, a kind heart, and an honest determination to see that justice is done. While the rights of the defendant are fully protected it is probable that actual justice is more nearly accomplished in these than in higher courts, where "reasonable doubt," the presumption of innocence, and kindred privileges, as interpreted by a sympathetic jury, intervene between the rights of the community and those of the prisoner at the bar.

FOOTNOTES:

[15] Of course if he has been indicted by the grand jury in the first instance, he is arrested on a "bench warrant" issued by a judge of the General Sessions and placed in confinement without any preliminary examination.

[16] This condition has been much improved in New York City by the institution of the "Night" Court in which one magistrate is always on duty. All minor offenders are at once arraigned before him, no matter what the hour, and thus may be disposed of without undue confinement.

[17] "Many persons are arrested under suspicious circumstances, such as well-known criminals mysteriously loitering about the streets at night, or frequenting crowded places, or persons having property in their possession for which they can give no good account, nor of themselves. Frequently such an arrest is the first step in the detection of some crime in which (after investigation), if the proper complainant is found, a formal complaint is taken, and the prisoner is held for trial. In many instances such an arrest prevents the commission of crime."

Comparison with Previous Years.

Number Arraigned and
Discharged.

YEAR.	Males.	Females.	Total.
1896	2335	120	2455
1897	1756	129	1885
1898	1628	154	1782
1899	2033	301	2334
1900	2023	293	2316
1901	2066	197	2263
1902	2337	200	2537
1903	2634	115	2749
1904	3734	224	3958

1905	3551	231	3782
1906	5483	180	5663
1907	2656	118	2774

[18] The nativity of the persons held for trial in 1907 or summarily tried and convicted in magistrates' courts was:

United States	30,261
Ireland	8,061
Germany	4,219
England	1,044
Scotland	473
France	869
Italy	8,243
Russia	9,254
Greece	3,039
Other countries	5,790
	———
Total	71,253

[19] In 1905 the number of persons so held in New York County by the magistrates of the first division, was 36,340.

[20] During 1907 there were arrested 1,669 persons on charges of burglary, of whom 1,055 were held for trial.

[21] See latter half of Subdivision 5, Section 278 New York Penal Code.

CHAPTER V

THE TRIAL OF MISDEMEANORS

One of the most efficient, effective, and important criminal courts in the civilized world is that established for the trial of misdemeanors in New York County. Three judges, each having an equal voice, act as arbiters of both law and fact. Originally this bench was filled by three regular police magistrates sitting in rotation, and in many cases the same judge before whom the prisoner had been arraigned in the first instance assisted in determining the final question of his guilt or innocence. But the old Court of Special Sessions acquired a very unsavory reputation for many reasons, the chief among them being its alleged susceptibility to political influence and the looseness with which its funds were handled, and it was finally legislated out of existence in 1895. Then a new court was created composed of three justices who, while they had the powers of police magistrates, did not sit in magistrates' courts, but devoted their entire time to the trial of misdemeanors. In the last eight years this court disposed of 65,579 cases, in which 40,894 persons were convicted of crime, either by trial or by plea of guilty. During the year 1907 alone 13,140 cases were disposed of, in which there were 7,960 convictions. The judges in this huge mill of justice rarely make mistakes, and few appeals are ever taken from their decisions. They have become, by virtue of long experience, experts in fact, and the training thus received has qualified several of them for higher office.[22]

As the reader is already aware, a defendant charged in a magistrate's court with the commission of a misdemeanor, say that of petit larceny, is given an immediate hearing, and, if there be reasonable ground to believe him guilty, is held for trial in the Special Sessions. The information or affidavit, to which the complaining witness has sworn and which contains a more or less succinct account of the facts alleged against the prisoner, is thereupon forwarded to the clerk of the court and in due course the defendant appears, if he be on bail, or is brought from prison, if he be in confinement, to "plead." This information, which is the basis of the proceedings against him and which is practically the only record in the case, is commonly called the "complaint" and corresponds with the indictment found by the grand jury where the defendant is charged with the commission of a felony.

After the prisoner has entered his plea, if he be in prison, he is given a trial almost immediately; if not, his case will probably come up within a week or two. The offences over which these three judges have jurisdiction are as many and as diversified as human ingenuity and the demands of modern civilized life, qualified by ineffective legislation, have combined to make them.

As might be expected, petty larcenies and assaults furnish together more than thirty per cent of the cases tried. The following table will show the more numerous and important offences for which defendants were held in 1907 for the Special Sessions and their relative proportions:

Petit larceny	2,890
Assault, third degree	2,097
Maintaining a disorderly house	674
Carry concealed pistol	988
Cruelty to animals	887
Failure to provide for minor	235
Possessing obscene prints	124
Malicious mischief	111
Indecent exposure	84
Unlawful entry	93
Adultery	11
Adulterated milk	252
Impure food	80
Possessing burglars' implements	35
Offence against trade-marks (364 P.C.)	6
Violation Liquor Tax Law	2,109
Violation Motor Vehicle Law	2,709

Violation Sanitary Code	321
Violation Labor Law	176
Violation Medical Law	48
Violation Dental Law	16
Miscellaneous	1,122
	———
Total	15,068

A spectator may in the course of a morning hear thirty or forty cases actually tried in which the charges cover almost every conceivable kind of sin, wrong, or prohibition. One prisoner is being prosecuted for assaulting a non-union workman, another for maintaining a public nuisance, another for a violation of the Liquor Tax Law, another for practising medicine without a license; a dozen cases will be rapidly disposed of wherein the defendants are charged with shoplifting or "illegal entry" (a charge frequently lodged against a suspected burglar who has made an entry without a "break" and has been caught before he has accomplished his purpose); others still will be tried for carrying concealed weapons, publishing or possessing indecent literature, violating trade-mark laws, breaking speed ordinances, or "malicious mischief"; while, if the student of institutions be patient, he may be rewarded by the exciting spectacle of one who is defending himself against the charge of selling skimmed milk, holding a mock auction, driving a spavined horse, writing a threatening letter, making a fraudulent assignment, pawning borrowed property, using a false weight, opening another's letter, keeping a cow in an unhealthy place, running a cock-fight, misrepresenting the circulation of a newspaper, divulging the contents of a telegram, impersonating a policeman, adulterating food; or, provided he be exceptionally fortunate, may hear the trial of a celebrated actress for her impersonation of "Sappho," or of a manager for producing "Mrs. Warren's Profession."

He will see every conceivable type of man, woman, and child, either as defendant or witness, and he may also study every variety of human failing or weakness. No mock defence or prepared lie can deceive these argus-eyed judges; short shrift is made of the guilty, while the "reasonable doubt" is recognized the instant it puts in the most furtive appearance. In fact defendants are often found guilty or acquitted almost before they are aware they are on trial,—and this with no detriment to them or to their cause.

The advocates of the abandonment of the jury system point to this court as their strongest argument. No time is lost in the selection of a jury,—a matter often of hours in the General Sessions in cases of no greater importance. There is no opening address on the part of the district attorney or counsel for the defendant,—the written statement or information sworn to by the complainant being entirely sufficient for the court. Cross-examination is cut down to its essentials and tests of "credibility" are almost unnecessary. At the conclusion of the case there are no harangues from either side, and the judges almost immediately announce their decision and generally impose sentence on the spot.

Of course in nine cases out of ten the evidence is conclusive and the merest glance at the complainant and his or her witnesses is enough to satisfy the onlooker that their claim is honest and the charge substantial. In such cases the trials proceed with lightning-like celerity. The owner of the stolen property is sworn while the defendant and his lawyer are pushing their way through the crowd to the bar.

"Mr. Blickendecker, are you a grocer, fifty-five years of age, residing at 1000-A-rear, First Avenue, and having a store at 666½ Catharine Street?" rapidly articulates the deputy assistant district attorney.

"Ya; I vas," answers Blickendecker heavily, trying helplessly to catch up.

"Did you, about 4:49 P.M., on Tuesday, the 17th of April, observe the defendant near your place of business?"

"Ya; I vas—I mean, ya, I did."

"What did you see him do?"

Blickendecker wipes his forehead and turns towards the court:

"Your honors, gentlemens, I see dot feller dere——"

"The defendant?" interrupts the presiding judge, patiently.

"Ya—the defender, I see dot defender mit a leetle vagon on two wheels, py mein store mit anoder feller, unt dey catch up ein crate of eggs unt put him in de vagon unt skip mit him, unt I hollers 'Tief!' unt runs, unt de officer——"

"That's enough. Any cross-examination? No? Call the officer."

The officer is sworn.

"Are you a member of the Municipal Police force of the city and county of New York, attached to the —— Precinct, and were you so attached on the 17th of April last, and did you see the defendant on that day near the premises 666½ Catharine Street?"

"Shure I seen him. Him and another feller. They were makin' off wid old 'Delicatessen's' eggs. I catched this young feller——"

"That's enough. Any cross-examination? No? Leave the stand."

"The People rest," announces the assistant.

"Take the stand," directs the lawyer, and his client shambles into the chair.

"Did you steal Mr. Blickendecker's eggs?"

"No, your honor; Cully Fagan asked me to go round and help him deliver some eggs. He said he'd gimme a drink. So I went along wid him. All of a sudden out comes this old guy and yells 'thief.' I gets scared and runs. I didn't mean no harm."

"That is our case," says the lawyer.

"No cross-examination," says the assistant.

The judges consult for a moment.

"We find the defendant guilty," announces the presiding judge, dipping his pen into the ink.

"Now, young man, have you ever been convicted?"

"No, your honor."

"I advise you not to steal any more eggs. One month in the penitentiary. Next case!"

Now here is a defendant given a perfectly fair, if not a very full, trial in less than three minutes. Of course it is in such a case practically a mere formality. Two witnesses who have had no previous acquaintance with the prisoner, whose eyesight is perfect, and who have no motive to swear falsely, identify him as caught *in flagrante delicto*. The defendant has merely put in his defence "on the chance." His sentence would be about the same in either case. The only disadvantage of so active a court is the fact that the multitude of the defendants render it almost impossible to make any very exhaustive study of the majority of them before sentence. However, as the sentences are all light, the defendant always gets the benefit of the doubt, and the court resolves all doubts in his favor.

Sometimes in such a case a criminal conspiracy between the complainant and the officer is disclosed to "do" a mischievous, but not criminal, youth who has fallen into their disfavor. Then the witnesses are subjected to such a fire of questions that they wilt and wither in the blast, the defendant is acquitted and the prosecution's witnesses sometimes held for the action of the grand jury on a charge of perjury. Many a *cause célèbre* has originated in the Special Sessions through the perspicacity of some member of that bench during a petty trial, and defendants there convicted often divulge in their confessions evidence which for a time sets the newspaper world by the ears. This is especially true of cases where some civil officer is accused of taking a bribe to influence his action or to make an appointment. He may be convicted, confess, and for a day or two the papers are full of the unearthing of a far-reaching conspiracy to debauch the city government, barter offices at wholesale, and deliver the city to a coterie of criminals. The next step in the proceeding is the unfortunate discovery that the defendant's confession, since it cannot be corroborated, is entirely worthless. Yet, as he has apparently done all he could to atone for his offence, he receives a mitigated sentence, while the uproar occasioned by his sensational disclosures subsides as suddenly as it began.

The bane of the Court of Special Sessions in New York County and very likely the bane of all similar courts, are the so-called "Liquor Tax cases." As one of the officers of this court recently said: "In this class of cases the court knows that it is being 'flim-flammed,' and, in addition, that it is helpless. We convict in about sixty per cent of the cases, but the judges know perfectly well that a considerable number of those convicted are men who, while not honest enough not to violate the law, are too honest to pay corruption money."

The possibilities for blackmail and the arbitrary and unequal way in which the law is enforced in different parts of the city (one section being allowed to be "wide open" while an adjacent district is "dry") render the judges loath to convict even in "straight" cases. When Liquor Tax cases are transferred, by order of the judge presiding in Part I, for trial in the General Sessions, the juries before which they are prosecuted will not convict at all.[23]

In the same way the court looks with grave suspicion on most cases where a defendant is arraigned charged with "assault" on an officer. They expect to see arraigned at the bar (and are usually not disappointed) a small man covered with bandages, while a burly officer without a scratch upon his rosy countenance takes the stand and swears that the defendant assaulted him. The policeman always has plenty of corroboration—the defendant none at all. The chances are that the relative sizes of the two men are such that if the officer coughed the defendant would drop dead. The proper charge in such a case would be, not attempted assault on an officer, but *attempted suicide*. The truth of the matter probably is that the small man, having done or said something to irritate the officer, has been pounded to a pulp and then ignominiously haled away to the station house, while his terrified companions, knowing full well that if they interfered theirs would be a similar fate, have retired to their homes privately to execrate a state of civilization where humble citizens can be subjected to such persecution.

Practically the Special Sessions is the final court of disposition for most misdemeanors. Except in automobile, theatrical, health, copyright, and trade-mark cases and a few others, a majority of the defendants do not have enough money even to hire a lawyer, to say nothing of taking an appeal. They are disposed of then and there just as in certain cases they are disposed of in the magistrates' courts. For them a sentence once imposed is final.

Occasionally the Special Sessions is the scene of a great trial, as celebrated as those fought out in the "Parts" upstairs or in the criminal trial term of the Supreme Court across the hall. A prominent druggist may have been accused of refilling bottles with spurious or diluted contents. He is being prosecuted by the owners of the trade-mark or label. They retain distinguished counsel to prepare the case for the prosecution. The accused engages equally able lawyers to defend him. The crime is highly technical and the evidence almost entirely a matter of chemical analysis and expert opinion. The battle goes on for weeks or even months. A jury would have become hopelessly confused and the issue successfully obscured, but the three judges are expert jurymen, and in due course, if he be guilty, the defendant is inevitably convicted. Such a trial may cost the parties tens of thousands of dollars for expert testimony alone, while the sentence of the defendant will very likely be not more than a two-hundred-and-fifty-dollar fine. Even so, the integrity of the trade-mark has been sustained and the swindler stamped as a criminal.

Fifty per cent or more of the work of the Special Sessions is practically amplified police-court business, but it is accomplished with an exactitude and efficiency that makes much of that done in the magistrates' courts appear crude indeed. The lesson of this particular court is that police business can be done speedily, effectively, and justly, provided the right men are selected to do it.

Fully seventy-five per cent of the criminals begin with petty infractions of the law. A driver for an iceman may "swipe" his comrade's horse blanket. If he be convicted and sent to the penitentiary he may learn to commit crimes of which he had never dreamed in his driver days, when his highest ambition was to get a ticket to a "chowder" or to a "grand ball." His next appearance may be in the General Sessions charged with burglary, and his last in the Supreme Court under indictment for murder. If, on the other hand, having been found guilty, he be merely reprimanded and paroled under a suspended sentence, he will in all likelihood never appear in court as a defendant again. Hence an opportunity, greater even than that of the police justice, for the exercise of a wise and humane discretion.

The multitude of prisoners who are unable to employ counsel have created a bevy of lawyers, abundantly able to look out for the interests of petty offenders, who stand or sit near the bar and are assigned by the court to the various defendants. A whispered fifteen seconds' conversation with their unfortunate client and they are enabled to take charge of the case. Long experience has made them almost as expert in estimating human nature as the judges themselves, and they are familiar with every trick of the trade which may raise a "reasonable doubt." The leaders among them have skilful "runners" who haunt the police courts and the corridors of the building, heralding the virtues and successes of their masters, handing cards to prospective clients, and currying business in every conceivable manner. Observing a forlorn person, who timidly responds when his case is called, the runner instantly offers him the services of the "biggest" lawyer in the court for a five-, three-, or two-dollar retainer. If the client escapes conviction he is supposed to pay twenty-five dollars more and is dunned until he does. This may seem petty business and small pickings, but when one considers that thirteen thousand odd cases are disposed of each year, one sees that at even the modest fee of ten dollars per case there is over a hundred thousand dollars a year in the Special Sessions waiting for somebody.

The best of these lawyers earn as much as five thousand dollars per year, including their outside and police-court business. The runner usually gets nearly as much. Sometimes there will be a one-hundred-dollar, a two-hundred-and-fifty-dollar, or even a five-hundred-dollar fee. In reality there is more money to be made in the police court than in the Special Sessions, for it is when the offender has just been caught and is in his first spasm of terror that he is most ready to "give up." Police-court fees are sometimes very high.

The most notable figure of this bar was Tom Cherry, otherwise known as "The Attorney-General of the Special Sessions." When sober he was a most capable, rough-and-ready, catch-as-catch-can, police-court lawyer. His fame extended to every magistrate's court, and his business was so constant that he never sat down, but stood at the bar from the opening of court to its adjournment, defending almost every prisoner who had money to pay a fee, and being assigned to practically all those who had not. His success was his undoing. Without any knowledge of law, although he presumably had passed the Bar examinations (Heaven knows how!), his judgment of character, his ready wit, and his quick tongue made him no unworthy antagonist for a well-trained youngster. But Cherry never took an unfair advantage, and his statement as to his client's past, and sometimes as to his innocence, was received without question by the court. It was a boon to a new assistant to gain Cherry's confidence; and it was a reproach to many that they did not do so.

Cherry finally succumbed to his closest friend and worst enemy—drink. His periodic absences became more and more frequent, and finally the word was sadly whispered through the building that Cherry had "passed." His memory is still green and his smiling face will never be forgotten by those who knew him. A rival attorney almost immediately succeeded to his practice and his particular place beside the bar, but the Court of Special Sessions is not the same.

The practices of the shysters are the curse of the lower courts, and their enormities are such that a special cycle in Hades should be reserved for their particular retribution. Preying upon ignorance and vice, they become hardened to every appeal of human sympathy and often deserve punishment a thousand times more heavy than the miserable wretches whom they make a pretence of defending. They pervert justice and prostitute a sacred calling, extorting from their clients the uttermost farthing by fear and false pretence. To show that this charge is not ill-founded, the reader may take as an example the practice of the shyster in dealing with those unfortunate women who are the common prey of the corrupt plain-clothes man and his conscienceless ally—the police-court lawyer.

Let us suppose that a certain section of the town is, as the saying goes, "wide open," and the police are regularly collecting protection money according to the approved method of "the system." The houses which pay up are left undisturbed—and all do pay up. So does the little street walker who plies her trade in the open. Some citizen or newspaper makes a complaint that the police are not doing their duty. There is a bare chance that political capital will be made of it and word is sent to the captain of the precinct to "get busy." He sends for the plain-clothes man, and tells him "there are not arrests enough." The officer answers that "everything is quiet." "Get busy," says the captain. A scapegoat is necessary and so the officer goes out and, leaving the bawdy-houses untroubled, tracks some miserable creature to her lonely room and there arrests her under the pretence that she is violating the "Tenement House Law." Now the worst that would happen to such an unfortunate would be, having "waived examination" before the magistrate, and pleaded guilty in Special Sessions, to be fined twenty-five or fifty dollars. The girl usually does not know this. When she is brought in under arrest the keeper "tips off" the runner for some lawyer, who first frightens her into believing that a long term of imprisonment confronts her, and then introduces his master. The latter in turn offers to get her out on bail, meantime determining by an expert cross-examination, at which he is a past master, exactly how much money she has in the world. He then proceeds to acquire this by every means at his command. An actual case will illustrate what follows.

A young girl who had fallen from virtue, but who had never been arrested before, was brought into the Jefferson Market prison. She had saved five hundred dollars with which she intended the following week to return to her native town in New Hampshire and start life anew. The keeper led her to believe that she would be imprisoned in the penitentiary for nearly a year unless she could "beat the case." One of these buzzards learned of her distress and offered to procure bail for her for the sum of fifty dollars. A straw bondsman was produced, and she paid him the money and was liberated. Meanwhile the lawyer had learned of the existence of her five hundred dollars. By terrifying her with all sorts of stories as to what would possibly happen to her, he succeeded in inducing her to pay him three hundred as a retainer to appear for her at the hearing in the magistrate's court. He had guaranteed to get her off then and there, but when her case was called he happened to be engaged in reading a newspaper and, looking up from where he was sitting, merely remarked, "Waives examination, your honor." The girl had only one hundred and fifty dollars left, and as yet had had no defence, but the shyster now demanded and received one hundred dollars more for representing her in the Special Sessions. She now had but fifty dollars. Immediately after the hearing in the police court the bondsman "surrendered" her and she was locked up in the Tombs pending her trial, for she had not money enough to secure another bail bond. Here she languished three or four days. When at last her case appeared upon the calendar the shyster did not even take the trouble to come to court himself, but telephoned to another buzzard that she still had fifty dollars, telling him to "take her on." Abandoned by her counsel, alone and in prison, she gave up the last cent she had, hoping thus still to escape the dreadful fate predicted for her. When she was called to the bar the second lawyer informed her she had no defence and the best thing she could do was to plead guilty. This she did and was fined twenty-five dollars, but, having now no money, was compelled to serve out her time, a day for each dollar, in the City Prison, at the end of which time she was cast penniless upon the streets.

Many an originally honest young fellow who, in a sincere attempt to build up a small practice, has haunted the magistrate's court and secured petty police business has been gradually drawn into the vortex of crime until he is even more tainted than those whom he defends. The Legal Aid Society, which, so far as the writer is aware, is the only bona fide charitable organization existing in New York for the purpose of assisting impoverished persons to secure legal counsel, does not undertake any criminal business. No greater service could be rendered to the community than by some society organized to protect helpless defendants who have fallen victims to the vultures who prey upon the prison pens. At the present time the official prosecutor himself is the only person to whom one charged with a criminal offence can turn with any hope of relief from his own lawyer, and if the number of cases were known where the prosecutor has befriended the prosecuted the eyes of jurors and of the public would be opened to the real spirit which animates a fair-minded district attorney.

A favorite trick of shysters if they have an imprisoned client who still refuses to "give up," is to plead "not guilty and not ready" and thus have the case adjourned until they squeeze their victim dry. A defendant who has any money is never permitted to go to trial or even to plead guilty before his money is entirely exhausted.

This is not romance, it is practice. The men who do these things can be seen any day in every police court in New York—heartless, cynical, merciless. Lying and deceit are their stock in trade, corruption their daily food. Within three months one of these gentry not only compelled an eighteen-year-old girl to give him a fine Etruscan ring which she had inherited, and which he pawned for five dollars, but stripped her of a new silk petticoat which he carried away in a newspaper as a fee. This woman served ten days because she could not pay her fine. Another woman who had *stolen an umbrella* gave a shyster her watch. He pawned it and then abandoned her, when she came up for trial. Each of these men has a special line of clients which he serves, either because he is supposed to be particularly expert in such cases or because he is regularly retained by the "trust" which they compose. Thus the East Side pickpockets have one attorney, the "green-goods" men another, the opium sellers a third, the abortionists a fourth, while every "short changing," "thimble rigging," or "flim-flam" case sees the same lawyer for the defence.

It is a fact of considerable significance that most retailers charged with selling adulterated milk are defended by the same lawyers. The large milk companies apparently invite the trade of the small dealer by offering him cheap milk, and a guarantee that if he is caught selling their product they will not only defend him but, if he be found guilty, will pay his fine. Who does the adulterating? The company or the retailer? It is almost impossible to say. Nevertheless, if lack of evidence prevents proceedings against the companies themselves, the next best thing is to punish the dealers who act as their agents, under the guise of doing an independent business. If prison sentences were invariably inflicted in such cases the dealers would soon find their miserable business as unhealthy as do the consumers who buy from them.

Some very disreputable, but, nevertheless, highly amusing tricks are invoked by wily practitioners in the Special Sessions to secure the release of their clients. One of the most adroit is to secure adjournments from day to day on various pretexts until the patience of the complaining witness is nearly exhausted. When the case is at last about to be called for trial the lawyer tells his runner to go into the corridor outside the court-room and send in word that some one desires to see the complainant. The complainant goes out to see what is wanted. In the meantime the case is moved for trial, and when his name is called he naturally fails to respond. The shyster, in a most aggrieved tone, then informs the court that the defendant "is a hard-working man who has already been dragged down to court four or five times," on each occasion being compelled to lose an entire day's pay; that he is the only support of an invalid wife, an aged mother, six children, and an imbecile brother; that the defence is and always has been ready to proceed with the case; that simply in the interests of justice he requests that the defendant be discharged on his own recognizance or acquitted. In many cases this motion is granted and the complainant hurries back into the court-room just in time to meet the defendant making a triumphal exit.

The tears and laughter of the police courts are the tears and laughter of the Sessions. The *Miserables* of Hugo are the miserables of to-day. Jean Valjean, Fantine, and Cosette haunt the corridors of our courts. As well try to paint the sufferings and experiences of mankind in a single picture as the ten thousand yearly tragedies of the Special Sessions in a single chapter.

FOOTNOTES:

[22] MISDEMEANORS DISPOSED OF DURING THE YEAR 1907.

Convicted	1,853
Acquitted	1,045
Plead Guilty	6,107
Discharged	502
Demurrers allowed	1
Forfeited	457
Actions dismissed	3,175

Total   13,140

CHAPTER VI

THE GRAND JURY

The constitutions and laws of most of the States of the Union provide that no person shall be tried for a felony unless he shall first have been indicted for his offence by a grand jury. The defendant may have been caught in the very act, have freely acknowledged his guilt to the officer who arrested him, have admitted it before the magistrate, and have signed a full and complete confession of his crime in every detail, yet he cannot be placed on trial or his plea of guilty received until a body of twenty-three intelligent, but exceedingly busy, gentlemen, sitting together in a secluded chamber, have solemnly deliberated upon the case. If they agree with the prisoner in his contention that he is guilty they thereupon file a diffuse and perplexing document to that effect, which they have not read, and probably would not understand if they had. The proceeding has cost the county some additional expense and the defendant a day or two longer in jail, and he has still to be tried before a petit jury, where the evidence must be presented again at the greatest length, and where the grand jury's action cannot be considered in any way as affecting the issue. If, on the other hand, the prisoner contends that he is innocent, and yet the magistrate who has heard the case thinks otherwise, the same twenty-three gentlemen, hearing, as a general rule, only the evidence in his *dis*favor, will almost inevitably return a true bill against him, and he will be put to his trial. Of all the features of modern criminal procedure, bar only the office of coroner, the grand jury, or "The Grand Inquest," as it is called, is the most archaic. While without any doubt in thinly populated districts it may still be of value, in crowded cities like New York, where the volume of criminal business is overwhelming, it has in large measure ceased to be either effective or desirable so far as the ordinary run of criminal cases is concerned.

Some States manage to dispense entirely with the services of the grand jury. The prosecutor receives the complaint against the accused directly from the committing magistrate, files an information and puts the prisoner on trial. Truly this would seem both cheap and expeditious.

Among the dusty archives of the Court of General Sessions lie a pile of parchment-bound volumes which contain the earliest minutes of criminal proceedings in the county. The first page of the most ancient of these presents an account of the empanelling of the first grand jury of which any record now remains in New York. It reads as follows:

PROVINCE OF NEW YORK. Att the General Quarter Sessions of our Lord the King held att the Citty Hall in the Citty of New-York for Our Sayd Lord the King, and the body of the sayd Citty and County of New-York, that is to say on Tuesday the 8th day of February, in the Six and thirtieth year of the Reigne of our Sovereigne Lord Charles the Second of England, Scottland, France and Ireland, King, Defender of the faith, & before Cornelis Steenyck, Esqr, May^r of the sayd Citty, and James Graham, Recorder, Nicholas Bayard, John Inians, Wm Pinho ... Guyl. Ver Plank, Jno Robinson and William Cox, Esq^{rs}, Aldermen and Justices of the Peace of the sayd Citty and County, Commisionated by Authority und^r his Royal Highness James Duke of York and Albany Lord Propriet^r of the Province afores^d.

The Grand Jury "which consisted of Nineteen [?],[24] was Called and Sworne According to An Oath Agreed On by the Court, and was as followeth, viz^{tt}.:

"You Shall diligently Enquire and true Presentm^t make of all Such things and matt^{rs} as shall be giuen you in Charge Or shall Come to your knowledge this Present Servise. The Kings, His Royal Highness Lord Propriet^r and this City Councell Yo^r fallows and you^r owne you shall well and Truely keep Secreet. You shall present nothing for Malace or Euill will that you Bare to Any Person, Neither shall you Leaue anything unpresented for Loue, favour, affection Reward Or Any hopes thereof, but in all things that shall Concerne this Present Servise you Shall Present the truth the whole truth and nothing but the truth, According to yor best skill and knowledge—Soe help you God."

M^r. Francis Rumbout was Apoynted foreman.

The Recorder ... read to them the^r Charge wh^{ch} was Deliuered in Writeing.

Then follows the quaint record of the first presentment or bill of indictment:

John Robinson,	} For Our Lord the Kings sworne to
Wm Cox,	} declare to the grand jury w^t they
Richard Elliott,	} know about the Burgulary Henry
Darby Bryan.	} Thomassen is Charged with.

The Bill Against him was Committed to the Grand Jury wth the Exam^ncon of the witnesses, and the Court adjourned till four in the afternoone.

In the Afternoone the Court being opened the Indictm^t ag^st Henry Thomassen was returned by the Grand Jury Billa vera.

Henry Thomassen being Called for the Sherriff returnes that he has Broak Prison and made his Escape, and Desires tyme till the next Sessions to Persue him.

Ordered That the Sherriff doe make Persuits after the prison^r to haue him att the next session to abide his Tryall. The Grand Jury was dismissed from further Attendance till ye next sessions and ye court dissolved.

It is interesting to observe that on the 13th day of the November following, in the first year of "the Reigne of our Sovereignee Lord James the Second of England, Scotland, France, and Ireland," etc., the "sherriff" having apparently made good "persuits" of Thomassen and effected his capture, the latter was brought to the bar and duly charged:

"For that he not haveing the feare of God before his eyes, but being Lead by the instigation of the divell ... by force and armes the Cellar belonging to and being parte of the dwelling house of William Cox of the Citty of New-Yorke merchant in the night Season, To Witt, between or about the houres of tenn or Eleven of the Clock ... feloniously and burgularly did breake and into the same did Enter with an intent to steale and spoile the goods and Chattles of the said William Cox contrary to the peace of our said sovereigne Lord the King his Crowne and dignity."

Having pleaded not guilty and put himself upon the county a jury was empanelled who swore:

> "That the said Henry Thomassen is guilty of the feleony and burgularly aforesaid in the said inditement above specifyed in manner and forme as above against him is supposed, Therefore it is considered by the Court, that the aforesaid Henry Thomassen be branded on the forehead with the Letter B, and be whipped on the bare back eleven Stripes on the fourteenth day of November instant in the morning by Eleven of the Clock, before the City Hall and pay all costs and charges of prosecution."

The oath of the grand jurors, their general procedure, and the form of indictment are practically the same up to the present day.

To appreciate fully just what part the grand jury plays in the administration of criminal justice the reader should remember that almost all defendants in criminal cases are brought immediately after their arrest before a police magistrate and given, if they so desire, an exhaustive hearing. If the magistrate thinks there is sufficient cause to believe the prisoner has committed the crime charged against him he is held (if the crime be a felony or a libel) for the action of the grand jury, or if it be a misdemeanor, for whatever court tries such offences,—in New York County the Court of Special Sessions. Of course it is the privilege of the defendant to be admitted to bail, save where the charge is one of murder, until the proceedings against him result either in his final discharge or his indictment, and, as has been said before, once he is *held* for the grand jury he cannot, even if he be a self-confessed criminal, be tried or punished until that body has deliberated upon his case.

The following table shows the number of arrests for felony in New York County each year since 1900, the number of persons so arrested who were "held" by magistrates for the action of the grand jury, and the number of indictments "found" by that body:

Year	Number of Arrests for Felony	Number of Persons "Held" for Action of Grand Jury	Number of Indictments Found	Population of New York County
1900	8,588	4,473	3,674	2,050,600
1901	8,435	4,395	4,210	2,095,116

1902	9,465	5,020	3,890	2,139,632
1903	9,939	4,372	3,898	2,186,017
1904	9,238	3,452	3,950	2,235,060
1905	11,688	4,751	4,199	2,468,046
1906	11,553	4,169	4,116	2,553,100
1907	13,913	5,879	5,295	2,687,800
Total	119,206	57,241	52,027	......

It may be of some interest to note how this inquisitorial body is brought into being. Every year a Board of Commissioners, consisting of the Mayor, the Recorder, the Presiding Justice of the Supreme Court, and others, meet and make up a list of a thousand names from which the grand jurors for the year are to be drawn. These names are placed in a wheel and each month fifty of them are drawn out at random by the County Clerk in the presence of one of the judges of the General Sessions. From these fifty names the grand jury of the succeeding month are chosen by lot. Of course the selection of jurors must perforce be made with ostensible impartiality, for a grand jury which was amenable to political influence would render the administration of justice worse than a farce. Such a condition has not been unknown.

Not so very long ago Recorder Goff observed that certain representative gentlemen who had served on the grand jury for years were no longer drawn. In view of the significance of the political situation at that time the fact seemed peculiar and he determined to make a personal investigation. Accordingly at the next monthly drawing the Recorder inserted his own hand in the wheel and found that some of the slips were heavier and of a different texture from the others, and could easily be separated by the sense of touch. The inference was obvious. Undoubtedly the opportunity thus to elect between the sheep and the goats had been made good use of. No excuse for this astounding situation was offered, and all the slips at once were destroyed by order of the court. Later on it was explained that the manufacturer *"had not been able to furnish all the slips of the same material."*

As but twenty-three grand jurymen are selected each month, only two hundred and seventy-six out of the total number chosen ever actually serve. The judge appoints a foreman, usually a man of some previous experience, and the jury are sworn. The court then delivers a charge and reads or calls to their attention certain sections from the Code of Criminal Procedure. If there is any matter of public notoriety which comes within their purvue, such as crimes against the elective franchise, or insurance, banking, or other frauds, he is likely to dwell upon the necessity of paying particular attention to this variety of offence. The jury then retire to the rooms prepared for them and begin their secret deliberations.

They are now prepared to hear the evidence against all persons charged with felonies or libel, who have been held for their action by the police magistrates. The original papers in all these cases have already been copied under the direction of the district attorney and the witnesses subpœnaed to attend and give their testimony. These subpœnas are served by attachés of the prosecutor's office, commonly known as "county detectives," or, more popularly, "sleuths." It should be observed that the district attorney in fact decides what cases shall be submitted, and prepares the daily calendar of the grand jury, which as a rule does not know in advance what business it is to consider. In addition to this, the district attorney draws, usually in advance, all the indictments.

The indictment may be said to be the most important individual paper in criminal procedure, for upon its sufficiency depends the question of whether or not a defendant may be tried, or if tried and convicted, sentenced to prison. The general form of these instruments has varied little during many centuries. They are as archaic as the grand jury itself. Originally the draughter of documents was paid by the word, and the more prolix he could be the better it was for him. This fact naturally influenced the form of all legal papers. His sins are still directly visited upon us. Moreover, not the best forms, but the worst are our inheritance, for usually only the sufficiency of the worst is questioned and tested by appeal. If an indictment is not absolutely defective, it is sustained by the higher courts, and having been passed upon and not found wanting, immediately becomes a model for all future draughtsmen. It may fairly be said that the more faulty an indictment is (so long as it be not actually void) the better its chance of immortality.

Probably the simplest indictment which the grand jury can find is one for larceny. Let us suppose that a servant, Maria Holohan, has stolen the teapot of her master, the Hon. Silas Appleboy. The grand jury present an indictment against her in the following terms:

> Court of General Sessions of the Peace in and for the County of New York. The People of the State of New York against Maria Holohan.
>
> The People of the State of New York, by this indictment, accuse Maria Holohan of the crime of grand larceny in the

second degree committed as follows: The said Maria Holohan, late of the Borough of Manhattan of the City of New York, in the County of New York, aforesaid, on the 1st day of April, in the year of our Lord, One thousand, nine hundred and seven, at the Borough and County aforesaid, one teapot of the value of $50, of the goods, chattels and personal property of one Silas Appleboy, then and there being found, then and there feloniously did steal, take and carry away, against the form of the statute in such case made and provided and against the peace of the People of the State of New York and their dignity.

A. BIRD,
District Attorney.

This is merely saying that "the grand jury charge Maria Holohan with stealing the silver teapot of Silas Appleboy on April 1, 1907." It is the shortest indictment possible. A complicated indictment may fill hundreds of pages.

Many interesting old indictments are on file among the records of the General Sessions; and if one can judge by the frequency with which the names of divers ungodly and reckless Philadelphians are inscribed upon their pages, "the general reputation" of the City of Brotherly Love for "peace and quiet" must have considerably improved during the past two hundred years.

As a usual thing we find among the papers filed with the indictment the original "information" sworn to by the aggrieved party. Give heed to the "unmerciful conduct" of Mr. William Miller:

CITY OF NEW }
YORK ss: }

Mathew O'Brien of the City of New York Mariner maketh Oath and Saith that on Sunday night the first Day of November instant he this Deponent being at the Tavern kept by Francis King on the Dock between the Hours of Ten and Eleven of the Clock and having a dispute with the Landlord relative to a French Crown dropped by this Deponent one William Miller who this Deponent heard and believes *is Marker to a Billiard Table in Philadelphia* immediately challenged this Dep*.* to fight him and stopped this Deponent from going out either at the Door or window altho. he made frequent attempts for that purpose and thereupon knocked this Deponent down, and beat kicked and wounded him in a desperate and unmerciful manner. This Dep^t. Saith he also lost out of his pocket the whole of his Money then about him consisting of five Guineas in Gold two Crown pieces and a Note of hand for ten guineas. And further saith not.

Mathew O'Brien.

Sworn the 1 Day of
Nov ^{r}. 1704 before me
Jn° Broome, Jus^t Peace.

The grand jury of to-day is the same old grand jury that indicted William Miller; and the cases are piling up,—piling up, at the rate of three, four, five, or even six hundred a month.

What would Mr. Francis Rumbout, who was "apoynted" foreman of that earliest grand jury, have said if he had been obliged to pass upon six hundred cases in a month? The time which could actually be given to the consideration of any particular charge under such circumstances would average about *six minutes*!

For example, Giuseppe Candido, having been summoned to appear suddenly, finds himself standing in the centre of a large room around which are arranged a semi-circle of inquisitors.

He states where he lives, what his business is, that he knows Michael Angelo Spaghetti, and that the latter cut him in the shoulder in a quarrel over a glass of beer. He is then excused. The grand jury take a vote and Spaghetti is indicted for "wilfully and feloniously committing an assault with intent to kill." Generally only one side of the case is heard. There is very little attempt made to hold the witnesses down to the strict rules of evidence. It is all *ex parte*. "*L'évidence at jurie est que cunque chose que serve le partie a prover l'issue pur luy,*" as Henry Finch put it at the beginning of the seventeenth century.

Once in a great while, if there is something a little peculiar in the charge or in the manner in which the witnesses give their testimony, the jurors may become suspicious and send out for other witnesses or possibly for the defendant himself. Of course he cannot be compelled to testify, but usually he is glad of a chance to explain away the accusation if he can. Perchance the inquisitors refuse to indict. But what a waste of time for twenty-three busy men! And as a rule what trivial matters are brought to their attention!

Most of the cases dismissed are so inherently weak that the district attorney would himself have discharged the defendants of his own motion, but the action of the grand jury saves him the trouble and the odium, if any, and diffuses it among an irresponsible body. The same thing is true of indictments found against influential persons,—the responsibility is with twenty-three, not merely one.

But if the grand jury is to exist at all, it must be constituted, and required to act, in accordance with the law. The indictment is invalid if there be on the grand jury one who has not the proper qualification to sit, or if an unauthorized person be present, or if the evidence is not legally sufficient. Even if the defendant be as guilty as the Father of Sin, he may make a motion to dismiss the indictment on any of these grounds, and, whether the point be well taken or no, the case may in consequence be delayed for weeks. Where the defendant has the means to employ astute and learned counsel, he may retard his trial for weeks, or even months, by questioning the proceedings of the grand jury which found the indictment against him.

For example, when Fire Commissioner John J. Scannel was indicted for conspiracy to defraud the city of New York, his lawyers ferreted out the fact that one of the grand jurors who had found the indictment lived a large portion of the year in the town of New Rochelle. When the defendant was called upon to plead to his indictment the lawyers offered "*a plea in abatement*," although the law expressly provides that no pleas save of "guilty" or "not guilty" or of "*autrefois acquit*" may now be entered. They insisted, however, on their right to such a plea and the matter was delayed for a long time. Their plea having been refused they then moved to dismiss the indictment because of the alleged irregularity in having this juror present who spent his summers at the seashore. The determination of this motion took months. How like the situation to that which existed in 1433, when a statute was enacted in order to remedy, if possible, somewhat similar abuses.

> " ... When the Grand Jury appears and is ready to pass, a tenant or defendant or one of the petit jury pleads false pleas not tryable by the Grand Jury, and so delays proceedings until this be tried. When this is settled for the plaintiff, another pleads a like false plea since the last continuance; and so each of the defendants, tenants, or jurors, one after another, may plead and delay the Grand Jury; and although all be false and feigned, the Common Law has no penalty. This has caused great vexation and travail to the grand juries, and plaintiffs have been so impoverished that they could not pursue their cases, and jurors are more emboldened to swear falsely."[25]

A substantial proportion of the delays in criminal procedure are due to the interminable motions based upon alleged irregularities in the constitution and action of the grand jury, and the insufficiency of indictments. Such delays would vanish with the abolition of that body.

But beyond its general power to investigate specific charges of crime laid before it, the grand jury constitutes the only general inquisitorial body that we have, and its value and services in this respect must not be overlooked. It is highly important that the power should reside in some responsible body to summon witnesses and compel testimony anent suspected offences, conspiracies, and official misconduct. This is precisely what the grand jury did as far back as 1300, when it acted as a "suspecting" jury. Only through some such power can a rumor of crime, unsubstantial and intangible in itself, be traced to its source and the knowledge of those who can testify as to the perpetration of it secured at first hand.

Acting within its legal powers as an investigating body, the grand jury has a vast power and can be immensely useful to the community, but when it attempts to do more, its action has no more validity and is entitled to no more respect than that of any other self-constituted inquisitorial body of intelligent citizens.

A belief is quite prevalent, however, among grand jurymen that it is their duty not only to ascertain what crimes have been committed and to find indictments for them, but to act as the censors of the public morals, as watchdogs of the public treasury, as the promoters of legislation, and generally as the conservators of the public interests. This impression is entirely erroneous, and yet it is surprising to what an extent grand jurors imagine that because of their office some particular sanctity attaches to their enunciation of opinions in matters that do not concern them.

A grand juror walking in the morning from his house to the corner to take a street-car, accidentally stumbles over a coal-hole cover; he reports it to his associates; many of them know persons who have stumbled over coal-hole covers; they talk the matter over and decide that there should be no coal-holes, since with the abolition of the coal-hole the coal-hole cover also would disappear. They call upon the commissioner of public works to appear before them and testify; upon the street-cleaning commissioner; upon the commissioner of buildings; they learn how many coal-holes there are in the city; what their covers are made of; how they are fastened or are not fastened in place; and some day when the grand jury comes down into court, the foreman arises and states that he has a presentment. The judge on the bench requests him to hand it up; he delivers it to the clerk, who passes it to the judge, who returns it to the clerk and directs him to read it. The clerk stands; the grand jurors stand; the clerk reads:

"To the Honorable John Smith, Presiding Justice of the Court of General Sessions: The Grand Jury of the County of New York respectfully present: Our attention has been called to the large number of unprotected and unguarded coal-holes existing in the County of New York; we have called before us a large number of witnesses and given much time to the taking of testimony relative thereto; we find that in the past year ten thousand persons have lost their lives through falling into improperly guarded coal-holes, and that the records of the hospitals show lists of over one hundred thousand others who have been severely injured by similar catastrophies; while it is beyond the capacity of the mind of man to comprehend the infinite number of those who have been wounded, bruised, lacerated and contused by similar accidents, to an extent not sufficient to render hospital aid necessary, etc." And such a presentment goes on with its statistics and figures and ends with the recommendation that the legislature pass a certain law, that the aldermen pass a certain ordinance, that certain laws or certain ordinances be repealed, or that other legislative interference be had, or legislative action should be taken, or that some city official or city officials do this or do that, or that some department make such and such an investigation and act thereon in such and such a way, and concludes with the signature of the foreman and secretary of the grand jury. The court then arises, bows to the grand jurors, says: "Gentlemen, we have heard your presentment; I now direct that it be placed on file in this court and that copies thereof be forwarded forthwith by the clerks to the heads of the appropriate departments." And the grand jurors retire, imagining that in some way they have contributed directly to the public weal.

An examination of the long list of presentments on file in the office of the clerk of the Court of General Sessions will show the diversified interests to which the grand jury, acting as we have shown as a merely self-constituted *censor morum*, has devoted its attention and in which it has consumed many of its working hours in the past. So far as we know, no action whatever has ever been taken upon any of these presentments. That at times they may have done some good through calling to the attention of the public press matters which otherwise would not be under scrutiny, may be admitted; but the discussion of them in the press has usually been as ephemeral as the existence of the grand jury by which they were filed; and in general it may be said that the only effect of a grand jury's meddling with these things is to detract from the dignity of its office and the importance of the work which it and it alone can lawfully do.

The lay reader will naturally be led to inquire why this archaic institution which it costs so much time and money to perpetuate, which causes so much unnecessary inconvenience to witnesses and offers so many technical opportunities for delay, which frequently is ineffective and officious, and for the most part concerns itself with the most trivial matters only, should not be abolished, and why prisoners charged with crime whose cases have been properly examined by committing magistrates should not be immediately placed upon their trial.

It is doubtful if any very convincing arguments in favor of retaining the grand jury for the purpose of indicting ordinary offenders can be advanced. That it should be continued for the purposes of investigation, with power of indictment, to be summoned when the need thereof arises, is indisputable. But the original necessity for the grand jury has disappeared with the onward march of the centuries.[26] In early days, when the influence of the crown threatened the liberties of the English freeman, and when judges and magistrates owed their positions to royal favor, it was often difficult if not impossible to secure the punishment of a criminal if he happened to be a retainer or under the protection of those in power. So, too, the defenceless subject might be accused of crime by an influential person and haled to the bar upon a baseless and malicious charge. Some barrier was needed between the powerful and the weak, and some tribunal before which the weak could accuse the powerful of their wrongs. This was supplied by the grand jury, which, ever changing its members and deliberating in secret, seemed well calculated to safeguard the people's liberties. But at present we need no such protection against a government of and by the people, and indeed such a body, deliberating secretly and hearing the evidence against an accused person without giving him the opportunity to be heard, seems strangely out of harmony with the spirit of our institutions.

To-day, the grand jury, initiating a proceeding against a citizen who may be ignorant that he is even under suspicion, may be led to accuse him of some foul crime upon the mere *ex parte* statement of malicious witnesses, without giving him an opportunity to explain or contradict the evidence. The mere charge of crime is often enough to ruin a man forever. The argument that a suspected person may escape before arrest unless the charge is considered secretly, has in these days of telegraphs, railroads and extradition treaties little of the force which it may have carried with it in cruder times. Moreover, the possibility of indicting public officials or others upon insufficient evidence for political purposes, or for "moral effect," would be done away with, and only those against whom legal testimony made the charge reasonably clear would be threatened with prosecution, and then only when their defence had been heard by a magistrate and held insufficient.

Prosecutors now prefer to take as few cases before their grand juries in the first instance as possible, and to send the man with a grievance, who thinks he has some political pull and "wants to get the fellow indicted anyway," into the magistrate's court to make good his charge.

Almost twenty-five per cent of the States in the Union have modified their procedure in this regard so as to conform to modern requirements. The State constitutions of Indiana, Illinois, Iowa, Nebraska, Oregon and Colorado give the legislatures the power to make laws dispensing with grand juries in any case, and in California, Connecticut, Kansas, Louisiana, Montana, South Dakota, Utah, Vermont, Wisconsin and Wyoming constitutional provisions exist permitting all criminal proceedings to be made by information, or dispensing with grand juries in certain cases. This is also true of the Federal Government. Experience has demonstrated that ample protection is afforded the accused where the State is permitted to prosecute those held to bail by an examining magistrate upon proof of probable cause. He is better protected than by a grand jury which hears in secret only the evidence against him and gives him no opportunity of explanation.

A system which would allow of the prosecution of all felonies by information would do away with the great and practically useless labor of our grand jurors in the ordinary run of cases, would save endless time and money to all concerned, and might still retain the grand jury for such purposes as necessity requires. Justice would be more speedy and just as effective if the prosecution of all crimes were instituted before an examining magistrate, and the grand jury would then, at the summons of the court, meet to perform only those important and peculiar functions of investigation that are consonant with its dignity and necessary to the public weal.

FOOTNOTES:

[24] Record illegible.

[25] The historical development of the grand jury is highly interesting. Originally the assize at which the knights assembled was not unlike a sort of county parliament and all manner of matters were submitted to them. Gradually as the jury developed out of this unorderly gathering together, the sheriffs got into the habit of summoning only enough men to form the grand jury and as many petty juries (when those came into existence) as might be needed.

In the beginning private vengeance was the moving cause of all criminal procedure. The aggrieved party made a direct appeal to the county and the issue was fought out, the complainant and defendant appearing in person or by champions. This was exceedingly unsatisfactory for many reasons, among others that not seldom a rich man would hire all the champions within reaching distance and the poor man be left without any, which suggests the somewhat similar practice of many wealthy litigants at the present day. But this mode of individual redress colored all English procedure and is the direct cause which makes English criminal trials in so many ways resemble private litigation. Private vengeance was at the bottom of it.

When the "county" or the public were the accusers, a mere accusation was practically equivalent to a conviction subject to the chance of the defendant's escaping by a favorable termination of "the ordeal of water." But "the ordeal" in time died out, just as did wager of battle, and something had to take its place. This was the jury.

From very early times we find "grand" or "accusing" juries presenting charges for the trial jury to dispose of, although the accusing jury frequently acted as trial jury as well. By 1212 it had become customary to submit a charge found by a presenting jury to a larger combination jury which included the original body which had presented the charge. This enlarged jury, usually composed of a jury from another "hundred" and "the four vills," delivered a unanimous verdict. By 1300 it had begun to be the privilege of an accused to "challenge" those who had presented the charge against him, but it was the approved practice to try an accused by some at least of those who had presented him.

"The four knights were called, who came to the bar girt with swords (above their garments) and were charged—to choose twelve knights girt with swords for themselves and the others—and the justices ordered the parties to go with the knights into a chamber to choose or to declare their challenges of the others chosen by the four, for after the return of the panel so made by the four knights the parties shall have no challenge to panel or polls before the justices." (1406) Y.B. 7 H. IV, 20, 28.

The idea seemed to be that unless there were a few on the jury who had already formed a provisional opinion as to his guilt the prosecution would not have a fair chance. In Willoughby's case in 1340, Parning, J. naively remarked, "In such case the inquest should be taken by the indictors (the accusors) and others. Certainly if the indictors be not there *it is not well for the King.*" In 1351 by St. 25 Edw. III, c. 3, it was enacted that "no indictor be put on an inquest upon the deliverance of one indicted for trespass or felony, if he be challenged for this cause by the party indicted." Persons "presented" or accused could "put themselves" upon different counties, that is to say, could submit their case to juries drawn from such counties, with certain limitations, as they might elect. Thus we find a case where one having been "presented" by an accusing jury "puts himself on the County of Surrey and on all men in England who know him." At Easter came riding twenty-four knights from Surrey at the king's summons who promptly found him to be a robber, and, says the record, "Since he put himself upon these, *let him be hanged.*"

There is a criminal case in Y.B. 30 & 31 Edw. I, 528, which throws a good light on the procedure of the time. W. was the stabler of J.'s horse and had been kicked, while trying to mount, so that he died. The horse thereupon became forfeit to the king as a *deodand.* The jury accused J. of keeping the horse in spite of this and also charged him with having buried W. without calling in the coroner. This he denied and "put himself on the county." The judge, addressing the jury, which was probably the same that had made the accusation, charged as follows:

> "If W. died from the kick of the horse, the horse would be *deodand.* If not it would be John's. If the king should lose through you what rightly belongs to him, you would be perjured. If you should take away from John what is his, you would commit a mortal sin. Therefore, by the oath you have made, disclose and tell us the truth, whether the said W. died of the horse's kick or not. If you find that he did, tell us in whose hands is the *deodand* horse and what he is worth; and whether the said W. was buried without a view of the coroner."

All things considered—a pretty good charge.

Gradually, and in large measure because the "ordeal" had disappeared and the grand jury as a distinct body had been fully established, no method of ascertaining the truth of an accusation was left, and a mere presentment in fact amounted to a conviction, so that the need of some other jury to pass upon the issue was apparent. Out of this need the modern petty jury developed.

In course of time the accusing jury became as it is now, a distinct and separate body, deliberating secretly, its members being no longer permitted to sit as trial jurors. They acted on common report, their own personal information, and upon the application of injured parties, and initiated most criminal proceedings. It was necessary for some one to ferret out crime and hold the perpetrators for trial, and the jury did practically the whole business. As the years went on the jury became more and more a purely *ex parte* accusing body with practically no judicial supervision and receiving about what it saw fit as evidence. From time to time the powers and the character of the grand jury has been fiercely assailed. Two centuries ago it came near receiving a knock-out blow, but it had become too firmly established. In Shaftsbury's case, 8 How. St. Tr. 759 (1681), they were in fact compelled to receive their evidence publicly in court, but their vigorous protests and the failure of the attempt left the body all the more securely entrenched in English procedure.—*Condensation from Prof. J.B. Thayer's masterly chapter on "Trial by Jury and Its Development" in his "Preliminary Treatise on the Law of Evidence."*

[26] Cf. "Reform in Criminal Procedure," H.W. Chapin, 7 Harvard Law Review 189.

CHAPTER VII

THE LAW'S DELAYS

"IF THE COOK SHOULD STEAL THE TEAPOT"

"I would have her locked up and punished!" the reader undoubtedly exclaims as he notes our title. It is hardly likely, however, that he realizes the possible significance of such an undertaking. For the edification, therefore, of those who have cooks and teapots, and in order to be forewarned, if not fore-armed, let us suppose that the worthy Mr. Appleboy has not only the domestic necessary for our case, but also a family heirloom which is worth more than twenty-five dollars, the requisite value to make its abstraction, with felonious intent, grand larceny in the second degree.

Mr. Appleboy, after a moderately hard day's work, has been for an hour at the club, and is now ascending his front steps. As he is about to place the key in the door, he observes his cook, Maria, making her exit from the area with some large object concealed beneath her shawl. A flash from the dying sun, setting over the elevated railroad tracks of Sixth Avenue, betrays a telltale protruding spout. Maria does not perceive her master, but the latter, being of an inquiring disposition, descends the steps and follows her down the street. She hurries along upon her journey until, reaching Eighth Avenue, she turns the corner and enters a pawnshop. Mr. Appleboy, puffing, follows hard, and opens the door just as Maria is in the act of receiving from the pawnbroker the sum of ten dollars. She has the money in one hand, the teapot in the other; she is caught *in flagrante delicto*, or, in the modern equivalent, "with the goods on."

Maria shrieks and calls upon the saints. Appleboy, purple from his exertions, pounds the floor with his gold-headed cane and fiercely inquires what she means by going off with his silver teapot. In reply Maria falls on her knees, breaks into tears, and confesses her crime, offering no excuse, and suggesting no palliating circumstance. She implores his forgiveness, but Appleboy, righteously indignant, is obdurate. She could have stolen anything but his grandmother's teapot, and he would have overlooked it. The pawnbroker, who takes but a mild interest in the proceedings, merely seizes the opportunity to remove from the cook's unresisting fingers the roll of bills.

Appleboy resolves to do his duty. He will set an example of good citizenship—he will have her arrested, locked up, and sent to prison.

"Summon a policeman!" he cries to the indifferent pawnbroker.

"Get one yourself!" replies the other.

Appleboy starts for the door, keeping one eye on the prostrate Maria. Two blocks distant he sees a stalwart officer in the act of conversing affably with a street cleaner. At this moment an urchin notices Maria couchant upon the floor. An expansive grin takes possession of his features, and, placing his fingers to his mouth, he emits a shrill whistle. Instantly, like a flight of vultures, a small army of boys descend upon Appleboy, who now decides that the only way to procure the policeman is to shout for him. In his embarrassment he yells: "Stop thief! Stop thief! Police!" but the officer pays no attention. He is discussing Tommy Sullivan's chowder party of the night before.

"Say, mister, I'll get the copper for ye," shouts some little fellow, and starts on a run up the avenue. A few follow him and quickly corral the officer, who, protesting, dawdles slowly in the direction of Mr. Appleboy, swinging his club, and apparently taking little interest in their remarks. Meantime, the pawnbroker has shut and locked the door. Maria, within, is still in a state of coma. The much-annoyed old gentleman is fast being surrounded by a dense throng of loafers, tradesmen, ladies of the neighborhood and pedestrians, while the street is blocked with vagrant cabs and grocery carts. He wishes he were at home in his comfortable library, but realizes that he is in for it now, and must stick it out.

"Well, what do you want?" demands the officer, pushing his way through the crowd until he confronts the innocent cause of the disturbance. "What are yer makin' all this row about, and blockin' up the street fer?"

"Maria, my cook, stole my silver teapot," answers Mr. Appleboy. "I caught her trying to sell it in *there*. I ask that you place her under arrest."

"What's yer name?" asks the policeman. "Who are yer anyway?" The crowd cheers delightedly, for while the copper is not popular in the neighborhood, an old swell like this is "nuts" for everybody.

"I am a citizen and a taxpayer," replies Mr. Appleboy stiffly, "and I insist upon your doing your duty and arresting this woman."

"Aw, come on now and give us yer name," continues the officer. "You can't expec' me t'arrest a person unless I know who I'm doin' it fer. How do *I* know yer ain't throwin' some game into me?"

At this moment one of the boys shies a banana peel at Mr. Appleboy's tall hat. The latter, seeing his disadvantage, responds:

"My name is Silas Appleboy, and I am a taxpayer and a freeholder. I demand that you arrest this woman." The policeman, somewhat impressed by the other's vehemence and the statement that he is a freeholder (the meaning of which the official naturally does not understand), inquires a little more genially where the lady is.

"In that shop," replies her master. The crowd, with a whoop, rushes at the door, but the pawnbroker is standing inside in an attitude of defence. The policeman, closely followed by Appleboy, pushes his way through the mob, and raps loudly.

"Stand back there, now," shouts the officer, waving his club. The small boys shrink back, leaving Appleboy in the centre of the ring. The pawnbroker opens the door. Maria is upon her knees, calling vaguely upon Heaven to defend her. The silver teapot reposes upon the counter. The officer grasps Maria roughly by the shoulder and yanks her to her feet.

"Get up there and pull yerself together!" he exclaims. "What's yer name?"

"Me name is Maria Holohan," she replies hysterically.

"Do yer know that man?" continues the officer, pointing at Appleboy.

"Shure, I know him," is the answer. "Haven't I worked for him for fourteen years?"

"Did you steal his teapot?" asked the officer.

"Oh, Holy Mother! Holy Mother!" wails Maria. "I took a dhrop too much, an' shure I didn't know what I was doin' at all, at all."

"Well, the first thing you'll do," remarks the officer, "'ll be to walk to the house. Come on, now!" And forthwith he drags Maria to the door, and, holding her firmly by the wrist, marches her upon the sidewalk. Mr. Appleboy, the teapot clasped to his bosom, follows immediately behind. Their appearance is greeted with vociferous approval by the waiting crowd, who fall in and escort the group towards the police station. But Maria's strength fails her, and, presently, with a groan she collapses. Perhaps the drop too much has taken effect in her legs. At all events, despite the efforts of the officer, she refuses to move, and remains limp. The crowd has now become so dense as entirely to obstruct all traffic in the street, long lines of electric cars leading in each direction up the avenue, motor-men and conductors forming a strong adjunct to those giving gratuitous advice. Two grocery wagons get their wheels locked in the throng. Some one telephones to the station house. At last the distant clanging of the patrol is heard. The crowd scatters, the carts and cabs extricate themselves, and the "hurry-up wagon" backs to the sidewalk with a flourish, two more coppers swinging on behind. They bundle Maria unceremoniously inside, escort her erstwhile employer with hardly more courtesy into the same vehicle, and toss in the teapot: the gong rings: and Mr. Appleboy starts upon his task of bringing an evil-doer to justice, and proving himself worthy of the proud title of citizen.

The drive to the station seems hours long, and the fumes of whiskey are very evident upon Maria. The officers are taciturn. The nose has been knocked off the teapot. Mr. Appleboy, holding himself tense in his seat, endeavors not to be jostled against the lady who has, previously, cooked his meals. Now and again she addresses him in no complimentary terms. She has by this time reached the belligerent stage, although she has no thought of denying her guilt.

The wagon draws up with a jerk in front of the precinct station house. Into a second crowd of gamins and loafers, Appleboy, still clutching the noseless teapot, emerges. He is followed by two policemen, half carrying, half supporting Maria. The doorman allows the party to enter, while repelling the inquisitive throng who would like to accompany them.

Once inside, Maria and her master, little distinction being made between them, are brought before the sergeant, who reclines behind a desk upon an elevated platform. This official interrogates Mr. Appleboy somewhat brusquely as to his name, address and the charge which he makes against the defendant, laboriously copying the answers in the "blotter." Maria, petrified with terror, absolutely refuses to answer any questions, and mutters incoherently to herself. The sergeant, satisfied of Mr. Appleboy's respectability by reason of his highly polished hat and gold-headed cane, commits the prisoner to a cell to await the hearing before the magistrate on the following morning. As the charge is one of felony, and as none of her friends as yet know of her detention or arrest, the question of her release upon bail does not arise, and after the sergeant has directed Mr. Appleboy to attend at the nearest police court the next morning at half-past eight punctually, that gentleman escapes down the steps of the precinct house, feeling that he has lived through untold ages of misery. The crowd cheers him as he descends, and he hastens homeward, the joy of release tempered only by the prospective agony of the morrow. The noseless teapot remains in the custody of the sergeant at the station house.

We can imagine Appleboy telling the story to his wife and children. How heroically he figures in his own account of the proceedings! How picturesquely penitent is Maria! How dramatic her capture in the very act of disposing of the stolen property! How the policemen cower at the majestic Appleboy's approach! By the time the old fellow has taken his coffee and lighted his perfecto he is almost restored to his former condition of pompous dignity. His intention to vindicate his position as a freeholder and to see that the law shall take its course is revived, and he dreams of Maria hurtling through the abyss with dozens of silver teapots tied about her ample neck.

DELAY THE FIRST

The next morning Appleboy orders his carriage and drives in state to the police court. His tall hat secures him easy access to a long room with a low ceiling, in which the air is full of strange odors.

Across the end of the court, two-thirds of the way towards the front, stretches an iron grating through which a gate admits police officers, local politicians, lawyers and the witnesses in any examination actually in progress. He enters the room exactly at eight-thirty. Already it is crowded, and, having no business inside the gate, he is forced to sit upon a bench in company with various friends of the divers defendants who have been committed during the night.

It is early as yet, and a substantial breakfast has put Mr. Appleboy in an optimistic frame of mind. Once the judge arrives how quickly the case will be disposed of and our hero receive the thanks of the magistrate for acting as he has done! But alas! Already a long file of officers is forming at the left of the desk behind the grating. Each officer has located at a safe distance one or more "drunks" or "disorderlies" whom he has gathered in during the preceding evening, and who have spent the night in the station house. The officers have recently come off post and now are waiting sleepily for the arrival of the magistrate to dispose of "The Watch."

By a quarter to nine the line has reached immense proportions. Twenty officers stand in single file and the procession of prisoners reaches to the doorway of the cells. In the meantime the jam in the room itself has become greater, and the heat and odors more oppressive. Mr. Appleboy wipes his brow with his silk handkerchief. He wishes he had brought his wife's smelling salts.

Presently he discerns amid the crowd inside the railing the now familiar features of Pat, the officer, who beckons him to come within.

Our friend rises to his feet to obey, but instantly another officer bawls: "Sit down there, you!" and Appleboy collapses.

"Hi, there, Rounds, let that old guy in, will ye?" asks Pat good-naturedly.

The roundsman condescendingly nods to the grizzled guardian of the gate, who holds it open just wide enough to allow our hero to squeeze through.

"Mornin'," remarks Pat, chewing vigorously.

"Good-morning, officer," replies Appleboy. "Where is the prisoner?"

"She came in the wagon half an hour ago," says Pat. "Step up while he makes out the complaint. After that we'll arrange her."

So Pat and his complainant join the mob which is besieging the clerk's desk, and finally secure enough of that functionary's scattered attention to induce him to draw up a brief statement of the facts in the case. Pat disappears into the cells to emerge in a few minutes, escorting the bewildered Maria. She is then "arranged," which in police parlance is to say she is arraigned. She has no counsel, and evidently supposes her interrogator to be the judge, for she insists on addressing him as "Yer onner." The clerk briefly warns her of her rights and puts the few necessary questions, which Maria answers in a quavering voice. It is obvious that she expects to be at once deported to Sing Sing or the "Island."

"Name?"

"Maria Holohan, yer onner."

"Address?"

"Two East Seventy-first Strate, yer onner, wid this man here." (Indicating Appleboy.)

"Occupation?"

"Shure, 'tis his cook, Oi am." ("Housework" puts down the clerk.)

"How long have you lived at this last address?"

"Fourteen year, yer onner, come St. Michael's Day."

"What have you to say, if anything, relative to the charge against you?"

(Maria mutters incoherently) "Shure Oi took the taypot, all right, all right."

"Guilty?" asks the clerk.

"Guilty," whispers Maria.

"That's all," says the other. "Stand back there and give some one else a chance."

Pat, holding the papers in his hands, escorts Maria to the end of the line, and Appleboy returns to his seat. In his deposition he has stated that his occupation is that of "Bank President" and he has instantly observed a change of attitude in those about him. "Rounds" even expels two unsavory characters for the purpose of making room for him in the front row.

In a moment more the judge enters hurriedly, takes his seat at the desk, and begins rapidly to dispose of the file of prisoners before him. One after another the officers press forward, make a brief statement of the circumstances of the arrest, and the prisoner is led away with a fine, a lecture, or a sentence of a few days in the workhouse. There is no opportunity for other cases until all the "disorderlies" and street-walkers have been dealt with. Half-past nine comes, quarter of ten and ten o'clock, the hour at which Mr. Appleboy usually makes a leisurely descent to his office, but still there is no respite. The monotonous business continues. But Mr. Appleboy's time is valuable, and he begins to fume and fidget. He thinks of the dollars he is losing by performing his duty as a citizen.

Pat has gradually neared the desk. At length there is but one more case to be heard, and the "Rounds" summons our hero once more inside. Maria is thrust in front of the platform and stands with her hands on the rail. It has seemed an easy thing to Mr. Appleboy for a complainant to tell his story, and he has smiled scornfully to himself at the wandering and unconvincing statements he has heard during the morning, but as he is pushed upon the platform under the sharp eye of the magistrate, his courage begins to ooze out of him. He wishes again for the hundredth time he had let Maria go off with the old teapot. The very thought of tea sickens him.

"Next," calls the "Rounds," as a dowdy young woman is led away, weeping hysterically.

Pat hands up the papers.

"Maria Holohan," mutters the judge, running his eye over the "information." "Stole a teapot,—um—um—Is this the defendant?"

"He indentifies her," answers Pat.

The judge turns to Appleboy.

"Are you the complainant?" he asks briskly.

"Y-e-e-s," answers our hero, "I am. This is my cook."

"That will do," says the magistrate. "Answer only the questions that are put to you. Do you swear that the statements contained in this complaint are the truth, the whole truth, and nothing but the truth, so help you, God?"

"I do," replies Appleboy with vigor.

Luckily for Appleboy, no lawyer appears for the delinquent Maria. Unfamiliar with all the vagaries and devices of the criminal law, this lady, realizing that she has been caught red-handed, foolishly supposes that there is nothing for her to do but to cry for forgiveness and beg for mercy.

"Do you desire counsel?" asks the judge.

Maria stares vaguely.

"Have ye got a lawyer?" interprets the nearest copper.

"Don't want no lawyer!" snaps Maria.

"I see you plead guilty," says the judge.

"Shure," she answers.

"Well," says the magistrate, "as she pleads guilty, I will not detain you further. Your cook, eh? Well, well, it's too bad! Why will they do such things? I am glad you did not lose the teapot. That is all."

Maria is led away, while Mr. Appleboy descends from the platform, to be followed by some other righteously indignant complainant.

The whole transaction has occupied less than a minute and a half. In order to accomplish it, Mr. Appleboy has remained in court from half-past eight in the morning until a quarter to twelve.

"Thank goodness," he says to himself, "it is all over now. The rest will be plain sailing." Ah, how little do the Appleboys know of the administration of criminal justice! Pat accompanies him to his carriage, expressing regret that the matter could not have been disposed of more speedily. Appleboy is not ungenerous. He always tips the colored porter in the sleeping-car most liberally, but although it is obvious, possibly, that Pat would like a drink and some cigars, Appleboy, believing that by accommodating him he would be committing a felony or, at least, a misdemeanor, coldly bids him good-afternoon, and Patrick, crestfallen, returns to the precinct house.

Meanwhile the magistrate fixes bail for Maria at five hundred dollars, and the teapot is tagged and returned to the custody of the sergeant at the station. Tired out, but feeling that "a duty well performed is a rainbow to the heart," Mr. Appleboy seeks the bosom of his family.

DELAY THE SECOND

Cookless, the Appleboys struggle through the following week. It is in the height of the season and cooks are scarce; they are also ill-tempered; and in five days Mrs. Appleboy has tried and dismissed three. The family, dinnerless, nightly seek a neighboring restaurant, and endeavor to console themselves with the theatre. But after the fourth night this bores them. They begin to long for Maria's omelets and Irish stew. After fourteen years one gets used to a particular kind of pudding.

"I almost wish," said Appleboy to his wife when they are alone, "that I had not done anything about Maria, but just let her come back and cook for us. I don't think she would have tried to steal the teapot a second time."

"But how do you know, Silas?" replies his wife. "Think of the orgies that may have been going on in the kitchen in the last fourteen years!"

"True, true," answers Appleboy, and again renews his determination to see the thing through to the bitter end. Then Mr. Appleboy receives at his office a green slip calling for his attendance on the morrow before the grand jury of the County of New York, promptly at ten o'clock. He has never been to the Criminal Courts building in his life. He only supposes vaguely that it is situated somewhere near the "wholesale district" and not far from the Italian quarter. He associates it with trips to Chinatown, the East Side and the Bowery.

After being thoroughly shaken up by a long journey over the cobblestones in his carriage, Mr. Appleboy finds himself on Franklin Street, between the Tombs, on the one hand, and the Criminal Courts building upon the other. Over his head runs "The Bridge of Sighs." A congregation of loafers, lawyers, runners, policemen and reporters linger upon the sidewalk. Unfamiliar with the means of entrance and exit, Appleboy turns the corner and climbs two long flights of stone steps upon the outside of the building instead of utilizing the side entrance upon the ground floor and taking the elevator. He enters an enormous hall around which, on all four sides, corridors reach to the top of the building. A motley collection of people are hurrying hither and thither. After some difficulty, Appleboy discovers a lift packed with odoriferous Italians, men with bandaged eyes and faces, small, half-clad children, and divers persons smoking enormous, evil-smelling cigars, whom he later discovers to be members of the legal profession. The car stops at the third floor.

"District attorney and grand jury," calls the elevator man. "Grand jury to the right."

Appleboy gets off with the rest of the mob, and wanders down a narrow corridor past rows of offices, until he comes to a policeman standing by the door of a small room crowded with people. There is hardly space to breathe, much less to sit down. From time to time a bell jingles in the distance, a door into another room opens, somebody comes out, and an officer calls out a name. Its owner hastily responds, is shot through the door into the other room, and the door closes again. This process goes on interminably. In a corner, clerks separated by a railing are busily engaged in making out subpoenas and filling in certificates of attendance. Police officers are everywhere. Appleboy takes his stand by the door. It is half-past ten o'clock. He has no means of knowing when he will be summoned before the august body who are deliberating in the next room. He has a craving to smoke, although he makes it a rule never to do so before six o'clock in the afternoon. He has left his newspaper at home, and has yielded up his subpœna to the officer at the door. There is nothing to occupy his attention except the sour visages of those about him. They belong to a class of people who instinctively fill him with disgust, being representatives of what Appleboy and his wife are accustomed to term the "masses."

Person after person is summoned into the other room, but no one seems to want the banker. Pat is there, to be sure, but he is at his usual pastime, enjoying the delights of mastication. He no longer has any "use" for Appleboy. At about a quarter-past eleven, the officer beside the outer door calls the name of Silas Appleboy. Our hero, believing that at last his turn has arrived, starts from his seat, only to be directed to "Come here!" by the officer. He discovers that he has been summoned to confer with a representative of the district attorney, who invites him into a neighboring office.

"Mr. Appleboy," says this young gentleman when the two are comfortably seated, "I see by the papers in the case that a Maria Holohan stole a teapot from you. Under what circumstances was the theft committed?"

Mr. Appleboy, who supposes that the merits of his case have been long since known personally to the district attorney, commences at the beginning and rehearses all his woes and difficulties. The assistant listens courteously, and then, without comment, bows Appleboy out, who returns once more to the ante-chamber of the grand jury. His seat has, meanwhile, been usurped by a corpulent lady in deep mourning, and its former occupant is forced to stand in the corridor for an hour longer. During this period he perchance has the annoyance of hearing Pat remark to a fellow officer in no uncertain tones that "the old guy is no good—a 'dead one'—I didn't even get a smoke off him."

The ante-chamber gradually has been thinning out. Finally Appleboy gets a seat. The bell keeps on ringing until only he and a man with a broken nose are left. At last a policeman hurries out of the open door, the bell rings again, and the clerk at the desk shouts "Appleboy! Appleboy!" Appleboy arises.

"Right in through that door," directs the clerk, and Mr. Appleboy, shrinking, enters timidly the chamber of horrors and finds himself in the centre of a semi-circle of gentlemen of varying ages and appearance. To Appleboy a thousand eyes seem peering at him from every side. The silence is appalling. He stands, silk hat in hand, feeling like a very small boy who has been called before the head master to be punished for some offence. A man in the middle of the semi-circle and directly in front of him, is scratching busily with his pen. The grand jurors whisper among themselves. Presently the foreman looks up, observes Appleboy standing, and remarks:

"Sit down, sir." Mr. Appleboy sinks into a chair beside the stenographer. The foreman glances at the indictment already prepared, and then says sharply: "Stand up, sir,—and be sworn!"

A Bible is forced into his unenthusiastic hand.

"You do solemnly swear the evidence you shall give to the Grand Inquest upon the complaint against Maria Holohan shall be the truth, the whole truth, and nothing but the truth: So help you, God!"

Mr. Appleboy replies faintly: "I do," and makes an ineffectual attempt to kiss the Bible.

"Sit down!" directs his interlocutor. "Ahem! You had a teapot worth over fifty dollars, and your cook stole it? Did you see her?"

"Yes," answers Appleboy, and in a few words describes the occurrence. The foreman sweeps the grand jury with his eye.

"Any questions?" he asks. There is no response from the others.

"That is all, sir," says the foreman. "I see that the woman pleaded guilty in the police court. Good-morning."

Appleboy takes his hat and retires. Two hours' wait for an examination occupying thirty seconds! He has heard of the "law's delays," now he knows what they are. The bell rings again as he is making his way out into the corridor, and the man with the broken nose stumbles in through the door by which our friend has made his exit.

DELAY THE THIRD

Mr. Appleboy now believes that his troubles are over, for he has consulted his family lawyer in order to make sure that everything is all right, and has learned that since Maria has pleaded guilty in the police court, she will, after her indictment, undoubtedly do likewise in the General Sessions.

Two days later Appleboy receives a subpœna to attend in "Part I of the Court of General Sessions of the Peace" as complainant in the case of "The People of the State of New York against Maria Holohan." Down he goes and sits for a full hour in an ice-cold court-room which is thronged with policemen, irate complainants, and sympathizing friends of the defendants, until, among the line of bedraggled prisoners, who are brought in batches of from four to six from the Tombs through a little door in the back of the room, he recognizes the erstwhile queen of his kitchen—Maria, the unapproachable. She looks much the worse for wear. The feathers of her hat hang disconsolate. In addition she is minus her collar and goes clumping around the room after the policeman as if she had never broiled a lobster or tossed a flapjack. As she turns the corner by the jury box she spies her lawyer, and immediately brightens. They hold an animated conversation in whispers as he takes his place beside her at the bar.

"Maria Holohan," says the clerk severely, "you have been indicted by the grand jury for grand larceny in the first degree. Do you plead guilty or not guilty?"

Appleboy starts from his seat almost ready to call out in explanation: "She pleads guilty, your honor," but before he has an opportunity to do so, or to suffer any of the uncomfortable consequences of such an act, the weazened-faced little attorney representing Maria responds sharply: "Not guilty."

Appleboy is stunned. Why, the woman has already confessed her guilt, after having been caught in the act! What absurdity! What nonsense! But the plea is taken; the lawyer asks that a date be set for trial not nearer than a week on the ground that he may conclude upon investigation to advise his client to change her plea, and because he has a witness living outside the State; and the court grants this application.

Not guilty! As Maria tramps out in company with other defendants, Appleboy makes up his mind that he will see what all this means, and steps forward through the gate to speak in person to the representative of the district attorney. A hand is laid upon his shoulder, and he is hauled back unceremoniously.

"Here! Where are you going?"

"I want to speak to the district attorney," he replies meekly.

"Sit down," replies the officer. "He can't speak to you now. Look him up in his office after court adjourns."

Mr. Appleboy, chastened by experience, makes no protest and retires from the room. He has lost too much money already by absence from his office to make it worth his while to wait until the adjournment of the court, so he goes down town to attend to his business, and at the first opportunity calls up his attorney to inquire what it all means. The lawyer responds briefly that the mere fact that the defendant has pleaded guilty in the police court does not preclude her from changing her mind and denying her guilt later when called upon to plead to an indictment. He regrets the inconvenience to which his client has been put, and suggests by implication that it would have been well if Mr. Appleboy had consulted him before taking any action in the matter. Appleboy has already come to this conclusion himself.

DELAY THE FOURTH

A week later Appleboy receives another subpœna which commands him under penalty to call at the district attorney's office at half after ten o'clock and "Ask to see" Mr. John Smith, whom he finds, after some difficulty, in a little office in the same building and corridor through which he passed when he appeared before the grand jury.

"Is this Mr. Smith?" he inquires.

"Yes," answers the young man. "What do you want?"

"I have a subpœna," replies the other, "to see you this morning."

"Oh, yes, I remember," remarks the assistant. "You're in the Holohan case, aren't you? Woman stole your teapot, didn't she?"

"Yes," mutters Mr. Appleboy, "she did, some time ago. What can I do for you?"

"Well, I want you to tell me about the case," mildly explains the assistant. "Who's Maria Holohan, anyway?"

So Appleboy begins at the beginning and tells the whole story through, while, from time to time, the assistant laughs softly to himself. When the history is concluded, the young man leans back in his chair, blows a ring of smoke towards the ceiling and exclaims: "That's always the way! Some miserable little shyster gets hold of 'em in the Tombs and swears that he can get 'em off, no matter how plain the facts are, or even if they have pleaded guilty in the police court. Well, I'll make a note of the case, and when it comes up for trial you'll get a subpœna. Sorry to have had to bother you. Good-morning!"

DELAY THE FIFTH

Appleboy departs. Three days later he gets another subpœna to appear before the Court of General Sessions. When the case is called, however, Maria's lawyer gets up and moves for an inspection of the grand jury minutes upon the ground that there was not sufficient evidence before that body to warrant the finding of an indictment. The judge denies this motion peremptorily, since there has already been a hearing in the police court. Upon this the attorney states that he is actually engaged in a trial of another action elsewhere. The case therefore "goes over," of necessity. Nearly three weeks have now elapsed since the theft. Presently Appleboy gets another subpœna. He trots down to court half an hour before the opening. The case is marked "Ready." He is told to remain in court, but some other case is already on trial, having lasted over from the day before, and at noon it is still in full swing. The court adjourns for an hour, from one to two.

Appleboy returns obediently at that time, but the case which was on trial in the morning continues throughout the entire afternoon. He departs at four o'clock, furious.

Next morning he is dragged down again. This time, however, the case against Holohan is adjourned without date, owing to the fact that Maria's counsel has applied to the court for a commission to take testimony in Boston. They intimate that they may interpose the defence of insanity, or at least dipsomania, and evince an unaccountable eagerness to examine Maria's great aunt, who is acting as general housework girl for a minister's family in Roxbury, Mass. The district attorney strenuously opposes this motion. The judge, however, "takes the papers," as he is obliged to assume that the request is made in good faith.

DELAY THE SIXTH

Appleboy hears nothing of the case for another week. At the end of that time he gets a subpœna of a different color, and again journeys down to court. But this time he first seeks out Smith in his office and asks if there is any likelihood of the case being tried that day. Mr. Smith, whose room is thronged with witnesses, tells Mr. Appleboy that he is no longer assigned to that part of the General Sessions on whose calendar the case appears, and that another assistant, Mr. Jones, will have to try the case. He therefore conducts Mr. Appleboy to an adjoining office and presents him to Jones.

The latter receives Appleboy courteously and assures him that he will try the Holohan case the very first of all. They talk the matter over and unite in their objurgations against defendants' lawyers in general. Jones, however, is confident that this time they will succeed in disposing of the matter. They adjourn together to the court-room. But on the call of the calendar Maria's lawyer claims that one of his most material witnesses is absent, and that without him his client's interests would be jeopardized. The judge, who by this time has correctly gauged the situation, nevertheless directs him to go on with the case. The lawyer then states that he has had a bad night and feels very unwell. The judge continues unsympathetic. The assistant is openly skeptical. The attorney thereupon is suddenly taken with great pain and retires for air to the corridor outside the court-room. Nothing can be done. Perhaps the lawyer really has a pain.

The assistant shrugs his shoulders and announces that he will move the case of Michael Angelo Spaghetti, indicted for assault; the defendant is ordered to the bar, and the court directs the clerk to announce that "no other case will be tried" that day.

Appleboy drags himself with the rest of the throng through the door into the corridor. This is the third time he has practically given up an entire morning to appearing as complainant in a case which seems fated never to be tried. He goes downstairs swearing vengeance against Maria and her lawyer. This performance is repeated possibly some four or five times more with variations. But he never gets nearer than having the case marked "ready," and something always intervenes, Maria's lawyer exhibiting an almost supernatural cleverness in the invention of excuses.

On all these occasions, while awaiting the call of the calendar, Appleboy is likely to sit in close proximity to the defendant, who has been released on bail pending her trial, and who casts withering glances in his direction. Her brother Terence also seizes the opportunity presented by the various adjournments to tell Appleboy what he thinks of him and what he intends to do to him after the case has been disposed of.

The district attorney has done everything in his power to force the defence to trial, but his every attempt has been unavailing. Nevertheless, Appleboy blames him personally for every idiosyncrasy of the law and for every delay procured by the defence.

DELAY THE SEVENTH

It was now the end of June. Mr. Appleboy has planned to take his family abroad, but, although the annual adjournment of court for vacation is at hand, through the dilatory tactics of Maria's pettifogging counsel, the case is still untried.

Appleboy had been in attendance at court eleven separate times, but the only satisfaction which he receives is the assurance that he will be paid fifty cents for each one of his subpœnas. He is by this time so disgusted with the whole business and has taken such a fierce dislike to all judges, district attorneys, policemen and lawyers, that he would long ago have thrown up the case had it not been for the fact that he has a vague idea that in so doing he might be compounding a felony. His desire to set an example as a model citizen has long since evaporated. Countless members of the Holohan family beset him at home and at the office, beseeching him for clemency.

It is possible that without consulting the district attorney, and under the assumption that he must remain at hand as a witness, he gives up Europe and takes a house on the mosquito coast instead. His wife is very unpleasant about it. She hints that Appleboy need not have been so vindictive in the first place. After he has cancelled his passage, and the whole family are safely ensconced for the summer, Appleboy discovers that cases in which the defendants have been released upon bail are not tried during July, August, and September. Appleboy's feeling can be easily imagined. It is needless to say that he does not impart the information to his lady.

The summer proves generally unsatisfactory. The visits of Maria's family and their efforts to persuade him not to prosecute are redoubled. Most of them are domestics on their evenings "out," plentiful of tears and reproaches. It is impossible to escape them. He also receives numerous letters from the lady's attorney suggesting that he call at the latter's office. These he has systematically ignored.

DELAY THE EIGHTH

October comes. The family return. Once more the familiar subpœna is served upon our hero at his office. At the sight of it he scowls fiercely as he watches the white smoke sailing up the air shaft into the azure of the sky. It is a beautiful autumn day. He recalls the police court, and the grand jury, the Criminal Courts building, the General Sessions, and Maria and Terence, and his miserable summer! Vestryman Appleboy mutters something very much resembling profanity. He thinks: "If I had not tried to punish that cook for stealing the teapot, why!—I might be spending to-day in Rome or Paris!" The next morning, however, finds him once more on his dreary way to court.

He consults Jones again upstairs, who promises by all that is holy that nothing shall prevent a trial. The case is marked "Ready," without opposition, and the assistant district attorney moves the indictment.

"Maria Holohan to the bar!" calls the clerk, as a jury is rapidly empanelled.

Appleboy is exultant. He is to reap the reward of virtue and fidelity to principle. At last the criminal is to be made to pay the penalty. He looks eagerly for Maria.

"Holohan! Maria Holohan!" reiterates the clerk.

But Maria comes not.

"Call her in the corridor," directs the judge to the officer at the door.

There is a sudden silence in the court-room. No response is heard outside.

The assistant district attorney says something to the judge, who nods to the clerk.

"Maria Holohan, come forth and answer pursuant to the terms of your recognizance or your recognizance will be forfeited," shouts that official.

There is no reply.

"Terence Holohan, bring forth Maria Holohan, for whom you are bound pursuant to the terms of your recognizance, or your recognizance will be forfeited," solemnly intones the clerk.

Terence arises and comes slowly forward from where he has been sitting.

"Are you the bondsman in this case?" asks the clerk.

"Oi am!" replies Terence.

"Where is the defendant?"

Terence looked sheepish.

"Where is the defendant?" repeats the clerk sharply.

"In Ireland! Bad cess to her!" answers Terence. "And divil a bit can Oi bring her forth," he murmurs, "whin she's in the ould country!"

"Forfeit the bail!" orders the judge.

Appleboy grasps the arm of the assistant.

"What's the trouble?" he asks anxiously.

"She's skipped!" answers the other with a grim laugh. "That's all."

"H—l!—I mean, thank God!" exclaims Vestryman Appleboy.

This, gentle reader, is what *might* happen to you if your cook should steal the teapot.

CHAPTER VIII

RED TAPE

Mr. Appleboy makes his way from the court-room to the corridor of the Criminal Courts building a sadder, wiser and more chastened member of society. He now has personal knowledge of the way in which our criminal laws are enforced and some idea of the administration of criminal justice in general in New York City. He has been dragged down to the Criminal Courts building, to the district attorney's office, the grand jury room, and the General Sessions not less than a dozen times, and he now takes a solemn vow that never, if he can possibly avoid it, will he be prevailed upon to go there again.

Our defeated hero on reaching home finds Mrs. Appleboy waiting luncheon for him.

"Well, Silas," she inquires, "has that woman been convicted at last?"

Her husband laughs somewhat shamefacedly.

"No; I'm afraid she has gotten the best of us," he replies, unfolding his napkin and beaming pleasantly upon his better half. "The fact is that she has skipped her bail—gone back to Ireland."

"What!" returns Mrs. Appleboy. "Do you mean to say that that woman has been allowed to get away after you have been doing nothing, apparently, for the last six months but spend your time in those miserable court-rooms down there? It's outrageous."

"Oh, you can't help that," he replies, "so long as prisoners are admitted to bail—they have the sacred privilege, guaranteed under our Constitution, of running away."

"Rubbish!" exclaims the lady.

"And do you know," continues Appleboy, "it really is a tremendous relief to feel that I shall not have to take the witness stand and be cross-examined as to my past career by some miserable little shyster lawyer from the Tombs."

"Why, Silas," interrupts his wife sharply, "what have you been doing that you are ashamed to tell of?"

"Oh, I didn't mean that," he adds hastily, "but they ask such embarrassing questions; I might have to tell how much property I own, and then the tax collector would get after us."

"Speaking of property," continues Mrs. Appleboy, "where's the teapot?"

Appleboy gazes at her blankly. In the excitement attendant upon Maria's non-appearance in the court-room, the family heirloom had completely escaped his mind.

"I forgot all about it," confesses Appleboy.

"Silas!" cries his wife. "I should think that after all your experiences you would have had sense enough not to leave the Criminal Courts building without bringing that teapot with you. How do you know Maria hasn't taken it with her to Ireland?"

"Oh, I'm sure she hasn't," answers her husband; "it's down at the police station; they tagged it, you know, and left it in the custody of the sergeant."

"Well, hurry through your dinner," commands his wife, "and go right down and get it. I am surprised at you."

Appleboy skips his usual demi-tasse and fragrant perfecto, the result of which omission is to leave him but half satisfied and with a feeling of incipient indigestion, and betakes himself as fast as possible to the police station, where he has last seen the teapot. Now the police station, as is a way with police stations, is located without any reference whatever to the conveniences of transportation, hence Vestryman Appleboy is obliged to walk some ten or twelve blocks towards the river after a heavy meal, and reaches his destination very much out of breath and in a distinctly ill humor. To his surprise the doorkeeper at once recalls him.

"How are you, Mr. Appleboy? Come right in," says that functionary in greeting.

"How do you do?" responds Appleboy. "I have come to get my teapot."

"Ask the sergeant about it," directs the doorman.

So Appleboy makes his way to the desk, where he is again recognized, this time by the sergeant on duty.

"Well, Mr. Appleboy," remarks the sergeant, "what became of that cook of yours? She was a bad one! I hope they convicted her."

"They did not," replies Mr. Appleboy; "they didn't even get a chance at her. She got away."

"Jumped?" inquires the sergeant with a grin.

"That's what she did," acknowledges Appleboy, "after she had kept me chasing up and down for nearly six months."

"Oh, she was a sly one," answers the sergeant sympathetically. "A little vacation up the river would have done her good."

"I suppose there's no objection to my having the teapot back, is there?"

"Sure not," answers the sergeant. "It's yours, ain't it? Of course you can have it back."

"Do you mind letting me have it then?" asks Appleboy.

"Oh, we haven't got your teapot!" exclaims the sergeant. "That was handed over to the property clerk at Police Headquarters. I suppose when the case was set for trial the pot was sent down to the district attorney's office; he's probably got it locked up in his safe,—I mean whatever assistant was going to try the case."

"Well, well," says Mr. Appleboy; "of course, I assumed it was right here, where I saw it last. What would you advise me to do?"

"Better go right down and see the assistant district attorney," says the sergeant. "Skipped her bail, did she? Well, that's a pretty good one, too!"

Although it is now three o'clock, Mr. Appleboy goes to the nearest elevated station and takes the train down town. This occupies about half an hour. He gets off at the corner of Franklin Street and walks to the Criminal Courts building. He is now thoroughly familiar with this lugubrious locality and finds the elevator without difficulty, ascending amid the usual odoriferous company to the floor upon which Mr. Smith, the assistant district attorney, has his office. Mr. Smith's door, however, is locked, and inquiry from a deaf attendant in a neighboring corridor elicits the fact that the assistant is engaged in trying a murder case in Part IV of the General Sessions. Appleboy now bethinks him of Jones and forthwith descends to the next tier of offices, but there finds to his chagrin that the latter also is trying a case.

Determined not to be thwarted by any such trifling matter, our hero takes the elevator to the second floor of the building, upon which the court-rooms are located. He first applies at Part I. The superannuated attendant at the door eyes him sharply, asks him for a subpœna, and upon his failure to produce it denies him admittance. Appleboy, naturally indignant, inquires the reason. The watchdog at the door brusquely replies that persons having no business in the court-room are not permitted to enter.

"But I want to speak to Mr. Jones."

"Well, he can't see you now, anyhow," replies the doorkeeper. "It won't do you a particle of good to go in; he's right in the middle of summing up the case to the jury."

This seems a sufficient excuse, even to our much-annoyed old gentleman, and he thereupon makes his way to the court-room in which he has been informed that Smith is disporting himself. Here he makes a second attempt to secure admission. On this occasion there is not even the question of a subpœna. No one can be admitted, because the judge is "charging the jury." The answer is definite and final.

The doorkeeper, however, is a good-natured, genial, warm-hearted Irishman, and notes with some sympathy the disappointment and chagrin of the weary little old man. Appleboy observes the benignity of the other's expression and tenders a cigar,—not what is commonly known about the building as a "cigar" (six for a quarter) or even a "good cigar" (a ten-center), but a bang-up, A-1, twenty-five-cent Havana, with a gorgeous coat of many colors. Being very tired he lights another for himself. The two converse amicably.

It now develops that the doorkeeper not only remembers Appleboy, but the case and the teapot, and finally, having become conversant with the entire situation, he pronounces judgment, namely, that Mr. Appleboy will find the teapot at the property clerk's office at Police Headquarters; that while it is possible that it might remain in the custody of one of the assistants, or in charge of the property clerk, attached to the district attorney's office, it is very unlikely that such is the case, since the defendant was never placed on trial. He therefore advises Appleboy to return with all haste to 300 Mulberry Street and secure the return of his property from the person there having it in charge. Appleboy is very much pleased; he begins to regard himself as quite a "mixer," while for a brief moment visions of running for mayor or perhaps for alderman hover in his mind; and after presenting the doorkeeper with a couple more Havanas he makes his way out of the building upon the Center Street side.

Appleboy supposes, as is not unnatural, that Police Headquarters must be somewhere in the immediate neighborhood of the Criminal Courts building. A laborer, in response to his question, waves his hand in a northerly direction, and Appleboy sets out, traversing what seems to him to be an interminable distance. Every one whom he addresses states that Headquarters is just a block or two farther on. Soon he finds himself on Mulberry Street; swarms of little children congregate upon the sidewalk and pass comments upon his appearance; Italian ladies in faded négligée look down upon him from upper windows; bunches of macaroni in a half-solidified condition stream from frame-works erected in the areas, and

Appleboy shudders as he thinks of the germs wafted down the side streets and from the open windows of the tenements which must, as he believes, collect and form a thick crust upon the surface of this unattractive variety of nutriment. From time to time he crosses the street for the purpose of avoiding a fight between small boys or a group of children dancing around an organ; occasionally he is obliged to walk in the middle of the street itself. After twenty minutes he comes in sight of an inhospitable-looking structure, which, he is informed by the peanut seller upon the corner, is that for which he seeks.

"Polica Headquarta!" chatters the Italian and grins; he knows well enough what it is, and "many there be that go in thereat."

Appleboy crosses the street and ascends the steps, meeting as he does so a squad of policemen who bang open the door and come marching down in pairs. He shrinks to one side, and then timidly makes his entry. An officer in the hall inquires his business.

"I desire to see the property clerk," says Mr. Appleboy, "and to secure the return of a teapot which was stolen from me."

"The property clerk's office closes at four o'clock," says the officer; "you'll have to come to-morrow morning, at nine."

Appleboy is disgusted; he has spent what is practically an entire afternoon in the pursuit of his teapot and has accomplished nothing.

"It's outrageous," he cries; "the idea of a public office closing at four o'clock in the afternoon! What do these fellows do, I would like to know, to earn their salary? Nine to four,—pooh! Why, it isn't half a day's work."

The officer has turned on his heel and walks slowly away, leaving Mr. Appleboy fuming by the door. The corridor is musty and dark, its stone flagging worn by the tread of millions of heavily booted feet. Poor old Mr. Appleboy is very tired; the dingy windows, the gloomy corridor, the unsympathetic policeman, the noise and smells of the Italian quarter, the weary trip to the district attorney's office and to the station house have brought him almost to the verge of tears. He is ashamed to go home and tell his wife that he has accomplished nothing,—he has not even *seen* the teapot. Feeling very small indeed Appleboy pushes open the door and passes out upon Mulberry Street. No one notices him; in this official world a bank president is but a unit among the countless multitudes of the public. He stumbles into a subway train, seeks sanctuary in his club and takes a Turkish bath.

Let us pass over the painful scene upon the return of Appleboy teapotless. His lady is hardly to be blamed for showing irritation over her husband's failure to recover that interesting relic and valuable domestic adjunct. She knows she could have done much better herself. At any rate she would not now calmly return home from the court with the humiliating admission that the prisoner had escaped and that the teapot had disappeared. Things are very unpleasant that evening, and no suggestion on the part of Appleboy that they go to the theatre or the opera will bring a smile over the features of his irate spouse.

The next morning Mr. Appleboy is up betimes. He does not wait for his wife to come down to breakfast, but pours himself a cup of coffee and snatches a roll at the sideboard. A quarter to nine finds him at Police Headquarters. In the clear morning sunshine the building does not look so repellent, and he trots up the steps, pushes open the door, and, avoiding his adversary of the afternoon before, saunters nonchalantly down the corridor until he sees a small door at the top of a couple of steps bearing the legend, "Property Clerk's Office."

The property clerk, whoever he is, is already there. Appleboy finds himself in a small room divided by a wire grating; this has a small opening through which he is obliged to converse with the official in charge.

"I have come to get a teapot which was stolen from me," explains Appleboy.

"What is the state of the case?" inquires the property clerk.

"The thief has forfeited his, I mean her, bail," replies our hero.

"What was her name?"

"Maria Holohan."

"When did she steal the teapot?"

"Last June."

"Where did you last see the teapot?" asks the clerk.

"At the station house, with a tag on it," Appleboy replies.

"Well, what makes you think we have it?" asks the clerk.

"Why, the policeman down at the court-room told me that you kept all the property which was retained as evidence," answers Appleboy.

The clerk rapidly turns over the leaves in a large book. Evidently he finds what he is looking for and, nodding, answers: "Well, here's the record of the case. One silver teapot, value fifty. Officer making arrest, Patrick McGinnis. Prisoner's name, Maria Holohan. Claimant's name, Silas

Appleboy. That's you, is it? Stolen property, teapot. Held for evidence, yes. There you are, and you say now she skipped her bail?"

"Certainly," answers Appleboy.

"And you want the teapot?"

"Of course I do," answers Appleboy.

"Well, first you have to get an order from the court to that effect," says the clerk.

Appleboy almost loses his temper. Has he got to make another trip down to that miserable Criminal Courts building?

"Look here," he exclaims rather angrily, "what is the sense of all this red tape? The case is over, I own the teapot,—why don't you give it to me and be done with it?"

The clerk smiles,—a trifle condescendingly, thinks Appleboy.

"My dear sir," he says, "are you aware that I have no means of knowing that you are the Silas Appleboy who owns this teapot, except your own say so?"

"Isn't that enough?" shouts Appleboy.

"It ought to be," responds the clerk, "but sometimes it isn't. I don't even know that the woman has skipped her bail."

Appleboy begins to see the force of the clerk's argument.

"I never imagined that a gentleman would be tossed about from pillar to post, as I have been since I lost that teapot. What is it you say I must do; get an order from the mayor?"

"No, no,—the judge," answers the clerk.

"How shall I get it?" inquires Appleboy rather huffily.

"Oh, ask the assistant district attorney; he will probably get it for you."

"Thank you," says Appleboy stiffly, and marches out. This time he takes the subway to Canal Street, reaching the Criminal Courts building a few moments after nine. Much to his surprise Mr. Smith is already down at his office hard at work.

"Ah, Mr. Appleboy, good-morning to you," he exclaims.

"How are you, Mr. Smith?" responds Appleboy. "I have come after that confounded teapot."

"Oh, the one your cook stole. I remember it well. Where is it?"

"At Police Headquarters," responds Appleboy, "and they want me to get an order from some judge or something before they will give it up to me."

"That's easily managed," responds the assistant, "but you have to get a waiver from this office of any claim that we may have upon the teapot as evidence. There is a regular printed blank. I think, inasmuch as Jones was actually going to try the case when Maria skipped her bail, that he had better fill it out. After you get it, come back here and I'll make the application for you."

Appleboy begins to feel better. Here is some one that knows his business. He lights a cigar and descends to the next floor, where he finds his old friend Jones. Jones is quite ready to give the desired waiver, and selects one from a pigeon-hole in his desk. He fills it out to read as follows:

New York, October 7, 1907.
District Attorney's Office,
County of New York.

The People of the State of	}
New York on the complaint of	}
Silas Appleboy	}
against	} For Grand Larceny in the Second Degree
Maria Holohan.	}

This office has no further use for the property taken from the defendant in this case, and now in the possession of the property clerk of the police department. No objection is therefore made by me to its delivery to any person who proves to your satisfaction his right to the possession of the same,—one silver teapot.

A. BIRD,
District Attorney.
Per William Jones, D.A.D.A.

To the Property Clerk of the Police Department, Borough
of Manhattan, City of New York.

"Now we'll go down and see if the judge will give us an order," says Jones.

"Why, is there any doubt about it?" inquires Appleboy, fearful that perhaps
after all he is going to lose his teapot.

"It all depends on circumstances," answers Jones. "Some of the judges are
perfectly willing to give orders while others are not. You see, the trouble in
your case is that the woman has never been tried, so that the question of
whether or not she stole your teapot has really not been decided at all."

"The wicked flee—!" murmurs Appleboy in his most approved Friday
evening manner.

They take the elevator down to the second floor, and make their way to
that part of the Sessions upon whose calendar Maria's case appeared at the
time she forfeited her bail. A trial is going on, and a pompous little lawyer is
cross-examining a stout lady who weeps and laughs hysterically by turns. As
the lawyer pauses for breath Mr. Jones arises and addresses the court.

"May it please your Honor, in the case of the People against Maria
Holohan, charged with grand larceny, the bail in which was forfeited before
your Honor about a week ago, I desire to apply for an order directing the
property clerk at Police Headquarters to turn over the property, namely a
silver teapot, to the complainant, who is here in court."

"But the case has never been tried, you say, Mr. Jones," objects his Honor.

"That is all very true," returns the assistant, "but the woman has run away,
her bail has been forfeited, and judgment entered and satisfied."

"Supposing, however, she were captured and brought back and tried, how
do I know but that the jury might acquit her? And they might acquit her on
the specific ground that the teapot belonged to her, and not to the
defendant. I should then be in a position of having directed its return to a
person to whom it did not belong."

"Of course what your Honor says is entirely correct," answers Jones, "but it
is unlikely that we shall ever hear of the case again."

"I don't know about that," answers the judge. "Your office might become
suddenly extremely energetic and try to extradite her."

"Well, it seems rather hard on Mr. Appleboy," responds Jones.

"Of course it's hard; he has my entire sympathy," replies the judge; "but I
cannot take the responsibility of deciding who owns property in a case

which has not been tried. I am not here for that purpose. Let him take the proper legal steps to secure the return of his property in the civil courts."

Appleboy, who has understood very little of this colloquy, but who supposes that, for some entirely insufficient reason apparently, the judge is trying to block his efforts to secure the return of his property, suddenly jumps to his feet and shouts:—

"Look here, your Honor, I would like to have a word about this, if I may! That teapot of mine was stolen last June; I caught my cook in the very act of selling it to a pawnbroker; I had her arrested on the spot; she admitted her crime, and acknowledged her guilt in the police court. My teapot is tagged and locked up in a room at Police Headquarters, and they won't give it to me unless your Honor will grant an order directing them to do so. Kindly tell me what I am to do."

The crowd in the court-room titters and the court attendant raps loudly with a paper-weight on the oaken railing for silence. The judge regards Mr. Appleboy good-naturedly.

"I am very sorry you have had so much trouble. My position in the matter simply is that I cannot personally take the responsibility of deciding to whom this property belongs, particularly when no jury has ever passed upon the guilt or innocence of the defendant. I shall be very glad, however, to approve any certificate which the district attorney may choose to give you stating that he has no further need or use for the property."

Appleboy brightens.

"Your Honor," says he, "Mr. Jones has already given me such a certificate, and I shall be much obliged to you if you will approve it."

Jones hands it to the judge, who writes the word "Approved" upon it, then returns it to the assistant.

"You will observe," says his Honor, "that all I do in the matter is to approve the statement of the district attorney that he makes no objection to the delivery of the property to any person who proves to the satisfaction of the property clerk his right to the possession of the same. My approval really does not amount to anything at all. I cannot grant you a court order. I am aware that several of my associates might do so under exactly similar circumstances, but I personally do not care to assume any such responsibility. Proceed with the case on trial."

Out in the corridor Appleboy inquires anxiously of Jones how on earth he is going to prove to the satisfaction of the property clerk his right to the possession of the teapot.

"Oh, you won't have any difficulty at all," says Jones; "this certificate from us, with the judge's 'O.K.' on it, is equivalent to a court order, even if it is not one technically."

"I don't know," answers Appleboy doubtfully; "this paper seems to leave it up to me to persuade the intelligence of the property clerk."

"You won't have any trouble," laughs the assistant. "Good-by."

Mr. Appleboy leaves the building once more, and again takes the subway to Police Headquarters.

"Back again?" inquires the property clerk pleasantly.

"I have a certificate from the district attorney, approved by the judge giving you permission to return the teapot to me," says Appleboy, shoving the paper through the wicket.

The clerk takes it.

"This isn't a court order," says he. "Still, if the woman has skipped her bail and the judgment has been satisfied, I guess we can take a chance and let you have your teapot, provided of course you are properly identified. You see, so far as we know, you may have picked this certificate up on the street. The thing for you to do is to get hold of the officer who made the arrest, and who knows all about the case, and have him identify you."

"How shall I do that?" asks Appleboy, very much irritated. "I don't know where he is; I can't go chasing all over the City of New York after police officers; I'm sick of this whole business; you know perfectly well I am Silas Appleboy, else I shouldn't have this paper, and I shouldn't be around here trying to get that teapot."

"Don't be too sure about that," replies the property clerk. "We have had three women here at the same time claiming the same pair of diamond earrings, and each woman looked absolutely respectable. One of them came in a carriage with a footman. We found out afterwards that the earrings didn't belong to any one of them, but to an entirely different person."

Appleboy loses all patience. Just as he is about to place his hands upon the teapot, *presto*, it vanishes. Two Italians and a Chinaman, escorted by an officer, now elbow past Appleboy, who disconsolately gives them place. He is "up against it" again; there is no help for it; rules are rules and the law is the law. How now to find Patrick, the officer! He begins to wish he had been nicer to Patrick;—if he had been a little more liberal in the way of cigars at the time the teapot was stolen, things might have been very much easier for him now. He utters an imprecation under his breath against all policemen and police red tape. Grinding his teeth, he goes to the nearest telephone booth and asks to be connected with the precinct to which Patrick is attached. The operator refers him to 3100 Spring, namely, Headquarters,—but there he is informed that private citizens may not be connected with police stations. He hangs up the receiver with something almost like an oath, Poor Vestryman Appleboy! Let us not be too hard upon him.

It is now half-past eleven o'clock. He takes the car uptown and returns to the station house, but the sergeant informs him that Patrick is down in the Criminal Courts building as a witness in a burglary case. This is the last straw. Frenzied, he rushes from the station house, takes another car and sits tensely until once more he is at the Criminal Courts building. Fortunately he has had the forethought to inquire of the sergeant to which of the four parts of the General Sessions Patrick has been subpœnaed, and he now finds that it is the same court-room at the door of which presides his friend of the day before. The doorkeeper greets him genially, and in response to Appleboy's inquiries replies, shure, that he knows Pat McGinnis;—that Pat has been there all the morning, but has just shtepped out over to Tom Foley's saloon. Although Appleboy has not been inside the portals of such a place since he was nineteen years old, he frantically inquires its direction, and, fearful lest he lose the object of his search, dashes across the street to the corner bar-room.

The little old gentleman with the shining silk hat sticks his head timidly through the door and observes Patrick at the end of the bar crooking his elbow in the customary manner. He draws an inspiration from the sight; with a bland smile he steps up to the bar himself, slaps the officer familiarly on the back and, pulling off his gloves, remarks, "Well, Pat, old boy, how do you feel? Have another on me!"

Patrick gazes at him open-mouthed. Can this be the stiff, little old bank president he knew six months ago? But there can be no question as to Appleboy's intention when he hears the latter order "two rye high-balls *and another-for-yourself*" of the astonished barkeeper. Appleboy toasts Patrick, Patrick toasts Appleboy. Patrick produces cigars; Appleboy replaces them with others, larger and thicker than any seen at Foley's.

"By the way," says Appleboy, "step up to Police Headquarters with me, will you, Pat? Now that I happen to be down this way, I might as well take that teapot home with me, don't you know."

"Shure," says Pat; "court's adjourned by this time, and I can get back by two o'clock all right."

The best of friends, they go up in the subway together to Police Headquarters. With a bold front and fearless eye Appleboy enters the office of the property clerk, produces his certificate from the district attorney, and demands his teapot.

"This officer will identify me," says he.

"Shure I indentify him," announces Pat.

The clerk takes the certificate, opens the record book and, with a rubber stamp, enters up on the back of the original report the words:

> "*Identified by officer*
>
> *as owner of the property.*"

"Write your name there," says he to Patrick, and McGinnis laboriously scrawls his name between the lines.

The clerk now disappears into an adjoining room, presently returning with an object about the size of a football, wrapped in coarse paper, tied with a multitude of strings and bearing a tag.

"Here you are, sir," says he, opening the door in the wire grating and passing the football to Appleboy, whose heart beats wildly.

The clerk then stamps the words "*Delivered on identification of officer*" upon his record book, closes the same with a slam and turns aside to other more important business. How simple it all is when you once know how to do it!

"Easy, ain't it?" remarks Pat.

"Easy as rolling off a log," answers Appleboy with a grim smile.

CHAPTER IX

THE TRIAL OF FELONIES

It is a fact, which may at first appear paradoxical, that the jury in the ordinary run of criminal cases passes upon the guilt or innocence of very few professional criminals. A moment's consideration will reveal the reason. The professional criminal usually has a "record" and he knows full well that in view of his past history, if there be any sort of a case against him, his own defence, however eloquent or ingenious, will go for nothing. An affirmative answer to the simple question, "Have you ever been convicted?" is, in three cases out of five, equivalent to a plea of guilty. Now it is an understood thing that any prisoner, who is willing to admit his guilt and save the county the expense and trouble of a trial, shall receive some consideration in return therefor when it comes time to impose his sentence, and usually he expects to receive in addition a guarantee of good faith from the assistant district attorney in the shape of the latter's acceptance of his plea to a lower degree of the same crime. The real "gun" is apt to have his life pretty well mapped out. He anticipates serving about so much time "in stir" and figures on beating about every other case before it reaches an actual trial. If worst comes to worst, and he finds he must face a jury of his peers, he dickers for the lowest plea he can get. Whole court terms often go by without a single professional crook being actually tried. If one of them is "caught with the goods" he generally throws up his hands and stolidly takes his medicine.

The ordinary citizen quite naturally gains his impressions of the administration of criminal justice by reading accounts of sensational trials. He imagines that the daily life of the prosecutor consists in demanding the conviction of hardened felons with sordid, crime-tracked features, varied by occasional spectacular "star cases" where counsel for the defendant and the prosecutor vie with one another in stupendous outbursts of oratory in which the bird of liberty screams unrestrained and Justice frantically waves her scales. He supposes, if he gives the matter any consideration at all, that defendants languish away their lives in the Tombs waiting for trials which never come, and that influential criminals walk the streets while the indictments against them lie accumulating an overcoat of dust in some forgotten pigeon-hole. He frankly assumes that the jury system is pretty nearly a failure, and knows of his own knowledge, or thinks he does, that any one with enough money can either avoid being tried for crime at all or, if by any mischance he be convicted, can easily escape punishment or at least delay it indefinitely by technicalities of procedure and appeals. In his customary dialect he "has no use" for the criminal or the criminal courts, and his only dread is that he may some time be drawn as a juror and be compelled to serve in a region of the city where he will be unable to find a satisfactory place to get his lunch and in the society of those whose companionship he fancies he is not likely to enjoy.

Let us assume that Mr. Ordinary Citizen has been so unfortunate as to receive one of those pink slips which call upon him to "all business or other matters lay aside" and to attend at Part I of the General Sessions of the Peace at ten o'clock on the first Monday of the month. He finds himself in a large and well-lighted court-room, at one end of which, on a dais, sits a judge more or less surrounded by various persons who continually approach and engage him in conversation. At a desk in front, a clerk and his assistant are busy with piles of documents, which "O.C." learns later to be indictments, and with big ledgers which are in fact the "Minutes of the Sessions." The room is crowded, all the benches being filled with a varied, but, on the whole, a respectable-appearing assortment of humanity. In front of the judge and clerk, wandering around inside an enclosure, at one side of which stands the temporarily empty jury-box, are several young men who are earnestly engaged in talking to the lawyers, complainants and policemen who throng at the bar.

Suddenly the clerk raises his voice and shouts, "Harken to the call of the calendar!" An officer pounds on a railing with a paper-weight, another bellows, "Find seats there! An' quit talkin'!" and the judge, gazing at a long sheet of foolscap in his hand, remarks inquiringly:

"People against Murphy?"

The young assistant district attorney at once answers:

"People are ready."

"If your Honor please," nervously exclaims a stout man pushing his way to the front, "this case has never been on the calendar before. I was only retained last night and I did not receive any notice that it was to be tried until this morning. I ask that it go over until next week."

"What do you say, Mr. District Attorney?" asks the judge.

"Oh, it's a very simple case," answers the assistant. "There's no reason why it should not be tried to-day."

"Well, I'll give you until to-morrow," says the judge. "You must be ready *then*."

"People against Smith?" he continues.

Both sides happen to be ready in this case.

"People against McCord?"

"Defendant's going to plead," says the assistant.

"People against Vermicelli?"

"We expect to make a recommendation in that case, your Honor," announces the assistant,—and so it goes until fifteen or twenty cases have been marked "Ready" or "Passed for the day" or adjourned to let the defendant get his witnesses or, in point of fact, for the lawyer to extract his fee.

The clerk then calls the roll of the jury, and after the rush which ensues to present excuses to the effect that the talesman's health or business is in a precarious condition, the court settles gradually down to its routine work.

A jury is empanelled and a lank, seedy-looking youth takes his seat at the bar between a spruce, bald-headed little man and a court officer. He is charged with having "policy-slips in his possession."

So far "O.C.," our juror, has been impressed with the business-like and cheerful manner in which the proceedings have been conducted. Most of the lawyers, instead of clamoring for a trial for their languishing clients, have exerted all their efforts to secure delays. Then he learns to his surprise that the average length of time which elapses between a defendant's arrest for felony and his trial, unless the prisoner be out on bail, is *less than one week*.[27]

"Jury satisfactory to both sides?" inquires the clerk.

"Entirely so," reply the little bald-headed man and the prosecutor together.

Suddenly the lank youth leans over and whispers to the lawyer, who after a moment's conversation beckons to the prosecutor. There is a brief consultation and the assistant tosses the indictment to the clerk with the announcement:

"He pleads guilty."

The defendant gets up and shuffles to the bar, where his pedigree is taken and a day set for his sentence, which, in the event of his never having been convicted before, will probably be a fine of twenty-five dollars or a month in the penitentiary.

"Call the next case," says the judge.

"People against Thompson," shouts the clerk. "Bring up Thompson."

The door in the back of the room opens and "Thompson" is "brought up." He is a good-looking young negro, defended by a member of his own race.

The jury say they have no prejudice against negroes and are sworn without leaving the box. The charge is one of assault in the first degree—that is to say, with intent to kill. The complainant is a flashily dressed young mulatto woman, who asserts that the defendant "done crack her head wif an ice-pitcher," and produces the fragments of pitcher, done up in a newspaper. She admits that at the time of the unfortunate occurrence she was living with the defendant as his wife. There are no other witnesses for the People, and the defendant is sworn without more ado. He explains that the complainant accused him of being too attentive to a "yaller gal" on the next street and when he attempted to go out of the house she attacked him with a pen-knife. In confirmation of this he exhibits a small cicatrix on his wrist. After hearing the evidence the assistant announces to the judge that the case ought in his opinion to have been disposed of in the police court and that the interests of justice will be subserved if his Honor will discharge the defendant on his own recognizance. This the judge does with an admonitory lecture, and the defendant and the complainant go away together. "O.C.," the juror, begins to conclude that the assistant is a pretty fair sort of a chap.

Trial follows trial with great rapidity. Gradually the crowd in the court-room thins out. By one o'clock only a dozen or fifteen witnesses and spectators remain, and by half-past three the benches are practically empty. "O.C." has heard a dozen different complaining witnesses tell the story of how as many defendants have wronged them. The Bowery merchant whose packing-cases have been broken into has followed as complainant the man who has been robbed in a saloon; the "clothes-line fight" has given place to the story of the actual abduction of a young girl by a "cadet"; the landlady who has received a bad cheque from a lodger can hardly wait to recount the history of her misfortunes, for the man who has lost a horse and wagon through a drunken driver, whom he charges with grand larceny.

Generally the "People's case" consists of the complainant's version of what has occurred, somewhat corroborated by another witness or two, and the officer who made the arrest. Then the lawyer for the defendant takes his client by the shoulder and with a gruff "Go 'round there, young man," or, if he be playing for sympathy, a gentle "Please take the stand, William," starts him upon that most dangerous of all adventures, a journey to the witness-chair in his own behalf. In two cases out of three the defendant's own testimony, if he is guilty, is what convicts him. Both sides "sum" up in short, disconnected speeches, and the judge delivers a brief charge. The jury file out and another is immediately sworn. As the next trial begins very likely the door from the "pen" will open and the proceedings be interrupted long enough to allow another prisoner to tramp around the court-room, take his stand at the bar, and plead guilty.

"John Keenan, alias Foxy Keenan, alias Gum-Shoe Jack, do you now desire to withdraw the plea of 'Not guilty' heretofore entered by you, and to now plead guilty to grand larceny in the second degree?"

The defendant acknowledges with no very amiable expression that this is his inclination, and his pedigree, which is taken by the clerk forthwith, discloses that he has served five times in State's prison and twice in the penitentiary. "O.C." looks at his fellow jurors and whistles under his breath. That was the real thing and no mistake. Very likely the jury upon which he is now serving will convict, it having thus been brought to their attention by a concrete illustration that all the defendants are not innocent persons unjustly accused of crime. "Remanded," says the clerk, and Gum-Shoe Jack tramps back to the little door and the interrupted trial goes on. The stream of complainants, witnesses and defendants is as varied as that in Balzac's "Comédie Humaine." "O.C." begins to take a keen interest and now and then to put a question himself. He has taken the opportunity to make the acquaintance of the assistant district attorney at the noon hour and now feels that he is really a part of the machinery of justice.[28]

Ordinarily in a full court day there will occur from two to four complete trials, while an equal number of pleas may be taken. Sometimes a hundred and fifty cases will be got rid of by trial or plea in a single term in one part of the General Sessions alone. On the other hand, if the calendar is made up of "old-bail cases," indictments for receiving stolen goods, misappropriation, and Italian or Chinese homicides, the office accounts itself lucky in getting rid of half a dozen cases in the month. Occasionally, when a brisk, business-like judge is sitting, a "homicide calendar" will be disposed of at the rate of one a day, but this is rare and can occur only when most of the cases are for manslaughter or criminal negligence.

When trials are rapid their speed always redounds to the benefit, not of the People, but of the defendant.

Such a performance in a court of justice as the following, recounted by Lord Brampton, could not take place to-day. It is worth reproduction as marking the progress of criminal procedure:

> The first thing that struck me in the after-dinner trials was the extreme rapidity with which the proceedings were conducted. As judges and counsel were exhilarated, the business was proportionately accelerated. But of all the men I had the pleasure of meeting on these occasions, the one who gave me the best idea of rapidity in an after-dinner case was Muirhouse.

Let me illustrate it by a trial which I heard: Jones was the name of the prisoner. His offence was that of picking pockets, entailing of course a punishment corresponding in severity with the barbarity of the times. It was not a plea of "Guilty," when perhaps a little more inquiry might have been necessary; it was a case in which the prisoner solemnly declared he was "Not guilty," and therefore had a right to be tried.

The accused having "held up his hand," and the jury having solemnly sworn "to hearken to the evidence," etc., the witness for the prosecution climbs into the box, which was like a pulpit, and before he has time to look around and see where the voice comes from, he is examined by the prosecuting counsel.

"I think you were walking up Ludgate Hill on Thursday 25th about half-past two in the afternoon and suddenly felt a tug at your pocket and missed your handkerchief, which the constable now produces. Is that it?"

"Yes, sir."

"I suppose you have nothing to ask him?" says the judge. "Next witness."

Constable stands up.

"Were you following the prosecutor on the occasion when he was robbed on Ludgate Hill, and did you see the prisoner put his hand into the prosecutor's pocket and take the handkerchief out of it?"

"Yes, sir."

Judge to the prisoner: "Nothing to say, I suppose?"

Then to the jury: "Gentlemen, I suppose you have no doubt? I have none."

Jury: "Guilty, my lord," as though to oblige his lordship.

Judge to prisoner: "Jones, we have met before—we shall not meet again for some time—seven years' transportation. Next case."

Time: two minutes and fifty-three seconds.

But to return to our juror. What strikes "O.C.," who has now become entirely disabused of his previous ideas of what criminal trials are like, is the fairness with which those trials are conducted in the General Sessions and the fact that the interests of the accused are safeguarded in every possible way. Plenty of time is taken to try out even a pickpocket case or a street-corner brawl. The judge always covers the law fully and accentuates the necessity of giving every reasonable doubt to the defendant. In his heart "O.C." begins to have a slight feeling that the devil is getting a little more than his due. He has acquitted so many of the persons who have been tried that when he now sees a head he is not at all unwilling to hit it. He is fast reaching that state of mind which the prosecutor has anticipated when he has told his chief that in a few days he will have the jury "knocked into shape," in other words, he no longer believes every hard-luck story that he hears, he knows that certain criminal attorneys are capable of almost any kind of misrepresentation, he realizes that practically every defendant has already had a pretty exhaustive trial in the police court before indictment, he is quite as anxious to see the guilty convicted as he is to see the innocent acquitted, and he has been properly disgusted with the attitude and actions of certain of his colleagues in the jury-room whom he regards quite properly as anarchists or idiots. The district attorney at the end of a week has found out who some of these are. They have been "excused" for the remainder of the term, and he can rely pretty safely on the others rendering a fair verdict in any important case which he now desires to move before them.

What naturally interests "O.C." and his fellow jurors most of all is the defendant's own story of how he came to be involved in the transaction out of which the charge against him arises. For the first few days he very probably gives such explanations rather more credit than they deserve, for he is sympathetically inclined to believe that the prisoner is more likely to be the victim of circumstances than guilty of an act of moral turpitude. The eager attitude of some of the complainants likewise gives him an excuse for believing them to be actuated by more than a mere desire to see justice done and to have the truth prevail. He is inclined to look for hidden motives for every prosecution. This gradually wears off and his attention becomes centred on the defendant himself. Will he put in a defence? Will he testify in his own behalf? What will he say? Little by little "O.C." gets to inventing defences to fit the facts established against the prisoner by the people's case. Meantime he is learning a little law. That "the people must prove the defendant's guilt beyond every reasonable doubt," and "that no unfavorable inference must be drawn as against the defendant from his failure to testify in his own behalf." "O.C." has some difficulty with the "reasonable doubt." Perhaps he says to himself, "I am a reasonable man,— hence any doubt I have must be reasonable." However, the judge's reiteration that not every doubt is a reasonable one and that the words do not mean "a mere guess or conjecture that the defendant may, after all, be innocent, but a substantial doubt arising out of the evidence in the case, for which a reason can be given," and of such a character as would influence him in the important affairs of his daily life, eventually clears his mind on this somewhat abstruse psychological problem, and he translates "beyond any reasonable doubt" into the more lucid and comprehensive "moral certainty" of ordinary existence.[29] But that he shall not permit himself to be prejudiced against a defendant by the latter's refusal to testify is a much more difficult matter. He knows it to be the law, and he tries hard to obey it, but in a majority of cases he cannot escape the sub-conscious deduction that if the defendant were innocent he would not hesitate to offer an explanation. As time goes on and he gains in experience it becomes even harder to follow the instructions of the judge in this respect. He discovers that the district attorney cannot prove the prison record or bad character of the defendant unless the latter subjects himself to cross-examination by taking the witness-stand, and hence is likely to suspect that any defendant who does not testify is an ex-convict. Three jurors out of five will convict any man who is unwilling to offer an explanation of the charge against him. How they reconcile this with their oath it would be hard to understand, if they were accustomed to obey it literally in other respects. The writer has heard more than one talesman say, in discussing a verdict, "Of course we couldn't take it against him, but we *knew* he was guilty because he was afraid to testify."

As the reader is doubtless aware, under the common law no defendant in either a civil suit or criminal prosecution could testify in his own behalf. He was regarded as a party in interest whose bias must necessarily render his evidence of questionable, if of any, value. This doctrine, along with many others, our fathers adopted on their severance from England, and it continued to be the law in New York for a long time,—in civil cases until 1849, and in criminal until 1869. Then, ostensibly for the sake of the defendant and for the protection of the innocent, the rule was abolished. That the change from the common law was not generally approved either by the bench or bar of New York is clear from the opinion of the Court of Appeals in one of the earliest cases which arose under the new practice.[30] The court expressed the opinion that the change would redound to the benefit of the glib, quick-witted and hardened criminal who could invent a plausible defence, and result in the confusion of the innocent man unjustly accused of crime who might from stupidity or timidity involve himself in apparent contradiction; to say nothing of the fact that if the defendant did not take the stand the jury, however much they were instructed to the contrary, would inevitably draw an unfavorable conclusion from his failure to deny his guilt.

Now to any fair-minded American it must seem almost rudimentary justice that the accused should have a chance to tell his own story. That in itself is a sufficient reason for the rule. Just why, theoretically, if a defendant does not see fit to give an explanation and subject himself to cross-examination, the jury should *not* be permitted to draw an unfavorable inference is not so clear.

Experience has demonstrated that an innocent man need have no fear about taking the stand. Jurors sympathize with a defendant who is subjected to a withering fire of questions, and do not expect him to be able to give a lucid account of himself since the day of his birth, or to explain without the minutest contradiction every detail in the evidence against him. But they do want him to deny his guilt and to have an opportunity to "size him up." On the other hand, the slightest word of explanation may suffice to change the whole complexion of a case.[31] In the old days the guiltiest of criminals could, almost with impunity, shield himself behind his lawyer's eloquent assertion that his client had a "perfect defence," but that the law "had sealed his lips." To-day in the vast majority of cases the prisoner who does not take the stand is doomed. Out of three hundred defendants tried by the writer's associate, Mr. C.C. Nott, twenty-three failed to take the stand in cases submitted to the jury. Of these twenty-one were convicted, one was acquitted, and as to one the jury disagreed. Had these men been prevented by law from testifying in their own behalf, the ratio would have been very different.

Thus a rule originally intended to benefit the innocent defendant by *permitting* him to offer his explanation of the charge against him has practically resulted in *compelling* all defendants, guilty or innocent alike, to testify. It goes without saying that this has resulted in a considerable benefit to the community. Its only disadvantage, and this is probably more theoretical than practical, is that ex-convicts on trial can no longer successfully conceal their pasts. If they do not testify they will probably pay the usual penalty, and if they do testify they are more than likely to be convicted "on their records." Clever criminals often seek to avoid this dilemma by declining the services of counsel and conducting their own cases, thus rendering it impossible for themselves to take the stand, for in such an event there would be no lawyer to examine them. This ruse is well calculated to deceive the ordinary juryman.

The jury are also far less inclined to draw an unfavorable inference from a defendant's failure to testify if, on the conclusion of the evidence of the prosecution, he merely "rests on the people's case" and puts in no defence at all, than if he puts in only a partial defence. They readily appreciate that his counsel may honestly believe that as matter of law no case has been made out against him, and they bend their energies to the determination of the simple and unobstructed issue of whether the uncontradicted evidence of the prosecution has of itself established the guilt of the prisoner beyond a reasonable doubt. If he puts in a defence and calls witnesses to contradict those of the people, the jury are apt to concentrate their attention upon the question of the relative truthfulness of the witnesses on either side. Juries, quite naturally, are quick to infer guilt from any attempt at deception on the part of the defence, and habitually visit the sins of his witness upon the prisoner. Every criminal lawyer has had the unpleasant experience of seeing his client convicted merely because the jury have caught one of the witnesses for the defence lying on an immaterial point. Whether the jury hear one or both sides of a case, they inevitably labor under the disadvantage of never being able to pierce the screen which the law has hung between them and the truth in every case. Many a jury is struggling manfully with the question of the defendant's guilt or innocence, while the latter sits in the pen chewing the cud of narcotic contentment and wondering whether the yarn he "framed" for them will be believed. He has figured out what he is likely to get, knowing that even if he were found guilty the judge would probably not "give" him "more than Elmira," and has resolved to "take a chance." As the Elmira sentence is indeterminate, the defendant has nothing to gain by pleading. Once there, he will be released in fourteen months if his conduct appears to warrant it. The only real "chance" that he takes, is, that the judge may send him to State's prison, but he usually has made a study of the judge's character and past performances. Similarly he may have offered to plead to a lower degree of the same offence and his offer may have been refused, yet the matter is confidential and the case has to be tried by the district attorney as though he had no knowledge of the defendant's guilt. So the jury retire and frequently end their deliberations by acquitting the defendant, who leaves the court-room triumphantly to the great chagrin of the prosecutor. The jury, on the other hand, are filled with complacent satisfaction at having restored to liberty a man unjustly accused of crime. But these trifling considerations are as nothing when compared with the limitations which the laws of evidence and procedure place upon the presentation of what is ofttimes a perfectly plain case.[32]

The prosecutor who has thoroughly investigated a case has a knowledge of its real merits which can never be brought to the minds of the jury. There is much evidence, not technically admissible, which properly should be considered by him in determining his official action, and there is usually an equal amount of evidence, the competency of which will depend on the course of the trial. He occupies a delicate and frequently a very difficult position, since he must prosecute the case without reference to facts which might conclusively prove the defendant guilty, could they be introduced in evidence. The real character of the accused can almost never be demonstrated, for unless he takes the stand in his own behalf his "record" is inadmissible, and even when he does take the stand, he can deny with impunity any allegation as to his past offences and conduct, since the law does not permit the prosecutor to disprove such denials unless they relate to actual convictions for crime. Similarly the excellent character of the complainant and his witnesses may not be shown, unless the defendant himself directly attacks it, so that it is probable that throughout the case the injured party and the wrong-doer appear to the jury to be of equal credibility. The district attorney is a "quasi-judicial" officer, who must be at one and the same time the friend and right arm of the court and the advocate of the public right. His official position gives him an influence with the jury which honor forbids him to abuse, and demands an impartial consideration of the evidence and a dignified method of conducting the case, irrespective of the tactics of the defence. He represents not only the public, but the defendant, who is one of the public. He should be glad to welcome at any stage of the proceedings credible evidence tending to establish the innocence of the accused, and if it convinces him that the defendant is not guilty, he should, even in the midst of a trial, arise and move that the jury be discharged and the prisoner set free. But this is by no means inconsistent with a vigorous insistence upon the people's rights, nor does it require that the prosecutor should refrain from using the advocate's customary weapons of attack and defence. While he is cross-examining the witnesses for the defence and arguing to the jury, he is for the time being the lawyer for the people, and the appellate courts have said that it would be manifestly unfair not to extend to him in summing up the case an equal latitude of expression and scope of argument with counsel for the defendant.

It is the consciousness that he is indeed sore let and hindered in really laying the truth before the jury that makes the accusation of "unfairness" so bitter to a prosecutor, and it is the cause of whatever "overzealousness" it is often popular to ascribe to the district attorney's office. One would think, to read the communications in the evening papers during a recent trial, that the community had no privileges at all. A prosecutor frequently reaches that conclusion from experience. The writer is not aware that the constitutional guarantees which protect the liberty of the individual were intended to deprive the public of an advocate. In the nature of things, if justice is to be done, the People should be entitled to the same rights as the individual. If we are to have respect for law, the law must be deserving of respect, and law which makes rather for the acquittal than for the conviction of the guilty is not of that sort.

But with a trained panel of jurors, at the end of the second week of the term, the chaff having been separated from the wheat, the prosecution may reasonably expect to see the mill of justice grinding smoothly and reasonably fine, the jury at home in the court-room, familiar with their duties, and appreciative of the fact that all the assistant is trying to accomplish is the disposal of as many cases as possible consistent with fair trials and just verdicts. By the middle of the term he must be a very indifferent sort of fellow if he has not made friends of the jury; and assuming that he has done his work disinterestedly and in a business-like fashion, he will find that he has now the good-will and respect of the entire panel,—a regard which may well stand him in good stead later on in his career. This is the prosecutor's reward,—to try cases before a body of men who know that he is anxious to do the right thing, ready to welcome any evidence that really tends to establish the innocence of the accused, but insistent that no guilty man shall go free unless his act is first stamped as wrong by a conscientious verdict on the part of the jury.

Yet, as the writer has already stated, when the jury disband at the conclusion of the term with the thanks of the court, they have seen few professional criminals, save for a fleeting glance as one or two are led to the bar to admit their guilt. One exception readily suggests itself,—namely, the prosperous swindler who, by means of the "wire-tapping," "sick engineer" or other similar device, has parted some gullible person from his savings. Yet these gentry always save plenty of money with which to engage able counsel and are only forced to trial after they have exhausted every means of delay known to the law. They never plead guilty, but fight until the last gun is fired, believing that as they have escaped punishment in the past, so they will in the future. Their records rarely make it possible for them to take the stand in their own behalf, and if the case goes to the jury at all they are immediately convicted. Almost every panel has the opportunity to hear at least one "sucker" tell his story and to render a speedy verdict in his favor. It needs little explanation from a prosecutor to convince the twelve hard-working tradesmen before him that the defendants in this class of cases are the "real" criminals,—systematic enemies of society.

The great bulk of cases, that is to say, nearly seventy-five per cent, are disposed of by plea, by direction of the court, or "recommendation," that is to say, on the written application of the district attorney that the defendant's bail be discharged. Hundreds of cases are thus "turned out" every year, and for the most part represent those instances where the magistrate and grand jury have not had either the time or the inclination to assume the responsibility of discharging the defendants, preferring to put the question "up" to the district attorney or a petit jury. These recommendations are made on numberless grounds, the principal being (1) that it is clearly apparent that a reasonable doubt exists on the evidence; in other words, that as a matter of law the case should not be submitted to a jury; (2) that the People's witnesses have disappeared or left the jurisdiction; (3) that the case has once been tried with the jury standing almost unanimously for acquittal; (4) that owing to the peculiar circumstances in the case it is quite unreasonable to suppose that any jury would convict,—such as where an entirely respectable young woman being out of work has, in a fit of despair, attempted her own life.[33] Two or three cases are disposed of in this manner in each part of the Sessions almost every calendar day in the year.

The defendants who plead guilty are professional criminals, ex-convicts, and prisoners whose guilt is so overwhelmingly clear that they have no hope of getting even a disagreement.

Thus most of the cases tried are neither "dead open and shut," as the saying is, nor exceptionally weak. They usually present some question of doubt,—usually only a conjectural one, however, or at least admit of a more or less logical argument for an acquittal on the part of the defence.

In trivial cases the jury are inclined to take the law into their own hands. Boys charged with attempting to pick pockets or burglarize small stores, with assaulting police officers, carrying concealed weapons such as knives and brass knuckles, having policy-slips in their possession, rioting, malicious mischief, etc., are usually acquitted. This is because the jury think that they have been already punished enough for the character of offence which they have committed,—not because they believe them innocent. Cases where the charge is a serious one and which are tried before trained panels on a substantial amount of evidence usually result in conviction. In so-called "important" or "star" cases, defendants are rarely acquitted. If the reader will recall the sensational first trials of the last ten years he will find that there is hardly a single acquittal among them.[34] It is the petty law-breaker who profits by the lawlessness of the modern jury.

The fact that the prosecutor appears every day before the general panel of jurors in the Part to which he is assigned throughout the term and soon gains among them the reputation of being fair, and that he on his side knows their peculiarities and idiosyncrasies is what makes the jury system in criminal cases work more accurately and accomplish better results than in civil trials, where the jury usually has never seen either counsel before and probably distrusts both of them. A prosecutor who knows his petit jury, its faults, virtues and foibles, can move an important case before it, even though it be composed of retail cigar and newspaper dealers and small tailors from the East Side, more safely and with a better expectation of a just verdict than before a "special" panel of bankers and architects with whom he is unfamiliar. The ordinary panel at its daily task during the last two weeks of every term illustrates the jury system at its best. Cases moved at the beginning of the term usually result in acquittals. Occasionally a jury will open a term with a rather unexpected conviction, but it takes three or four days before they realize that a reasonable doubt is not meant to include "a mere guess or conjecture that the defendant may, after all, be innocent." Wily criminal practitioners seek if possible to have their cases put on the calendars at the opening of a term, and to secure adjournments at the end of the term in order that they may go over to the beginning of the next.

Court officers often win fame in accordance with their ability as "plea getters." They are anxious that the particular Part to which they are assigned shall make as good a showing as possible in the number of cases disposed of. Accordingly each morning some of them visit the pens on the floor below the court-room and negotiate with the prisoners for pleas. The writer suspects that the assistant in charge of the Part is usually depicted as a fierce and relentless prosecutor and the jury as a hardened, heartless crew who would convict their own mothers on the slightest pretext. The joys of Elmira as contrasted with other places of confinement are alluringly described and a somewhat paradoxical readiness to accept any sort of plea, in view of his bull-dog character, is attributed to the assistant.

The writer has known of the entire population of a prison pen pleading guilty one after another under the persuasion of an eloquent bluecoat assisted by an opportune conviction. Of course the prisoners expect to be treated with a considerable degree of leniency, and if one of their comrades goes up to plead and returns with the story that the judge is "easy" and the assistant "all right," and a sentence to Elmira, the others are apt very quickly to follow suit. If, however, the first of the batch called for trial does not come back at all (having been acquitted), the remainder will not "plead" under any circumstances. The same thing is true if the first prisoner who pleads gets a severe sentence. Prosecutors anxious to dispose of business hope for light sentences at the beginning of the term.

Most of the homicide cases are tried in the Criminal Term of the Supreme Court, and a great many pleas to "manslaughter" are accepted by the judge where the technical charge is murder in the first degree. The grand jury indict for murder in almost every homicide case on the theory that some evidence may possibly be given at the trial which will warrant such a verdict. A very large proportion of these defendants plead guilty to manslaughter, and are encouraged in all legitimate ways to do so. About two years ago, in the Supreme Court, the first defendant called to the bar concluded that discretion was the better part of valor and pleaded guilty. The judge, who had never sat in Criminal Term before, promptly gave him eighteen years,—only two less than the maximum, although the shooting had occurred during a quarrel over a game of "craps." Not a single other prisoner offered a plea to any degree of crime during the remainder of the term.

A great deal of interest is felt everywhere in the practical results of the jury system, and particularly in the proportion of convictions to acquittals. Figures purporting to show such ratios should be scrutinized with great care, as they usually include among "verdicts of conviction" pleas of guilty voluntarily offered by the defendant, and similarly include among "acquittals" all cases where defendants are discharged without trial on the motion of the prosecutor. The only figures which have any particular bearing on the question of how far the jury system is efficacious are those drawn from the results of actual trials in which verdicts have been rendered.

The following table shows the comparative number of convictions, pleas, acquittals, etc., in New York County during the last eight years:

Year	Convictions	Pleas	Acquittals by Jury and Direction	Discharged on Own Recognizance	Bail Discharged	Indictment Dismissed	Forfeitures	Declared Insane	Sentenced on another Indictment	Superseded Indictment	Dismissed by Grand Jury	Discharged on Writ	Discharged (Comp.)	Total
1900	424	1,672	733	366	185	76	74	13	60	19	1,093	4	141	4,860
1901	551	1,838	688	434	192	165	113	8	77	36	1,045	4	116	5,267
1902	419	2,009	698	351	457	257	97	5	67	62	863	2	73	5,360
1903	485	1,918	615	321	299	92	62	12	65	40	807	7	86	4,809
1904	495	1,971	700	363	272	50	63	8	63	37	898	20	99	5,039
1905	489	2,001	602	352	207	57	51	8	82	38	1,035	5	93	5,020
1906	464	2,079	560	428	344	99	47	11	137	45	980	2	69	5,265
19	582	2,2	656	493	202	100	45	12	179	38	1,52	4	131	6,2

07	66									9			37
Total	3,909	15,754	5,252	3,108	2,158	896	552	77	730	315	8,250	48	808	41,857

During 1907 in New York County out of 4,573 indictments .62 per cent. (including pleas of guilty) resulted in convictions. The following table shows a gradually increasing percentage of such convictions for the past eight years:

Year	Number of Indictments Disposed of	Total Convictions	Ratio
1900	3,620	2,096	.5790
1901	4,096	2,389	.5839
1902	4,410	2,528	.5506
1903	3,909	2,403	.6144
1904	4,022	2,466	.6131
1905	3,887	2,490	.6405
1906	4,214	2,543	.6035
1907	4,573	2,848	.6228

During this eight-year period 32,731 indictments were finally disposed of either by trial, plea, direction of the court or on the recommendation of the district attorney. These dispositions bear the following ratios to each other:

Year	Convictions by Verdict	Pleas of Guilty	Acquittals by Verdict	Acquittals Directed	Discharges	Minor Dispositions
1900	.1171	.4619	.1013	.1012	.1707	.0478
1901	.1345	.4487	.0840	.0840	.1831	.0657
1902	.0950	.4556	.0792	.0791	.2324	.0587
1903	.1239	.4905	.0786	.0785	.1770	.0515
1904	.1231	.4901	.0887	.0853	.1685	.0443

1904	.1231	.4901	.0887	.0853	.1685	.0443
1905	.1258	.5148	.0769	.0779	.1585	.0461
1906	.1101	.4934	.0584	.0745	.2067	.0569
1907	.1273	.4955	.0577	.0857	.1739	.0599

What the reader is naturally most curious to discover is in what proportion of cases (where they had any say in the matter at all) the jury let the defendant go. Roughly speaking, the proportion of convictions to acquittals *by actual verdict* is considerably more than two to one,—the ratio for 1907 being as 69 is to 31:

Year	Number Convictions by Verdict	Number Acquittals by Verdict	Convictions Per Cent	Acquittals Per Cent
1900	424	367	54	46
1901	551	344	62	38
1902	419	349	55	45
1903	485	307	61	39
1904	495	357	58	42
1905	489	299	62	38
1906	464	246	65	35
1907	582	264	69	31

The writer desires very particularly not to be understood as suggesting that because the district attorney in all these cases thought the defendant guilty or even *knew* him to be guilty, the action of the jury was necessarily improper. So far as his opinion may be worth anything he believes thoroughly in the jury system in criminal cases, with some trifling modifications. In a vast proportion of the cases in which acquittals resulted there was undoubtedly room for an honest difference of opinion as between reasonable men,—men in the long run better qualified to judge of the defendant's guilt *on the evidence* than the prosecutor himself, who is always at the disadvantage of knowing the "inside" or "unprovable" elements of the People's case, a fact which is apt to lead him to believe that the record establishes his own contention more than it appears to do so to the jury. The propriety of any jury's action must be determined only upon the basis of the evidence presented to them, and upon which they are permitted to act. The writer is inclined to believe that nearer eighty than seventy per cent of the defendants tried should be convicted. In the heat of conflict he might even claim ninety per cent and maintain that if a majority of eleven on each jury could render a verdict, nine out of every ten defendants, after a hearing in the magistrate's court, an examination by the grand jury, and a careful investigation by the prosecutor's office, should be convicted. The writer submits that the increasing percentage of convictions shown on the opposite page is evidence of the effectiveness of the jury in criminal cases in New York County.

FOOTNOTES:

[27] This is a vast improvement over the conditions which existed in this regard six or seven years ago, when defendants in prison could count themselves fortunate if tried within three weeks, or, if on bail, within a year. It was by no means unusual to have cases appear upon the calendars from three to five years old, the backs of the indictments being covered with the names of assistants long since departed from official life. The writer once tried a case that had appeared on the calendar TWENTY-EIGHT times, and cases which had appeared there from ten to twenty times were the rule, not the exception. In the days when the present district attorney was a deputy, indictments were so carelessly found and treated that in order to clear the calendars bushel baskets of them would be brought into court and dismissed "on the recommendation" of the district attorney. A house-cleaning process of this sort would ordinarily occur just before it became necessary to make an official report on the number of cases "disposed of." To-day there are very few indictments not tried within the year, and almost any defendant who wants one can get a speedy trial, such delays as arise being generally caused by the defendant himself. Of course during the summer months when but two courts are open, and the judges sit from only ten-thirty to one o'clock, action is somewhat less speedy, and as homicide cases usually require more time for trial than others, and are tried *seriatim* in order of age, the defendants may have to wait a little longer than in cases of less gravity. Even in such cases defendants generally have to be "forced to trial" against their will.

[28] The writer's colleague, Mr. Charles Cooper Nott, Jr., has recorded, as follows, the actual proceedings of an ordinary court day:

"Maria Dzialozindky takes the stand and swears that after a brief acquaintance she married (as she supposed) the defendant before a rabbi of his choosing; a man in charge of an officer is identified by her as the rabbi;

- 121 -

he is brought over from the penitentiary on Blackwell's Island where he is serving a sentence for larceny, being a thief and not a rabbi; Maria then goes on to relate how the defendant then procured from her one hundred and forty-nine dollars, and disappeared, leaving her alone in the Suffolk Street tenement which was to have been their connubial bower of bliss; it further appears that the defendant had a wife living at the time that he went through the ceremony of a mock marriage with Maria. Defendant takes the stand, modestly admits that he is possessed of such unusual attractions that Maria persecuted him into this marriage; that she forced the one hundred and forty-nine dollars upon him, and that he unfortunately slumbered in a saloon and it was stolen from his person. The jury fail to give credence to his tale, and promptly convict him. The next defendant is smooth and well dressed, a hanger-on in the region known as the Tenderloin. Testimony is given that he and another did take and carry away and sell certain typewriting machines from an office in Thirty-fourth Street. Defendant with an engaging smile tells how his companion had just been discharged from the office in question, and had enlisted his (defendant's) aid to remove the machines, which he informed defendant were his own, and how shocked he was later to learn that this wicked companion had no right or title to them. His smile is so engaging, and his looks so respectable, that the jury acquit him, and are somewhat chagrined when the judge, in discharging him, states that in the court's opinion he is a smooth and plausible thief and guilty beyond a doubt—which is the fact, as previous to the trial he had offered to plead guilty to a lower degree of the crime charged. Next comes a stalwart Irishman who describes with much feeling how the defendant (unfortunately a much smaller man), without any provocation whatever, viciously assaulted him in the hallway of the West Side tenement-house where they both lived, and cut him in various vital parts with a pocket knife. Defendant (bandaged to no less a degree than complainant) describes how he had "an argument" (a term embracing any affray ending in anything short of murder in the first degree) with complainant and his brother over a game of cards, whereupon they followed him to the hallway, threw him down and kicked him, and then struck at them with a large key. His talk sounding reasonable and being corroborated by several neighbors, defendant is acquitted. Lastly, an unsuspecting passenger and an alert trolley-car conductor tell how defendant, a shifty-looking young gentleman, while sitting next to the unsuspecting passenger, kept with one hand a newspaper shoved under the latter's chin, while with the other he abstracted a fine diamond scarf pin adorning his cravat. When their tale is completed, the defendant and his counsel put their respective heads together, and counsel then announces that his client, the sole support of a widowed mother, did, in a moment of temptation induced by filial anxiety, endeavor to acquire this pin, and he therefore desires to throw himself upon the mercy of the court and plead guilty, which he does. It appears, however (of course to counsel's astonishment), that his portrait has for several years ornamented the Rogues' Gallery, and that his record as a son is not all that it might be, whereupon he is sentenced upon the spot, and court adjourns. This is the summary of the actual record of a court day presenting no unusual features"—*"In the District Attorney's Office," Atlantic Monthly for April, 1905.*

[29] Cf. "Reform in Criminal Procedure," by Everet P. Wheeler, 4 Columbia Law Rev. 356.

[30] Ruloff vs. The People, 45 N.Y. 221.

[31] Mr. Nott cites the following case:

"The complainant, A, a well-dressed bartender, testified that he had known the defendant, B, for some time; that on the night in question B came to A's rooms, and shortly after B's departure, A found that his watch was missing; the watch had been in the pocket of A's vest, which A had left hanging on a chair, and A had stepped out of the room for ten minutes, leaving B alone there. B afterwards admitted to A that he had "hocked" the watch. Of course this testimony, if believed, made a case against B, and it is difficult now to realize how any one could ever have believed that the chance of explaining or contradicting it could be more dangerous to B than the certainty of having A's testimony go to the jury uncontradicted. B took the stand and testified that he was getting a good salary as manager of an "intelligence office"; had never been even arrested before; that A had obtained a loan of fifteen dollars from him and had left the watch with him on the understanding that B was to pawn it for fifteen dollars and give A the ticket; B did pawn it in his own name and was shortly thereafter arrested. This case is a fair illustration of a puzzling class. On the one hand, no motive or reason was shown why A should cause the arrest of his friend on a false charge (unless that of getting the watch back from the pawnbroker without payment of the fifteen dollars, on the ground that it had been stolen, is an adequate one). Upon the other hand, B's character and position in life seemed to make it unlikely that he would commit such a theft, and his act in pawning the watch under his true name gave color to his story. The jury acquitted, and who can say that there was not at least a reasonable doubt?"

[32] Mr. Nott gives the following illustration from an actual trial:

"Take, for example, a certain case tried in the Criminal Branch of the Supreme Court in the January term of 1902. The jury saw the defendant, a stalwart, open-faced laboring man of nearly sixty years, on trial for murder in the first degree; they heard a bartender and a smooth-shaven, bullet-headed witness describe how the defendant in the saloon became involved in a dispute with the deceased, caused by the defendant's bad taste in reminding him that he had done time for killing his own father; and they heard him of the bullet-head admit on cross-examination that a scar adorning his neck had been inflicted by the deceased some two years before; they heard the two witnesses describe how the deceased left, breathing threatenings and slaughter, and how a few minutes later the defendant, in the room back of the saloon, was approaching the rear door, cutting a plug of tobacco with his knife, which he had providentially drawn for that purpose, when the deceased leaped upon him from the door and tried to stab him, whereupon a fight ensued, in which the defendant was cut, and after which the deceased left, followed a few minutes later by the defendant and the bullet-headed, who saw naught further of him. To mar the symmetry of this tale of self-defence (proved by the prosecution's own case), but two jarring facts appeared—first, the saloon proper (not the rear room) was found soaked in blood, and, second, the deceased was found shortly after the defendant's departure at three A.M. lying on the sidewalk in plain sight of the rear door, with his throat cut from ear to ear. No evidence was put in for the defence, the defendant modestly refrained from taking the stand, and of course an acquittal was inevitable.

"From behind the scenes, however, the facts assumed a different aspect. The frank-faced defendant was one 'Red,' who had served time for robbery and other offences; the bullet-head surmounted shoulders upon which rested a heavy load of crime and violence, their owner having served the State several times and been implicated in numerous crimes, including murder; the bartender would have considered it quite as safe, and far more comfortable, to put a bullet through his head than to testify against this choice pair; while it was true that the deceased had killed his own father, the act was performed while parent and son were in a drunken fight, by striking the old man on the head with a water pitcher, and had occasioned great mortification to the son when he became sober; and it was true that defendant and the bullet-headed were both bitter enemies of the deceased. On this statement of facts, there is little doubt that the deceased was murdered in the saloon where the blood was found, and his body thrown out on to the sidewalk, and the story arranged, the defendant shouldering the quarrel because he had received a cut in the course of the fight. As the defendant did not take the stand, his record and character could not be shown; as the State was compelled to call the bartender and the other witness (they being the sole witnesses to the occurrence), it could not impeach their veracity nor attack their character. To the prosecuting officer, therefore, was presented the choice of recommending the 'turning out' of a desperate criminal without a trial, or of putting in what facts the law permitted to be shown, and leaving the jury to acquit, while marvelling that such a weak case should be presented to them."

[33] The number of these cases is one of the saddest commentaries upon the conditions of life in a great city. Upon this charge during the year 1905, 268 males and 114 females, a total of 382, were arrested. Thirteen males and no females were held for trial and the others were discharged.

Comparison with Previous Years

	NUMBER ARRAIGNED			NUMBER HELD FOR TRIAL		
YEAR	Males	Females	Total	Males	Females	Total
1896	147	72	219	30	6	36
1897	228	130	358	42	12	54
1898	202	159	861	26	15	41
1899	257	140	397	40	13	53
1900	251	173	424	40	12	52
1901	244	143	387	24	3	27
1902	244	158	402	23	6	29
1903	374	156	530	15	4	19
1904	234	123	357	15	..	15
1905	268	114	382	13	..	13
1906	269	136	405	20	2	22
1907	258	136	393	13	1	14

[34] Peo. *vs.* Molineux, Peo. *vs.* Bissert, Peo. *vs.* Glennon, Peo. *vs.* Mills, Peo. *vs.* Patrick, Peo. *vs.* Ammon, Peo. *vs.* "Al" Adams, Peo. *vs.* Hummel, Peo. *vs.* Wickes, Peo. *vs.* Wooten, Peo. *vs.* Rothschild, Peo. *vs.* Kanter, Peo. *vs.* Summerfield, Peo. *vs.* Sam Parks, Peo. *vs.* Weinseimer, Peo. *vs.* Burnham, Peo. *vs.* Gillette, Peo. *vs.* H. Huffman Browne.

CHAPTER X

THE JUDGE

The two principal functions of the judge of a criminal court are, first, to preside at the trial, declaring the law and seeing to it that the rules of procedure and of evidence are properly observed and, second, to impose sentence in case of a conviction. In the first case he is a judge of the law; in the last he becomes a judge of the facts. It would be impossible to say which of these duties is the more important, but the latter is certainly vastly the more difficult. An unjust sentence is as bad, if not worse, than an unfair trial, for the defendant does not have a chance of escape and, since punishment is a matter of discretion upon the part of the judge, it cannot be considered or reversed on appeal. It must be of precious little satisfaction to a convicted prisoner to know that he has had a perfectly impartial trial, if at the same time he receives a sentence four times longer than he deserves, and equally little consolation to a prosecutor when, after a fair contest, he has convicted a political rascal of influence if the judge "suspend sentence" and the defendant is permitted to walk the streets in spite of his offences.

The amount of learning requisite to preside with efficiency at an ordinary criminal trial is comparatively small, and provided the judge be honest, impartial, possessed of common-sense and what is known as "backbone," neither prosecutor nor defendant's counsel need, as a rule, complain, but the trouble, time, courage and discrimination necessary adequately to determine what punishment should be meted out to a particular offender for a given offence cannot well be overestimated. It is not a difficult matter to preside with dignity at a trial, preserve order, exclude hearsay testimony, apply the other simple rules of evidence that are ordinarily involved in a case of assault, larceny, burglary or homicide, and instruct a jury as to "reasonable doubt," "good reputation" and the "presumption of innocence" in words of one syllable. We may fairly assume that it is no harder for the ordinary judge to try a man for picking a pocket than it is to dress himself in the morning. It must in time become automatic if not almost subconscious. He could probably do it in his sleep. Most petty criminal cases "try themselves." The trouble begins when the same judge is compelled to decide whether the convict shall be sent to the Elmira Reformatory (where he may reasonably expect to be discharged in fourteen months) or to State's prison for twenty years.

Let us consider first the conduct of the judge during the trial itself. Theoretically it is his duty, at least in most States of the Union, simply to declare the law governing the case and to rule impartially upon the questions of evidence presented. He is supposed to give no hint of his own opinion as to whether or not the defendant should be convicted and to refrain from any marshalling of the facts claimed to have been proven by either side in such a way as to influence the verdict of the jury. In England he may and generally does "sum up" the case; in America such a course would usually be a ground for reversal, his function being limited to an abstract discussion of the law involved, with little reference to the facts save in so far as it may be necessary for purposes of illustrating the way in which the jury shall apply it. He is supposed to sit upon his dais serenely, indifferent as to whether a murderer be convicted or acquitted, whether an inexperienced assistant district attorney be "trounced" by an astute criminal lawyer with a couple of generations of trial experience, or, on the other hand, a bulldozing prosecutor bedevil a miserable prisoner, defended by an ignorant and untutored counsel, into State's prison,—provided either be done within the strict rules of evidence and proper court behavior.

This may be all very well in theory,—but it is very far from what is either followed in practice or, to speak frankly, desirable. What the people want in our criminal courts is, of course, a "fair trial," but they want a "fair trial" that results in the acquittal of the innocent and the conviction of the guilty,—so long as he is convicted by what they deem fair means. The people do not expect a judge to be more than human. Did he appear as indifferent to results as theory might seem to require the jury would quickly infer that the case was of slight importance and their action a matter of utter indifference to the court. Juries need to be kept in order and made to behave themselves, and, if judges did not from time to time exert a disciplinary influence, would easily run wild and become hopelessly demoralized. It is almost impossible to overestimate the awe with which the ordinary juryman regards the judge presiding at a criminal trial. He may have a supreme contempt for his personality or private conduct, but once let the judicial ermine enshroud the individual and he sees only the judge,— the personification of the law, the autocrat of the court-room, the "boss" of the particular "job" upon which he is temporarily employed. He knows nothing of the abstract theory of the situation. He wants to do well as a juryman and believes, quite naturally, that an improper verdict will be visited by the judicial wrath and a just one be acknowledged by a look of benignant commendation. If he thought the judge did not care he would take little interest in the business himself, and the apprehension of the court's approval or disapproval is an ever-present factor in keeping him doing conscientious work,—quite as important in its results as his own lightly murmured oath as a juror.

The judge, in addition to his theoretic duties, is in effect the individual who must keep the gang at work and see that every one of them earns his two dollars a day. If he appeared to them to be star-gazing or studying Epictetus they would soon rest on their shovels. Many juries take their cue from the court, laughing when he laughs, and frowning when he frowns, and instinctively, however much he may admonish them to the contrary, trying to determine from his manner and charge what his own impression of the case may be.

Now, a judge who has sat for ten or fifteen years on the criminal bench is usually keener to detect a liar or see through a "faked" defence than any twelve men drawn indiscriminately from different walks of business activity. A timely question from him may demolish a perjured explanation which, but for his interference, would have acquitted a guilty criminal. Theoretically it is none of his business. Practically it is. An inexperienced prosecutor may be so inadequate to the task of coping with some old war-horse of a lawyer that save for the assistance of the court a rascal would be turned loose upon the community; or, turn about, a stupid lawyer may convict his own client if not prevented by a considerate presiding justice. Theoretically the judge must let the parties fight it out by themselves. In point of fact it is his business to even things up. The old country judge was not so far wrong when on being assigned to the criminal term of the Supreme Court in New York City he said to the prosecutor:

"Mr. District Attorney, I reckon that, between us, we shall let no innocent man be convicted,—and no guilty man escape."

Practically this expresses in a nutshell the popular idea of what a criminal judge is for, and it is certainly the idea which pervades the minds of the jury. Nothing can eradicate it. It is a fact,—an existing condition, which the court must inevitably take into consideration in determining his course of conduct upon the bench. By this it is not meant that a judge should be either counsel for the defendant or district attorney, nor that he should force his ideas upon the jury, but simply that to be effective he must be more than a nonentity, a mere law book, or an ornament, must guide the course of the trial, and, in default of its being done by the counsel on either side, test by his questions the truth or falsity of the testimony. More than this, he should in his charge indicate the tests which the jury should apply to the various phases of the evidence and, while not influencing them upon the questions of fact which they are to determine, should nevertheless so elucidate their task that they may be guided in their deliberations and not go astray among the tangled underbrush of an adroit counsellor's "requests to charge."

The writer has endeavored in the preceding paragraphs to set forth briefly the theoretical function of the judge as opposed to his proper practical function if he is to be of any value in the actual administration of criminal justice. One more step is necessary, namely, to comment on the actual conduct of some judges who from natural disposition or a conscientious purpose to "do justice" are inclined to usurp the function of the jury and practically to direct either an acquittal or a conviction.

Under our prevailing doctrines the court has no right to influence the jury on the facts in the slightest degree, and indeed most judges expressly direct the jury to disregard absolutely any idea they may have obtained of what the court's opinion may be. This, in the face of the balance of the charge, must often seem paradoxical to the talesman, for few judges entirely succeed in concealing their own views of the case, however hard they may honestly try to do so.

It is quite as foreign to the spirit of our institutions for a judge to interfere with the jury on questions of fact as for a jury to arrogate to itself the decision of points of law. The system is designed to do "justice" by means of its several parts working harmoniously together, but neither part "working justice" by itself. If the judge arrogate the jury's function, the jury becomes superfluous. This is not the intent of the Constitution. There is no real trial by jury when the judge decides the whole matter, and it would be far more dangerous for a single man to act as arbiter of the defendant's fate than for twelve. Yet more or less consciously there is often a tendency upon the part of the criminal bench to lend itself to the success of one party or the other, however positively it may declare and direct to the contrary. The actual amount of suggestion needed to give the jury an effective hint is infinitesimal. The almost imperceptible accentuation of a word, the slightest lifting of an eyebrow, and a verdict has been determined—by the judge.

Now a printed record on appeal fails utterly to disclose the tone of the voice or the stage effects of a judge's charge. A distinguished member of the bench, now long since deceased, was accustomed to deliver charges so drastic that a defendant charged with a serious offence rarely, if ever, escaped. Upon appeal absolutely no exception could be taken to his remarks, yet nothing more unfair could be conceived of. The record would show that the judge had charged:

"If you believe the defendant's testimony you will of course acquit him. He is presumed to be innocent until the contrary is proved. If you have any reasonable doubt as to his guilt you must give him the benefit of it. On the other hand, if you accept the testimony offered by the People you may and will convict him."

Now, nothing on its face would seem to be fairer. What the jury actually heard was:

"If [scornfully] you *believe* the defendant's testimony you will of course acquit him. He is *presumed* [with a shrug of the shoulders] to be innocent until the contrary is proved. If you *have* [another shrug] any *reasonable* doubt as to his guilt you must give him the benefit of it. *On the other hand,* if you accept the testimony offered in behalf *of the People* you may *and will convict him!*" [The last few words in tones of thunder.]

Sometimes a judge becomes known as a "convicting" judge, although, perhaps, at the same time as a learned one. This usually occurs where a man of pronounced opinions with the advocate's temperament is elevated to the bench. Very likely by inclination he is a "prosecutor," with strong prejudices against law-breakers and bitterly intolerant of technicalities. The powers that prey may cower inert in their dens of darkness knowing full well that if one of them be haled before this Jeffries he will pay the uttermost penalty. Yet the spectacle of such a judge does not increase the public respect for law, and juries sometimes revolt and acquit out of sheer resentment at such dictation. But happily these men are of the past, and the more enlightened sentiment of to-day would frown as much upon a "hanging" judge as upon a jelly-backed wearer of the gown who was afraid of the displeasure of some politician if a "heeler" were convicted and who ruled systematically against the people because they had no appeal and could take no exceptions to his conduct.

Nothing strikes so sharply at our conception of liberty as the failure of criminal justice, and the conviction of a defendant not legally proven guilty or the acquittal of an influential criminal has a more disastrous effect upon the body politic than ten thousand bales of anarchistic propaganda. The partisan judge, who makes up his mind to convict or acquit if he can, may be right nine times out of ten, but the other time he commits an outrage. The judicial temperament is a jewel above all price. The writer recalls a certain case of a variety subject at the time to great public condemnation, where the judge before the indictment was moved for trial, inquired casually of the clerk what the defendant was charged with. When he learned the nature of the accusation he exclaimed audibly:

"Ha! He's one of those ——s, is he? Well, I'LL try *this* case." And he did. Unfortunately judges often "try" cases, either for the defendant or against him.

Nothing is more unfortunate for the judicial equilibrium than the fact that the prosecution has no right of appeal in the event of a verdict of acquittal. The judge may persistently prevent the district attorney from putting questions which are both competent and proper and rule flatly against him on the most obvious points of law without any redress on the part of the people. A weak judge will take no chances on being reversed and will pursue this course, while at the same time he is allowing every latitude to defendant's counsel and is ruling in his favor in defiance of the established doctrines of law.

A criminal lawyer of great adroitness, learning and probity, after he had concluded an argument of the most utter absurdity to which the presiding judge had listened with much attention and apparent consideration, frankly stated to the writer:

"You think my argument was nonsense? Well, you are quite right, it was. But no proposition of law is too far-fetched or ridiculous to be advanced in behalf of a defendant without some prospect of success in our criminal courts." The lawyer in question will undoubtedly recognize his dictum in these pages.

The attitude and disposition of the various judges becomes speedily known among the members of what is popularly known as the "criminal bar," and heroic efforts (often successful) are made to bring certain cases before the "right" judge.

"Do you think I'd try the Smith case before ——?" one will say. "Not on your life!"

In similar fashion lawyers retained by complainants will seek to have their cases put on the calendar of such and such a judge.

"Put it before ——," they will say. "He's *hell* on larceny!"

Some judges are supposed to be more lenient in the matter of sentences than their brothers of the bench, but the writer, after six years of observation, believes this to be a fiction. They are all lenient,—entirely too much so.

Much of the impression among criminal lawyers that they will fare worse at the hands of one member of the judiciary than another is due to the obvious fact that some judges are by reason of their training better suited to sit in certain classes of cases than others. One may have had an exhaustive experience in commercial matters and thus be better qualified to pass upon the questions of law involved therein. Another may have heard many complicated cases involving expert testimony, etc., etc. Of course as a rule the less well equipped a judge is to hear a certain kind of case the more apt he will be to listen to ill-founded argument on the law or the facts. No insurance swindler would want to be tried before an expert on insurance law. He would very naturally prefer a judge whose experiences had converged upon assault and battery. It must be admitted that occasionally a judge is to be found who seems to feel that every complainant who has lost money in a commercial transaction has no standing in the criminal courts but must be relegated to civil tribunals. This is but another way of saying that such a judge does not believe that the criminal law is meant to cover cases where there has been fraud in commercial transactions. This is hardly to be wondered at considering the present ineffectiveness of our statutes governing such classes of crime.

The writer recalls prosecuting such a case before a certain judge who, after hearing some rather complicated evidence in regard to certain written instruments, called abruptly for the defendant. The latter took the stand, and the judge inquired with a smile:

"You didn't intend to cheat this man, did you?"

"Certainly not!" cried the defendant.

"Gentlemen of the jury!" said the judge. "This is not the kind of case that should be brought before a jury at all. This court is not the place to collect civil debts. I instruct you to acquit."

Learning wisdom by experience, the writer moved the case of the co-defendant for trial before another judge and convicted him, although he was, if anything, less guilty than the first. He was sentenced to a substantial term in State's prison.

As a rule, however, little fault can be found with the conduct of our judges at criminal jury trials. In some instances it may seem to one side or the other that a judge shows bias, but these cases are comparatively few and seldom result in any actual miscarriage of justice. If some judges are inclined to rule against the People upon doubtful questions of law, this in the long run has at least the beneficial effect of reducing the number of cases reversed upon appeal. The judges are almost invariably courteous, long-suffering, and given to allowing the greatest latitude to each side in getting its evidence before the jury. In addition they are practical men of common-sense, most of them of long and profitable experience, and experts in the rapid disposition of business.

Let us now turn to the other and no less important function of the judge,—the imposition of sentence. It is a platitude that the chief failing of modern criminal justice is the inequality of punishment. It may well be and often is the case that in one branch of the General Sessions a prisoner is being released upon "parole" under a "suspended" sentence at the precise moment that some other and no more guilty defendant in another branch of the same court is being sentenced to prison for three, five or even ten years at hard labor.

That most able and practical of English criminal judges, Sir Henry Hawkins, has this to say in his reminiscences in the matter of sentences of convicted persons:

"The want of even an approach to uniformity in criminal sentences is no doubt a very serious matter, and is due, not to any defect in the criminal law (much as I think that might be improved in many respects), but is owing to the great diversity of opinion, and therefore of action, which not unnaturally exists among criminal judges....

"The result of this state of things is extremely unsatisfactory, and the most glaring irregularities, diversity and variety of sentences are daily brought to our notice, the same offence committed under similar circumstances being visited by one judge with a long term of penal servitude, by another with simple imprisonment, with nothing appreciable to account for the difference.

"In one or the other of these sentences discretion must have been erroneously exercised.... Experience, however, has told us that the profoundest lawyers are not always the best administrators of the criminal law...."

Sir Henry likewise speaks of the great intellectual difficulty of a conscientious English judge in trying to determine for himself the amount of punishment he should inflict in any given case. The English bench occupies an altitude practically unknown in this country. Access to it is far less easy than with us, and the personal, familiar, and off-hand method of communication between the judge and the bar, not to mention interested outside parties, witnesses, and relatives of the defendant, in vogue in our trial courts would hardly be viewed there with favor. It is the wholesale attempted interference with the action of the judges in our criminal courts that imparts a flavor of indecision and arbitrariness to so many scenes upon a sentence day. It is not unheard of to see a prisoner actually at the bar awaiting sentence while the judge upon the bench holds a sort of open levee, free to all comers, in which the prisoner's lawyer, his wife, the officer who made the arrest, the complainant, and the district attorney (and sometimes others who have far less claim to be heard) endeavor to bring the judge to their own particular way of thinking, and harangue him and each other in tones by no means always either deferential or amicable. Meanwhile the judge who will permit any such performance sits with an expression of exasperated indecision, and usually finally ends the matter by "remanding" the prisoner for further investigation. Such scenes are calculated to bring the administration of justice into contempt. Snap-shot judgments formed in the midst of an altercation may be unfair to the defendant and frequently are so to the People. A judge who tries to please everybody ends by pleasing nobody and makes a farce of justice. The administration of the criminal law is not a pleasing matter nor is it conducted for the purpose of pleasing the various parties. The judge is there to attend to his own business and make his own decisions. The writer once heard a judge inflict sentence in the following manner:

"Your counsel says sentence ought to be suspended upon you. The district attorney says you ought to get five years in State's prison. Well, I'll split the difference and send you to the Elmira Reformatory."

The sentence may have been the result of a conscientious and careful attempt upon the part of the judge to decide the question, but the phraseology in which it was couched will hardly commend itself as a standard.

A thousand indefinite factors enter into the determination of the exact amount of punishment to be meted out to an offender, and relatively trivial circumstances may eventually decide whether the stroke of the judge's pen in his sentence book shall swerve from a "three" into a "five." Assuming that the judge have the rectitude of a granite monolith and be impervious to influence of every sort, he is nevertheless compelled when inflicting sentence to depend in large measure upon "hearsay" testimony and evidence that could not possibly be admitted upon actual trial. He seeks to find out if he can what the past record and reputation of the defendant have been, and in so doing often is forced to rely almost entirely upon the word of the officer who originally made the arrest. If the latter be vindictive he can easily convey the impression that the defendant is a man of the worst possible character who has hitherto had the luck to escape being caught. In most cases the prisoner has little opportunity to traverse these vague and generally unheard allegations. Again it often happens that he has been previously arrested. This fact is of course excluded upon the trial for his present crime upon the common-sense doctrine that the fact of his former arrest of itself proves nothing whatever as to his guilt or innocence of the charge upon which he was thus arrested. When, however, he comes up for sentence it is frequently considered by the court, no matter what the subsequent disposition of the case against him may have been, on the general assumption that "where there is so much smoke there is generally a little fire." If he has actually been convicted before, the fact weighs heavily against him.

Almost anything may be presented for the consideration of the judge, however remote its connection with the crime of which the defendant has been convicted, and either as militating for or against the prisoner. Affidavits, letters, newspaper clippings and memoranda are submitted tending to show that he is of either good or bad character, has had a reputable or a disreputable past, has or has not committed or attempted to commit other crimes, or is or is not likely to "reform." Often these may have a good deal of weight, but the persons who present them are almost never sworn or placed upon the witness-stand or the defendant or prosecutor given a chance to cross-examine them as to their accuracy.

The mere attitude of complainants, obviously an entirely immaterial matter, is also often a considerable factor in determining how the prisoner shall be disposed of. If they are vindictive and anxious to "make an example" of the offender it may happen that they will persuade the judge honestly to believe that a heavy sentence should be inflicted, whereas if they are sorry for the prisoner and his family and are willing to "give him another chance," and intercede strongly for him, the judge may "suspend sentence" upon the same man. Now the attitude of the parties wronged is largely determined by the character and disposition of the parties themselves, and of course in many cases has no relation whatever to the real rights of the case. For example, a half-drunken laborer lacking the money to buy liquor may wander into an area and cut away a strip of copper water-spout belonging to some old lady. He sells it for a few cents and then is arrested and is convicted of petty larceny. No one has any particular interest in the case and the old lady comes into court and begs for the defendant's "parole." He has hitherto led a decent life and the judge lets him go. Now, if the same man, instead of stealing a piece of pipe out of an area, finds himself in the vicinity of a freight yard and cabbages a piece of iron belonging to a railroad company, he is no sooner convicted than the attorneys for the company swarm about the judge demanding that "this wholesale pillage of corporation property" be put an end to, that an example be made of such thieves, and insisting that it is an important case where a severe sentence should be inflicted. The judge cannot be blamed if his mind is, to a certain extent, affected by the representations of these gentlemen and he may easily give the defendant six months or a year in the penitentiary. The moral guilt of the prisoner is precisely the same and so will be the significance of his punishment so far as its serving as a deterrent to himself or to others is concerned.

Another instance is where a young clerk in a banking, express, or insurance office is caught pilfering. He has, to be sure, violated the trust reposed in him, but if the officers of the company are disposed to intercede in his behalf and express the belief that he "has learned his lesson" it is probable that they can persuade the judge to give the boy another chance, whereas if their attitude were otherwise he would, and perhaps very properly, be sent to Elmira or to State's prison. It thus, in many cases, lies within the power of the lawyer for a defendant, if he be assiduous, persuasive, or have influence which can be exerted upon the complainant in the case, to lessen materially the sentence of his client, who without his services would perhaps receive the maximum of punishment. The poor or friendless prisoner, who cannot pay for able or indefatigable counsel, inevitably suffers in consequence, for his *defence to punishment* after trial cannot be adequately presented. His guilt is the same.

Another matter, frequently entirely fortuitous, which yet may affect the question of punishment, is the fact of restitution. Where a prisoner has been guilty of embezzlement or theft and afterwards returns the money it is almost inevitably taken into consideration when sentence is imposed. Naturally it is apt to affect the attitude of the complainant in the highest degree. Now, if the offender be merely foolish, he very probably has spent the money he has stolen in gambling or feasting, while if he be shrewd and cunning he has laid it by until he can accumulate enough to go to South America. In the latter case he can be made to disgorge; in the former he cannot, and is often far worse off when he comes to be sentenced than if he had been more criminally minded.

From what has been said the reader should not infer that the majority of sentences are excessive. In point of fact the leniency of most of our judges is surprising, and when they err it is invariably upon the side of mercy.[35] The sentences actually inflicted are often so short that they must seem to the average layman almost trivial, and the number of cases in which sentence is "suspended" and the offender paroled in the custody of the Prison Association is almost seventy-five per cent of the total number of first convictions.

The reasons for this leniency are varied. Primarily it is because the judge realizes that it is not so much the length of imprisonment as the fact that the defendant is imprisoned at all that, in the majority of cases, acts as a deterrent upon that particular offender and upon those to whom his conviction is calculated to serve as an example; secondarily, it is due to the sentimental attitude of society towards criminals of all varieties; and, lastly, to an appreciation of the unfortunate inequality of punishment, and the difficulty in adequately and justly determining what weight should be given to hearsay evidence as to the convict's past history. In some instances leniency may arise from other and less creditable sources, such as sheer cowardice in defying influence, political or otherwise, the desire to curry popular favor in the hope of subsequent preferment in office, or possibly from the hope that if a light sentence is inflicted the case will not be appealed and the conviction reversed. This dread of reversal in the case of some judges amounts almost to hysteria, and there are well-known instances in which judges in the criminal courts have stood heroically by the district attorney and the People with the result that some scoundrel of great political influence has been convicted, and have then completely nullified the effect of their good conduct by weakly suspending sentence or by inflicting one so slight as to arouse the amusement and contempt of even the defendant himself.

The ultimate object of the proper administration of criminal justice is to sustain and increase the general respect for law. If it result in a lessened regard for law by engendering a belief that its officers are weak, cowardly, venal, or ineffective, it is a failure. The adjuration therefore to avoid even the appearance of evil applies strongly to all members of the bench. Nothing conduces more to lawlessness than a popular impression that criminal judges are incapable, "easy," or are subject to influence. A judge who, it is supposed, can be "reached," is an incentive to crime. Now it is highly improbable that any judge is ever "reached." Our judges are honorable men. But once let an impression to the contrary get abroad among criminals and the same result follows as if the judge were actually "crooked." If a judge is supposed to be amenable to influence, the criminal will assume that his own particular pull will be effective.

As an illustration, let us suppose that one of a band or "gang" of young toughs has been apprehended in making a vicious assault which might well have resulted in murder. Perhaps he has been paid fifty or a hundred dollars to "knock out" (kill) his victim. He receives a fair trial and is convicted. He deserves all he can get—ten years. Instead he is sent to the Elmira Reformatory. The rest of the gang, with their hangers-on, amounting in number very likely to forty or fifty youths and men, are immediately convinced either that they have been able to influence the judge through their political friends or that he and his associates are "easy." "Going to Elmira" is nothing in their eyes; and the conviction of their comrade results in no deterrent effect upon them whatever. He becomes a clever hero. Any one of them is ready to undertake the same job at the same price. If his conviction be reversed and he be set at liberty they conclude that in addition the authorities are incapable and that they can "beat the case" any time they happen to be caught. The effect of an important conviction reversed in its effect upon lawless sentiment cannot be overestimated.

A sense of judicial propriety is one of the most to be desired qualities in a judge. The slightest suspicion that he is giving ear to voices from behind the dais nullifies his effectiveness and destroys popular respect for the law which he may perhaps in fact enforce with ability and justice. The sight of a politician emerging from a judge's chambers may baselessly destroy the latter's influence for good. Actual infractions of judicial propriety should be visited with the utmost severity. Prescott speaks of the jealousy of the Aztecs of the integrity of their bench:

"To receive presents or a bribe, to be guilty of collusion in any way with a suitor, was punished in a judge with death. Who or what tribunal decided as to his guilt does not appear. In Tezcuco this was done by the rest of the court. But the king presided over that body. The Tezcucan prince, Nezahua Epilli, who rarely tempered justice with mercy, put one judge to death for taking a bribe, and another for determining suits in his own house,—a capital offence, also, by law." Perhaps this was going too far.

"The judges of the higher tribunals," he continues, "were maintained from the produce of a part of the crown lands, reserved for the purpose. They, as well as the supreme judge, held their offices for life. The proceedings in the courts were conducted with decency and order. The judges wore an appropriate dress, and attended to business both parts of the day, dining always, for the sake of despatch, in an apartment of the same building where they held their session; a method of proceeding much commended by the Spanish chroniclers, to whom despatch was not very familiar in their own tribunals."

We can appreciate to a considerable extent the emotions of the Spanish chroniclers. Judges often dine together, but not always for the sake of despatch. The writer has no hesitation in affirming that disregard of the comfort and time of jurors and witnesses is the most obvious fault of certain of them. Some judges occasionally adjourn court from one until two and make their own appearance any time before three. It is small consolation to a juror nervously distracted by waiting to find that the judge expects conscientiously to make up the time thus lost by keeping the jury at work until five. In most instances, however, the judges are more punctual and business-like than the jurors and counsel who appear before them.

Some judges occasionally seem to feel that the benefit of the "reasonable doubt" to which a prisoner is entitled before the jury remains with and should be given to him even after conviction. This sometimes manifests itself in the extraordinary phenomenon of a defendant who has stood trial and perjured himself in his own behalf receiving a less severe sentence than his co-defendant who has pleaded guilty and saved the county the expense and labor of a trial. There was once a case where this occurred in which two of the perpetrators of a brutal robbery pleaded guilty and received seven years apiece, while their "side-partner," after being convicted before a jury, was given five years by another judge. It was not in this case, but an earlier one, in which a judge, obviously on the theory of reasonable doubt, addressed the prisoner substantially as follows:

"Young man, you have been convicted by a jury of your peers after a fair trial. Your offence is a heinous one. You took the stand and perjured yourself, asserting your innocence. I might inflict a severe punishment. Still, under all the circumstances, *and in view of your claim that you are not guilty*, I will suspend sentence."

The reader should not and will not assume that these instances of unequal punishment and erratic clemency are set forth for the purpose of illustrating the usual course of justice. They are the exception, not the rule. That they sometimes occur cannot be denied. They should never occur. They are probably due frequently to utter weariness on the part of the judge, coupled with the realization that it is sometimes practically a human impossibility to get at the true inwardness of a case or know *what* to do. Seemingly arbitrary sentences on close observation are sometimes found to be erratic only in the language in which they are phrased,—not in the amount of the punishment. The table on the opposite page shows, the writer believes, that the average sentences imposed in the various classes of crime bear a remarkably sound relation to one another.

Could, however, the separate sentences be examined, an astonishing and lamentable inequality would be discovered,—an inequality which is an actual injustice, but an injustice which cannot be prevented under our present system. Unless all offences should be tried before a single judge of unvarying disposition and physical condition absolute equality could not be secured. Where they are tried before four or five different judges there will be four or five different and constantly varying factors which must be multiplied into the constants shown by the record. Some judges regard certain crimes as more detestable than others do, and some judges see greater possibilities of reformation in any given criminal than others. Some are more affected by the immorality, as distinguished from the illegality, of a given crime than others, and certain judges will take into consideration features of the case that would be entirely disregarded by their associates.

===
============================

Classified list of the number of persons convicted, and the average term imposed for each particular crime during the year 1907 in New York County.

MALES

Offence	No.	Aggregate Term of Sentences		Average Term Each Person	
		Years	Months	Years	Months
Abduction	4	32	..	8	..
Abandonment	2	4	..	2	..

Assault, 1st degree	4	27	1	6	9
" 2d degree	48	161	7	3	4
Bigamy	6	20	10	3	6
Bribery	1	3	6	3	6
Burglary, 1st degree	5	94	7	18	11
" 2d degree	30	187	5	6	3
" 3d degree	120	385	2	3	2
Blackmail	4	17	6	4	4
Carrying burglar's tools	6	23	4	3	11
Carrying concealed weapons	9	34	..	3	9
Election law	8	26	1	3	3
Extortion	6	14	6	2	5
Felony (N.C.)	2	12	..	6	..
Forgery, 1st degree	2	10	6	5	3
" 2d degree	13	63	2	4	10
" 3d degree	3	10	3	3	5
Grand larceny, 1st degree	38	209	8	5	6
" " 2d degree	146	478	..	3	3
Kidnapping	3	44	1	14	8
Maiming	1	2	..	2	..
Manslaughter, 1st degree	11	165	1	15	..
" 2d degree	3	30	9	10	3

Offence	No.	Years	Months	Years	Months
Murder, 1st degree	3	Sentenced to be executed			
" 2d degree	13	260	See note	20	..
Attempted murder, 1st degree	1	24	6	24	6
Perjury	2	19	5	9	8
Rape, 1st degree	1	18	..	18	..
" 2d degree	10	80	6	8	..
Receiving stolen goods	11	42	..	3	10
Robbery, 1st degree	23	245	7	10	8
" 2d degree	6	59	2	9	10
Seduction	1	4	9	4	9
Sodomy	3	29	1	9	8
Total	550	2,845	7	5	2

NOTE.—In preparing the above table, the maximum terms of all indeterminate sentences are computed, except in convictions of murder in the second degree, in which the minimum terms of twenty years are used. (Section 187. Penal Code.)

STATE PRISON—FEMALES

Offence	No.	Terms of Sentences		Average Term Each Person	
		Years	Months	Years	Months
Assault, 2d degree	5	13	10	2	9
Grand larceny, 1st degree	7	40	3	5	9
" " 2d degree	7	23	8	3	4
Manslaughter, 1st	1	7	5	7	5

degree					
" 2d degree	1	13	6	13	6
Receiving stolen goods	1	5	..	5	..
Robbery, 1st degree	1	3	6	3	6
Total	23	107	2	4	8

This divergency of mental attitude accounts in part for the great curse of the inequality of sentences. Two cases suggest themselves vividly as examples.

A conductor on a surface car took the place of the motorman and carelessly ran into a wagon, throwing out the driver, who died in consequence. He was convicted of manslaughter in the *second* degree and sentenced to ten years in State's prison.

Another defendant who had killed a woman by cutting her throat and hacking her up with a razor was convicted of the *first* degree of the same crime and sentenced to *the Elmira Reformatory*. Both defendants were of approximately the same age. In each case the particular sentence seemed just and fair to the judge who presided at the trial. It was conscientiously imposed. Yet the thing speaks for itself.

It has sometimes been suggested that all sentences should be imposed by all the judges sitting *en banc*. While this would entail great labor and expense it would undoubtedly, if it were practicable, do much to obviate the present unfortunate condition. Assuming that four judges composed this sentencing board, the vote of the justice who had presided at the trial might, by virtue of his greater familiarity with the facts, be given a weight equal to that of the other three combined. Had the two sentences just named been imposed by such a board it is far from probable that they would have been inflicted in the same terms.

An effort has been made in the preceding pages to set forth some of the failings of criminal justice on the part of the court which seem open to honest criticism. The members of the bench themselves would be the last to minimize the injustice of the inequality of sentences which under our present system seems inevitable, and are continually endeavoring to remedy it so far as possible. They also recognize the fact that it is often difficult, if not out of the question, to preserve in the face of overwhelming evidence an imperturbable serenity of demeanor when the fact of the defendant's guilt is clear and the details of his crime are revolting to every moral sense, and they are equally ready to acknowledge that on occasion they may inadvertently disclose their impression that while they may "let a case go to the jury," the defendant should be acquitted. Judges are, after all, but men, and to err is human. But there is hardly a judge upon the bench who does not conscientiously strive to perform his duties in such a way that justice may be secured in the manner provided by the Constitution,—by leaving the jury untrammelled in their function of determining upon the sworn evidence in the case the guilt or innocence of the defendant. Finally it should be said that it is not the weak but the strong judge that is most apt to transgress in this direction, and that it is the strong judge who is most likely to serve the best interests of the community. For the weak judge there is no place in the administration of criminal justice. His presence upon the bench is an incentive to crime and a reproach to his fellows.

FOOTNOTES:

[35] Cf. "Light Sentences and Pardons," by Frederick Bausman, 39 American Law Rev. 727.

CHAPTER XI

THE JURY

Is trial by jury successful in criminal cases? Certainly it is popularly so regarded. Even lawyers and prosecutors will usually agree that it "works substantial justice," but this does not answer the question. In about three cases out of five "Judge Lynch" himself works "substantial justice." The function of the jury is not to "work justice" at all, but to decide a limited question of fact. They are there for the purpose of determining the issue without prejudice on the one hand or sympathy upon the other, and having no regard for the consequences of their verdict; they must accept unquestioningly the law from the judge upon every point and base their conclusions solely upon the sworn evidence in the case. This they swear that they will do. Yet they do not. Why? Is it want of intelligence, lack of regard for law, or vital misconception of their function?

Certainly it is not from want of intelligence. There can be no question as to the capability of the ordinary juryman to perform his duties. The independent American is singularly adapted to just this form of investigation. If the English be "a nation of shopkeepers," we are a nation of natural cross-examiners. You will find fully as good verbal fencing in a New England corner grocery store about mail time as you will in most courts of justice. But the very innate capacity of the native American to perceive the truth and get to the bottom of things, leads him to believe that he knows equally well, if not better than the judge, what ought to be done about it and what punishment, if any, should be inflicted upon the defendant under the circumstances. It is not that our jurors are incapable or uninterested, but, paradoxical as it may seem, that they are too capable and too interested. They want to be not only jurors, but district attorney, counsel for the defendant, expert witness, and judge into the bargain.

Your shopkeeper in England makes a less intelligent, but a far more satisfactory juror. There they will empanel a jury in a few moments in a capital case, and so deeply implanted in the bosom of each juryman is a respect for the law as such and an inherited reverence for the judiciary, which its uniformly high character has done so much to foster, that, provided the facts are sufficiently established, the sex of the defendant, the condition of his or her family, the character of the motive for the act, will not be the subject of discussion or even of consideration in determining the verdict. It is enough that they are sworn to decide the facts and the facts alone. They are told by the judge what evidence they may consider, and what facts they *may not* consider, and did they not obey his instructions they would receive the severe censure of the public and the press.

There is an historical reason for this. In 1666, when a jury found a verdict of manslaughter after having been instructed that the evidence showed that it was murder, Kelyng, C.J., promptly fined them five pounds apiece. On petition, he reduced it to forty shillings, "which they all paid." In 1667 he fined eleven of the grand jury twenty pounds apiece for refusing to indict for murder. The judges of the King's Bench said he was quite right, adding, "and where a petty juror, contrary to directions of the court, will find a murder manslaughter, ... yet the court will fine them" (King *vs*. Windham, 2 Keble, 180). For centuries it was the common practice to punish severely by imprisonment, fine, and attainder juries who refused to convict on what appeared to the court to be sufficient evidence. Perhaps Throckmorton's case in 1554, when the jury acquitted the defendant of treason, is the most famous illustration of this. The court committed the jury to prison, eight being confined from April 17 to December 12, and on their discharge fined them, some sixty and some two hundred and twenty pounds apiece. The reasoning under the circumstances was obvious. If a jury found a man guilty improperly, he could be pardoned, but "if, having pregnant evidence, nevertheless, the twelve do acquit the malefactor, which they will do sometime ... the prisoner escapeth...." It is refreshing to observe that even English juries "will do [this] sometime." All this naturally created, as it was designed to create, a tremendous regard for the judge and his instructions.

There is at the present time little of this wholesome regard for law in America. The jury realize that the judge's elevation to the bench is often a matter of politics alone, and sometimes have comparatively little respect for his character, learning, or ability. They frequently feel by no means confident that the punishment will fit the crime, and are anxious, so far as they can, to dispose of the case for themselves. For example, in one case where three defendants were found guilty of stealing in company a single article of value, the jury rendered a verdict of grand larceny in the first degree against one, grand larceny in the second degree against another, and petty larceny against the third. They did this because of the varying ages of the defendants, but in so doing obviously violated their oaths and usurped the functions of the judge. Very likely "substantial justice" was accomplished.

There are hundreds of jurors who, having in all honesty taken the oath to "a true verdict find," will, once in the jury-room, frankly turn to their fellows and exclaim: "Oh, let him go! He's only a kid. Give him another chance!" "Substantial justice," again at the expense of our regard for law.

As an example of what may occur, the case of Rosa di Pietro, tried for murder before the Recorder, in December, 1904, is illuminating. The defendant was a young Italian woman of good repute charged with shooting and killing her brother-in-law, who, the evidence clearly showed, had endeavored to persuade her to yield to his desires. She claimed to have shot him in self-defence. Her story was so obviously a fabrication that no jury could have believed her, and must have found (if they had considered the matter at all) that she pursued her would-be seducer down the stairs and shot him in a dark hallway, as he was leaving the building. A "special" jury of perfectly intelligent men promptly acquitted her. The writer presumes that after this all the Italian residents will get their wives to do their killing for them.

In a well-known case the jury found the defendant guilty of manslaughter, instead of murder, because one of their number had read that the prisoner had been a "Rough Rider" in the Cuban campaign. After they had returned their verdict they learned that he had been nothing of the kind.

The action of the New York County jury in a criminal case is right as to the defendant's guilt or innocence about four times out of five, but less frequently as to the appropriate *degree* of crime.[36] The percentage of proper verdicts differs, of course, in different varieties of crime. In cases of common felony, such as larceny, burglary, rape, robbery, arson, forgery, etc., it is usually high; in homicides and gambling much lower; and in commercial frauds and liquor-tax cases smaller still, the number of convictions being inconsiderable. Making due allowance for the unconscious prejudices, sympathies, and idiosyncrasies of mankind, we have still, as citizens, a right to demand a far higher degree of accuracy in the verdicts of our juries—to expect the murderer to be found guilty of murder and the thief to be stigmatized as a thief. What is the explanation for this?

The fundamental reason for the arbitrary character of the verdicts of our juries lies not in our lack of intelligence as a nation, but in our small regard for human life, our low standard of commercial honesty, our hypocrisy in legislation, our consequent lack of respect for law, and the general misapprehension that the function of the jury is to render "substantial justice"—a misapprehension fostered by public sentiment, the press, and even in some cases by the bench itself, to the complete abandonment of the literal interpretation of the juror's oath of office.

The writer has heard judges from the bench congratulate juries upon having rendered a "merciful verdict"! They are popularly expected "to temper justice with mercy," "exercise a wise discretion," and "to be moved to magnanimity." But the jurors who satisfy their emotions at the expense of their honesty, and the judge who countenances the performance, are worse law-breakers than the defendant himself.

We carry upon our statute books laws which we have no intention of enforcing, and which, in our present state of development, are actually unenforceable. Even law-abiding, law-loving, and (ordinarily) conscientious jurors will become lawless when compelled to sit in a case of this character. Thus while the three judges of Special Sessions find guilty some sixty per cent of those brought before them for violations of various phases of the liquor-tax law, a conviction by a jury in the General Sessions is practically unheard of. The grand jury have now reached the point where they practically refuse to indict at all in liquor-tax cases.[37] Just as long as we have hypocrisy in religion, in business, and in legislation, so long shall we have hypocrisy in our courts of justice.

Of course, as we live in an age when violence is found inconvenient and annoying, your jury naturally condemns by its verdict crimes of a violent character, and will make but short work of highwayman and thug. Burglars are unpopular both with the public and with the juror; and it needs no burst of rhetoric to induce a jury to find a verdict against a "firebug" or a "cadet." But once step into that class of cases, the subject of which is commercial fraud, and the jury look upon the prosecution with averted eye. Just so long as dishonesty of one kind or another is openly countenanced in business, just so long it will be practically impossible, except under unusual conditions, to convict the fraudulent bankrupt or the retailer who has secured goods and credit upon false representations. Mayhap there is upon the jury some tradesman who has "padded" his own credit statement; some one who has placed a fictitious valuation on his stock, or has told alluring but unsubstantial stories as to his "orders on hand," "cash in bank," and "bills receivable." What chance under those circumstances of a conviction?

"The jury, passing on the prisoner's life,
May have in the sworn twelve a thief or two
Guiltier than him they try."

"Why," says a juror, "here they are trying to convict this fellow Einstein of what everybody does every day in the year. Rubbish! Am *I* a thief! *I* don't have any *criminal intent*. He was just tryin' to boost his assets a little. He's no criminal." And out he goes to the jury-room and persuades the other eleven that the defendant is no worse than everybody. Of course, everybody isn't a thief. The syllogism is irrefutable.

"I suppose you didn't believe that Mr. Einstein made those false statements?" says the writer, approaching him as he steps into the corridor. The juror pauses in lighting his cigar.

"*Sure*, he made 'em!" he remarks. "Of *course* he *made* 'em! But, H——l, he's no *criminal*!" This is an actual experience.

Our distaste for physical violence has had a rather paradoxical result so far as the jury is concerned, for it appears to be coupled with a small (and what seems to be a decreasing) regard for human life. Verdicts of murder in the first degree are exceedingly rare, and it requires a crime of a peculiarly atrocious character to induce the jury to send the defendant to the electric chair. This is due in part to cowardice and in part to the misconception of their function already dwelt upon, since in almost all murder cases the jury regard themselves as fixing the penalty. Inasmuch as most persons who meet death from violence are themselves of violent character, the jury frequently seems to believe that the defendant is entitled to a certain amount of consideration for ridding the community of his victim, and this often finds joyful expression in a verdict of manslaughter.

Totally distinct, however, from this trifling with justice, whether it be wilful or voluntary, is the unconscious bias of each member of the human family due to race, religion, education, and character. Hence jurors are examined with an elaborate care and minuteness of investigation which in practice is often shown to be ridiculous. In fact certain maxims having almost the force of legal doctrines have grown up about the selection of a jury. A defendant's counsel will invariably challenge an Irishman if his client be a negro, and vice versa. This is likewise apt to be the case if the client be an Italian. Talesmen with wives and children are generally supposed to be more susceptible to arguments directed to their sympathies. Hebrews are presumed to make particularly undesirable jurors for the defence where the crime charged is one of violence or arson, and are likewise usually challenged when the defence is self-defence. Old men are popularly supposed to make indulgent jurors, although the writer's own experience is to the contrary, and he has noticed that persons with long, drooping mustaches are invariably excused. Neither side as a rule cares for missionaries or persons engaged in philanthropic enterprises, since the prosecutor feels instinctively that their eleemosynary tendencies will extend to the prisoner, while the defence has a presentiment that they will lead him to favor the damaged complainant. Writers, editors, and publishers are generally excused by the defence as *too intelligent*, *i.e.*, too prone to theoretic arguments as distinguished from a "broad view," which from the prisoner's standpoint means one including every sympathetic reason that can be suggested. Artists are distrusted by prosecutors as romantic and imaginative. Butchers, coffin-makers, sextons, grave-diggers, undertakers, and dealers in electrical supplies are invariably excused for obvious reasons by the defendant in homicide cases. Liquor dealers are believed to be prone to take a lenient view of the shortcomings of humanity in general, while persons of brisk, incisive manners naturally suggest heartlessness to the cowering defendant. The writer knows an assistant who will not try a case if there is a man with a pompadour on the jury, and neither prosecution nor defence cares for long-haired jurors of the "yarb doctor" variety, while the dapper little man with the "dickey" and red necktie is invariably excused by the defence unless the defendant be a woman.

The frivolous character of these rules needs no comment. Almost every lawyer and every prosecutor believes himself to be a past master in the study of character from external evidence, and upon the most trivial and unnatural of pretexts will challenge a talesman so unfortunate as not to suit his fancy. Yet when all is done and when, after the most exhaustive examination and cross-examination of several hundred special talesmen, wrenched from their places of business or the bosoms of their families, twelve men have been finally selected and sworn, it is probable that they are in no respect superior to the first twelve who might have been chosen.

In murder cases each side may challenge peremptorily thirty talesmen, and numerous are the legal "jumps" over which they must successfully ride before they can qualify for service. Thus it is unusual in a homicide case to select a jury in less than two days, and in some instances it has taken two weeks. On the other hand, equally satisfactory juries have occasionally been selected in such cases in less than an hour.

The general futility of trying to secure a jury of particular capacity or intelligence, or one which will contain no juror of pronounced idiosyncrasies, is rather well illustrated by the following incident: The defendant's counsel, a man of considerable repute at the criminal bar, had spent over two days in the elaborate selection of a jury. It had taken him two hours to get a foreman to his fancy, but at last he had accepted a solid-looking old German grocer. After a trial lasting several days the jury convicted the defendant in short order, greatly to the disgust of the eminent lawyer, who vented his indignation rather loudly in the presence of the foreman as he was leaving the box. The old German leaned over good-naturedly and remarked, pointing to the door in the back of the court-room leading to the prison pen: "Vell, Mr. ——, if you vant to know vat I tinks, I tells you. Ven I see him come in through dot leetle door back dere, den I *knows* he's guilty!"

This lawyer now selects a jury in thirty minutes.

Of course, some examination into the general qualifications of jurors and their possible bias in the case is imperative, and frequently the interposition of a peremptory challenge is not only justifiable, but absolutely necessary. A talesman will sometimes betray by an inflection of his voice a sentiment or prejudice which his *words* deny, or suggest to the vigilant counsel for the defendant the juror's susceptibility to the insidious flattery of the prosecutor in making him a part of the "organization of the court."

During the selection of a jury to try Moran, the dynamiter, in March, 1906, before Judge Foster, in the General Sessions, a little old man took the stand who qualified satisfactorily as a juror so far as the prosecution was concerned. Daniel F. Cohalan, attorney for the defendant, then took him in hand somewhat as follows:

"Have you any prejudice against a man accused of crime?"

"I have not," replied the little old man.

"Or against this defendant?"

"I have not."

"Do you think you would make an absolutely fair and impartial juror?"

"I do."

"Do you know of any reason to the contrary?"

"I do not."

Cohalan turned to another line of examination.

"Do you read the papers?"

"Yes. Yes."

"What paper do you read?"

"What paper?"

"Yes. What paper do you read in the morning?"

The little old man settled himself in his chair and, eyeing Cohalan suspiciously, replied:

"I read the *Herald, Times, World, Journal, Sun, Tribune, Press, Staats Zeitung, Telegraph*———"

"Stop!" cried Cohalan feebly; "that's quite enough. Don't you do anything but read the papers?"

The little old man regarded the lawyer scornfully.

"I spend six hours a day keeping myself informed of what is going on. I flatter myself that there is nothing in the whole world with which I am not fully acquainted. Knowledge is power!"

Cohalan collapsed into his seat.

"That is all. You are excused. You know too much for us!"

As the little old man shuffled off he whispered to the prosecutor:

"I'd have given the —— twenty years!"

On the other hand, the hyper-sensitiveness of counsel renders it easy for talesmen to escape who do not wish to serve. The writer knows an estimable man who is regularly drawn about four times a year upon the special jury. He has never served. His method is as follows: Having taken his seat upon the witness-stand he wrinkles his forehead and looks fiercely at the defendant. When asked if he has any objection to capital punishment he thrusts out his under jaw and exclaims: "I should *say not!* I think hangin's too good for 'em!" In reality he is the mildest, the most sympathetic and the "easiest" of human beings. Another observant talesman who appears periodically has learned, the writer believes, his trick from the first. His stock reply to the same question relative to capital punishment is, "I have *not.* I believe in the Biblical injunction of 'an eye for an eye,' and 'a tooth for a tooth,' and, 'Whoso sheddeth man's blood by man shall his blood be shed.'" Needless to say, he leaves the stand with the same alacrity as the other. Jurors readily enter into friendly relations with the prosecutor and defendant's counsel, but rarely with any effect upon their verdicts. In the first trial of Mock Duck, a Chinaman indicted for murder, where the defence interposed was an alibi, to wit, that the prisoner had been buying a terrapin in Fulton Market at the time of the commission of the crime (whence the prosecutor claimed that it was the case of a Mock Duck with a *mock turtle* defence), a juryman met the defendant's counsel during recess and told him that there was no further need for him to call any more witnesses for the defendant, as the jury "understood the situation perfectly." The lawyer took the hint, and upon the reopening of court closed his case, feeling sure of an acquittal or at least of a disagreement. When the jury had retired the talesman in question made a long speech in favor of murder in the first degree, and refused to vote for any other crime. Such performances are rare. Of course, it not infrequently occurs that a juror by his manner of asking questions shows plainly his state of mind. The feelings of a prosecutor can be easily imagined when a juror turns in disgust from one of the People's witnesses, or those of a defendant's counsel when another, looking towards the prisoner, grinds his teeth as the evidence goes in and ejaculates, "Brute!"

The jury offers a fertile field for the study of human nature, and lawyers and prosecutors learn to look regularly for certain characters. Of these may be mentioned the too officious juror who asks hundreds of incompetent and irrelevant questions to which the lawyers are naturally afraid to object, and whose inquisitiveness has to be curbed by the court itself. Such a juror usually shows much conviction one way or the other in the early stages of the case, and before he has heard the evidence. Unfortunately his executive abilities usually fill the balance of the jury with such disgust that to have a juror of this sort on one's side is more of a misfortune than a boon.

Jurors of this variety frequently at inopportune moments interrupt counsel during their addresses. In one case an aggressive talesman broke in upon a burst of carefully prepared eloquence with the brutal interrogation: "How about the *knife?*" The counsel stopped, bowed to the juror, smiled, and said calmly: "Thank you, Mr. Smith, I'm *glad* you spoke of that. I am coming to it in a moment." The juror, satisfied, leaned back contentedly, but the lawyer has not "come" to the knife yet.

Practically the thing most desired by prosecutors and lawyers who are both convinced of the justice of their cause is homogeneity of some sort in the jury-box. Naturally antagonistic elements are undesirable, and a wise selector of juries will try to get men of approximately the same age, class in society, nationality, religion, and general character. Of course, this is a difficult matter, but without a friendly and helpful spirit among the jurors cases will result frequently in disagreements. This is naturally less objectionable to the defendant than to the People, for ordinarily it may be said that "two disagreements are equivalent to an acquittal."

The common idea that juries are prone to leave their decisions to chance, as by flipping a coin, or to act upon impulse, whim, caprice, or from a desire to get away, is grossly exaggerated.

It was Pope who sang in the "Rape of the Lock":

"The hungry judges soon the sentence sign,
And wretches hang, that jurymen may dine."

Unfortunately, if the jury is hungry or exhausted and anxious to dispose of the case, the defendant invariably gets the benefit of it. The "wretches" don't "hang," but instead are turned out with a rush. Instances of verdicts being determined by such considerations are in fact rare.

Much of the seeming misguidedness of juries in criminal cases is due, just as it is due in civil cases, to the idiosyncrasy, or the avowed purpose to be "agin' the government," of a single talesman. In an ideal community, no matter how many persons constituted the jury, provided the evidence was clear one way or the other, the jury would always agree, since they would all be honest and reasonable men. But just as a certain portion of our population is mentally unbalanced, anarchistic, and criminal, so will be a certain portion of our jurors. In addition to these elements there will almost invariably be found some men upon every panel who are so obstinate, conceited, and overbearing as to be totally unfit to serve, either from the point of view of the people or the defence. It is enough for one of these recalcitrant gentlemen that eleven other human beings desire something else. That settles it. They shall go his way or not at all.

The writer believes, therefore, that some allowance should be made for the single lunatic or anarchist that gets himself drawn on about every fifth jury, for if he once be empanelled a disagreement will inevitably follow. This could be accomplished by reducing the number necessary for a verdict to eleven.[38] Hundreds of juries have been "hung" by just one man.[39] The trouble, as Professor Thayer points out, began a long, long time ago in a case reported in the Book of Assizes in 1367.

"In another assize before the same justices at Northampton, the assize was sworn. They were all agreed except one, who would not agree with the eleven. They were remanded and stayed there all that day and the next, without drink or food. Then the judges asked him if he would agree with his associates, and he said never,—he would die in prison first. Whereupon they took the verdict of the eleven and ordered him to prison, and thereupon a day was given upon this verdict in the Common Bench.

... And afterwards by assent of all the justices it was declared that this was no verdict. It was therefore awarded that this panel be quashed and annulled, and that he who was in prison be enlarged, and that the plaintiff sue a new venire facias.... *Note, that the justices said they ought to have taken the assize with them in a wagon until they were agreed.*"

How much happier would not only the eleven, but the twelfth juror, who swore he would "die first," have been if, unanimity not being required, they could comfortably have agreed to disagree and yet returned to court and rendered a verdict.

A jury naturally tends to lean towards the defence—to let the accused go if they can conscientiously do so; to find somewhere a reasonable doubt as to the prisoner's guilt—and it is only because the cases are so well sifted before they come to trial at all, and the wheat separated from the chaff (the defendants in very weak cases being frequently discharged on the recommendation of the district attorney himself), that the percentage of acquittals is not vastly greater.

This natural feeling of sympathy for the accused makes it all the easier for juries to be affected consciously or unconsciously by considerations they have sworn to disregard. Then if the defendant be a woman, or a poor man with a large family, or his crime has injured no one's purse, or restitution has been made, or if the offence charged is merely that of swindling by means of false representations as to credit, or the defendant is very young or very old, or wears a clean collar, or has an attractive personality, or, better, a beautiful wife, he is turned out with a cheer.

"For twelve honest men have decided the cause,
Who are judges alike of the facts and the laws."

Yes, the jury system in criminal cases is a "practical success"—and it "works substantial justice." It works the exact justice that we want—the exact justice that we deserve. As we grow to have a greater respect for human life and a higher regard for law and honesty, the verdicts of our juries will continue to keep pace with our condition. Then we shall want something better, and we shall have it. The day will come when dishonesty in business will lead to the ball and chain as assuredly as arson and rape. But the time is not yet.

Then juries will decide the issues submitted to them upon the evidence alone, without prejudice or sympathy, in accordance with the laws which they are sworn to uphold, without truckling to popular sentiment or fear of newspaper disapproval; then they will allow the judge to perform the functions vested in him by law without usurpation by their verdicts; and will "true deliverance make" between the People on the one hand and the defendant on the other. Then there will probably be no need for juries—for there will be no criminals.[40]

FOOTNOTES:

[36] This estimate does not apply to the actions of juries outside of New York County. In other cities and in other states, particularly in rural districts, the percentage of convictions is often shockingly small.

[37] The following figures may be of interest to those readers who are interested in the question of amending the laws governing the sale of liquor:

In the year 1907, out of a total of 1,237 cases which came before the Court of Special Sessions, there were 334 convictions, 7 pleas of guilty, 223 acquittals, 18 discharges and 116 transfers to the General Sessions. During the last eight years, out of a total of 7,416 cases, there were 3,129 convictions, 244 pleas of guilty, 2,143 acquittals, 395 discharges, 361 demurrers allowed and 1,144 cases transferred, on the defendants' motion, to General Sessions, to be tried under indictment. During this period, very nearly half the cases have resulted in convictions.

These cases were tried, as the reader is aware, by a bench of three judges, who decide both law and fact. Compare this record with the result of 91 transfers, taken as illustrative, from the Special to the General Sessions in 1905. Of course, each case had to be taken first before the grand jury.

Eighty-four of these cases were summarily dismissed by that body. In the remaining seven instances, indictments were secured. Four of these seven defendants pleaded guilty, two were acquitted by the jury, one was discharged on his own recognizance and none were convicted. In other words, out of the whole bunch of transfers, less than four per cent of the defendants were convicted, as against nearly fifty per cent of convictions in the Special Sessions, in all liquor-tax cases in the last eight years. In the same period, out of a total of 1,241 cases presented to the grand jury, 987 were dismissed by that body. Of the balance, viz., 254 in which indictments were secured, 25 pleaded guilty, 36 were discharged on their own recognizances, in 12 cases the bail was forfeited, and of the 181 cases which actually were tried before juries, 165 defendants were acquitted and 16 were convicted.

In 1906, out of 85 cases transferred, 79 were dismissed, and of the remaining six, 5 defendants were acquitted and 1 was discharged. In 1907 there were 98 transferred and *all were dismissed* by the grand jury.

The significance of these figures becomes evident when it is realized that the defendants whose cases are thus transferred are those who are the actual holders of licenses. They can afford to pay for the services of counsel, and their conviction is of vastly more importance to the community than that of their hirelings who actually sell the liquor over the bar. The barkeeper who violates the law and is caught, comes to trial in the Special Sessions, either pleads guilty or is convicted, and receives a fine which his employer promptly pays. The owner of the saloon thereupon discharges the defendant from his service and secures another barkeeper. This process can be continued indefinitely. But when the owner himself is caught and convicted, he is either driven out of business or has got to operate under another name. These are the men who apply for and are apparently able to secure transfers of their cases to the General Sessions, although any judge granting such motions is, or, at least, should be, aware of what the practical result of his action will be. The transfer of a liquor-tax case upon the order of the judge sitting in Part I of the General Sessions is practically tantamount to a dismissal of it.

[38] Whatever the actual origin of the number twelve for this purpose there certainly lingered in olden times a feeling that it had a sacred or foreordained character, and in Duncomb's Trials *per pais*, the following illuminating explanation is to be found:

"And first as to their number twelve: and this number is no less esteemed by our law than by Holy Writ. If the twelve apostles on their twelve thrones must try us in our eternal state, good reason has the law to appoint the number of twelve to try our temporal. The tribes of Israel were twelve,

- 155 -

the patriarchs were twelve, and Solomon's officers were twelve. Therefore not only matters of fact were tried by twelve, but of ancient times twelve judges were to try matters in law, in the Exchequer Chamber, and there are twelve counsellors of state for matters of state; and he that wageth his law must have eleven others with him who believe he says true. And the law is so precise in this number of twelve, that if the trial be by more or less, it is a mistrial." (Cf. Thayer's Preliminary Treatise, as cited, p. 90.)

[39] Cf. "Criminal Law and Its Administration," by Robert Earl, 2 Columbia Law Rev. 144.

[40] Many cases result in mis-trials owing to the sickness or death of a single juror. In persecutions which it can be foreseen will be long the swearing of an *extra juror* would obviate this difficulty. Cf. "Newspapers and the Jury," Clarence B. Smith, 17 Greenbag 223.

CHAPTER XII

THE WITNESS

The probative value of all honestly given testimony depends, naturally, first upon the witness's original capacity to observe; second, upon the extent to which his memory may have played him false; and third, upon how far he really means exactly what he says. This is just as true of testimony in cases of so-called circumstantial evidence as in cases where the evidence is direct, for the circumstances themselves must be testified to by witnesses who have observed them, and the authoritativeness of everything these witnesses have to say must lie in their ability to see, remember, and describe accurately what they have seen.

The subject of perjury is so distinct and far-reaching that it deserves separate consideration. The crime is easy to commit and difficult to establish by competent proof, for it is a highly technical offence and one which juries seem to find it easy to condone. The brother or friend of the accused has but to take the stand and swear to an alibi and lo! he is free. The chance of detection is small in comparison with the immediate benefit secured, while the temptation to swear falsely must, at least in the case of the immediate family of the prisoner, often be overwhelming. Where convictions for perjury are secured heavy sentences are invariably imposed and a wholesome apprehension instilled into the hearts of prospective witnesses, yet the amount of deliberate false swearing in our criminal courts would be inadequately described as shocking. To estimate its quantity would be difficult if not impossible, for it varies with the character of the case and the nature of the defence. When the latter is an alibi the entire testimony for the prisoner is frequently manufactured out of whole cloth, and it is probably not very wide of the mark to say that anywhere from a quarter to seventy-five per cent of the testimony offered by the defendant's witnesses *upon the direct point in issue* in the ordinary run of criminal trials is perjured.

Yet a careful scrutiny of even the honestly given testimony in such cases gives rise to the belief that the amount of strictly accurate evidence adduced is relatively small, so small as probably to stagger the credulity of the layman and to give the lawyer ground for reflection. It must be borne in mind, however, that this refers to criminal trials only and to testimony of a character closely relevant to the issue.

The first consideration is how far the witness was originally capable of receiving correct impressions through his senses. Naturally this depends almost entirely upon his physical equipment and the keenness and accuracy of his general observation, both of which are usually evidenced to a considerable degree by his appearance and conduct upon the stand.

Children are proverbially observant, and make remarkable witnesses, habitually noticing details which inevitably escape the attention of their elders; while various classes of persons by reason of their professional requirements are, of course, better qualified than others to observe certain facts or conditions, as a gem merchant the shape and cutting of a diamond, or a doctor the physical condition of a patient.

Witnesses are often honestly mistaken, however, as to their own ability to observe facts, and will unhesitatingly testify that they could hear sounds and discern objects at extraordinary distances. Lawyers frequently attempt to induce aged or infirm witnesses to testify that they could hear plainly what was said by the defendant, in an ordinary tone, at a distance, say, of forty feet. The lawyer speaks in loud and distinct tones during the preliminary examination, and then gradually drops his voice to that usually employed in speaking, in the hope that the witness will ask him to repeat the question. This ruse usually fails by reason of the fact that the lawyer, in his anxiety to show that the witness could not possibly hear the distance claimed, lowers his voice to such an extent that the test is obviously unfair.

For similar reasons counsel often call upon such witnesses to state the time by the clock which usually hangs upon the rear wall of the court-room. A distinguished but conceited advocate, not long ago, after securing an unqualified statement from an octogenarian, who was bravely enduring cross-examination, that he "saw the whole thing as if it had occurred ten feet away," suddenly challenged him to tell the time by the clock referred to. The lawyer did not look around himself, as he had done so about half an hour before, when he had noticed that it was half after eleven. The old man looked at the clock and replied, after a pause, "Half-past eleven," upon which the lawyer, knowing that it must be nearly twelve, turned to the jury and burst into a derisive laugh, exclaiming sarcastically, "That is *all*," and threw himself back in his seat with an air of having finally annihilated the entire value of the witness's testimony. The distinguished practitioner, however, found himself laughing alone. Presently one of the jury chuckled, and in a trice the whole court-room was in a roar at the lawyer's expense. The clock had stopped—at half-past eleven.

The professional actor upon the stage presents the *illusion* of nature by exaggerating those details of action which ordinarily would escape the attention of the observer.

In daily life we are quite as likely as not to be deceived by what we have seen, and this fact is so familiar to jurors that they are apt to distrust witnesses who profess to have seen much of complicated or rapidly conducted transactions. They want the main facts stated convincingly. The rest can take care of themselves. The extraordinary extent to which the complex development of modern life has dwarfed our powers of observation is noticeable nowhere more markedly than in the court-room. Things run so smoothly, transportation facilities are so perfect, specialization is carried to so high a degree, and our whole existence goes on so much indoors, that it ceases to be a matter of note or even of interest that the breakfast is properly cooked and served, that we are whisked downtown (a little matter say of five miles) in ten or twelve minutes, that we are shot up to our offices through twenty floors in an electric elevator, that there is a blizzard or a deluge, or that part of Broadway has been blown up or a fifteen-story building fallen down. We pass days without paying the remotest attention to the weather, and forget that we have relations. Instead of walking home to supper, pausing to talk to our friends by the way, we drop into the subway, bury ourselves in newspapers, and are vomited forth almost without our knowing it at our front doorsteps. The multiplicity of detail deprives us of either the desire or the capacity to observe, and we cultivate a habit of not observing lest our eyes and brains be overwhelmed with fatigue. Observation has ceased to be necessary and has taken its place among the lost arts.

Compare the old days when a Greek could go to hear the "Œdipus," and on returning home could recount practically the whole of it from beginning to end for the benefit of the wife, who was not allowed to go herself, or even the comparatively recent period when the funeral oration over Alexander Hamilton could be reported in the "Evening Post" *from memory.*

Much the more difficult problem, however, is to determine how far the witness is the victim of his memory and is unconsciously confusing fact with imagination, or knowledge with belief. It is a matter of common experience that almost all cases are stronger in court than they give the impression of being when the witnesses are first examined in the private office. Time and again, cases which in the beginning have seemed hopeless to prosecute have resulted in verdicts of conviction, and defences originally so fragile as to appear but gossamer have returned many a defendant to his despairing family.

The reason is not far to seek. Witnesses to the events leading up to a crime are acquainted with a thousand details which are as vivid, and probably more vivid, to them than the occurrence in regard to which their testimony is actually desired. It may well be that the immaterial facts are the only ones which have interested them at all, while their knowledge of the criminal act is relatively slight. For example, they *know*, of course, that they were in the saloon; are *positive* that the complainant and defendant were playing cards, even remembering some of the hands dealt; are *sure* that the complainant arose and walked away; *have a very vivid recollection* that in a few moments the defendant got up and followed him across the room; are *pretty clear*, although their attention was still upon the game, that the two men had an argument; and *have a strong impression* that the defendant hit the complainant. In point of fact, their evidence is really of far *less* value, if of any at all, in regard to the *actual striking* than in regard to the events leading up to it, for at the time of the blow their attention was being given less to the participants in the quarrel than to something else. Their ideas are in truth very hazy as to the latter part of the transaction. However, they become witnesses, pronouncing themselves ready to swear that they saw the blow struck, which is perhaps the fact. Their evidence is practically of no value on the question of justification or self-defence. But finding, on being examined, that their testimony is wanted principally on that aspect of the case, they naturally tell their entire story as if they were as clear in their own minds upon one part of it as another. Being able to give details as to the earlier aspect of the quarrel, they feel obliged to be equally definite as to all of it. If they have an idea that the striking was without excuse, they gradually imagine details to fit their point of view. This is done quite unconsciously. Before long they are as glib with their description of the assault as they are about the game of cards. They get hazy on what occurred before, and overwhelmingly positive as to what occurred towards and at the last, and on the witness-stand swear convincingly that they *saw* the defendant strike the complainant, exactly how he did it, the words he said, and that the complainant made no offer of any sort to strike the defendant. From allowing their minds to dwell on their own conception of what *must* have occurred, they are soon convinced that it *did* occur in that way, and their account flows forth with a circumstantiality that carries with it an irresistible impression of veracity.

The witness remembers in a large proportion of cases what he *wants* to remember, or believes occurred. The liar with his prepared lie is far less dangerous than the honest, but mistaken witness, or the witness who draws inadvertently upon his imagination. Most juries instinctively know a liar when they see and hear one, but few of them can determine in the case of an honestly intentioned witness how much of his evidence should be discarded as unreliable, and how much accepted as true.

The greatest difficulty in the trial of jury cases so far as the evidence is concerned lies in the fallibility of the human mind, and not in the inventive genius of the devil. An old man who combines a venerable appearance with a failing memory is the witness most to be feared by either side.

In a recent case a patriarch of some eighty-five years positively, convincingly, and ultra-dramatically identified the defendant as a man who had knocked him down and robbed him of a ring. The identification was so perfect that on the evidence of this aged witness alone the jury convicted the defendant after but a few moments' deliberation. He was sentenced to ten years in State's prison, although he denied vehemently that he had ever *seen* the complainant. As he was being led from the bar, the real criminal arose among the audience and gave himself up, stating that he could not sit by and see an innocent man receive *so great* a punishment. The inference was, that had the sentence been lighter his conscience would not have pricked him sufficiently to sanction his act of self-sacrifice. In cross-examination lies the only corrective of this sort of specious testimony, but it would be manifestly inadequate to prevent injustice in such an instance as that just described. Juries must and do take the evidence of most well-intentioned witnesses with a grain of salt.

Both men and women habitually testify to facts as actually occurring on a specific occasion because they occurred on most occasions:

Q. "*Did* your husband *lock* the door?"

A. "Of course he did."

Q. "How do you know?"

A. "He *always* locks the door."

Witness after witness will take the stand and testify positively that certain events took place, or certain acts were done, when in point of fact all they can really swear to is that they usually took place or usually were done:

Q. "Did he put on his hat?"

A. "Certainly he did."

Q. "Did you *see* him?"

A. "No, but he *must* have put on his hat *if he went* out."

And the probability is that the whole question to be determined was whether or not "*he*" *did go out* or stay in.

The layman chancing to listen to a criminal trial finds himself gasping with astonishment at the deluge of minute facts which pour from the witnesses' mouths in regard to the happenings of some particular day a year or so before. He knows that it is humanly impossible actually to *remember* any such facts, even had they occurred the day before yesterday. He may ask himself what he did that very morning and be unable to give any satisfactory reply. And yet the jury believe this testimony, and because the witness swears to it it goes upon the record as evidence of actual knowledge. In ninety-nine cases out of a hundred counsel's only recourse is to argue to the jury that such a memory is impossible. But in the same proportion of cases the jury will take the oath of the witness against the lawyer's reasoning and their own common-sense. This is because of the fictitious value given to the witness's oath by talesmen who attach little significance to their own. "He *swears* to it," says the juryman, rubbing his forehead. "Well, he *must* remember it or he wouldn't swear to it!" And the witness probably thinks he *does* remember it.

Yet who of us could state with certainty the guests at a particular dinner six months ago? Or the transactions of a morning only a week ago, with any accuracy as to time? What the witness frequently does is to discuss the matter with his friends who were present on the occasion in question, and, as it were, form a sort of "pool" of their common recollections, impressions, and beliefs. One suggestion corrects or modifies another until a comparatively lucid and logical story is evoked. When this has been accomplished the witness mentally exclaims: "Of course! That was just the way it was! Now I remember it all!" The time is so distant that whatever the final crystallization of the matter may be, it is far from likely that it will thereafter be shown to be inaccurate by any piece of evidence which will present itself to the witness and his friends. The account thus developed by mutual questions and "refreshing" of each other's recollection becomes, so far as the parties to it are concerned, *the fact*. The witness is now positive that he did and said exactly so and so, and nothing will swerve him from it, for inherently there is nothing in the story or its make-up that affords any reason for questioning its accuracy. This story repeated from time to time becomes one of the most vivid things in the witness's mental experience. He repeats it over and over, is cross-examined by his own attorney upon it, incorporates it in an affidavit to which he swears, and when he takes the stand recounts these ancient happenings with an aggressiveness and enthusiasm that bring dismay to the other side.

But what a farce to call this recollection! What is this circumstantial romance when it comes to be analyzed? Jones, a friend of Smith the prospective witness, is anxious to establish an alibi, and asks Smith if he doesn't remember meeting him in the club on February 12, two years before. Smith has no recollection of it at all, but Jones says: "Oh, yes, you were going to the theatre with Robinson." Of course, if Jones is so sure, Smith naturally begins to think it is probably the fact, and he does remember vaguely that he and Robinson spent an evening together. So he consults his diary and finds it recorded there that he did attend the theatre on the day in question with Robinson. He does not remember the play, but Robinson recalls that it was "The Chinese Honeymoon," and believes that they dined together first at the club. Smith now thinks he remembers this himself. Then Robinson suggests that they probably went to the theatre in a cab. They look in a file of old papers and find that it was raining. That settles it—of *course*, they went in a cab. The next question is the hour. They have no recollection of being late, so they must have arrived on time. Well, the paper says the play commenced at eight, and it takes a cab about twenty minutes to get from the club to Daly's Theatre, so it is reasonably clear that they must have started a little before eight. Smith unconsciously is persuaded to believe that if Jones was right about their going to the theatre, he *must* also have been in the club at the time he says he was there. Both he and Robinson recall that Jones was always hanging round the club two years ago, and as neither can remember an evening when he wasn't there, they decide he must have been there *that* night. Robinson has a dim recollection that they had a drink together. That is a pretty safe guess and has all the air of verisimilitude. In an hour or two Smith is ready to swear positively from *recollection* that he dined with Robinson at the club on February 12 two years ago, met Jones, had a drink with him, that this occurred at seven fifty-five, that it was raining, that they took a cab, etc., etc. In its elements this testimony is entirely hearsay upon the only vital point, *i.e.*, Jones's presence in the club at that time, and the immaterial remainder is made up of equal parts of diary, newspaper, play-bill, weather report, usual custom, reliance on Robinson's alleged recollection, and belief in Jones's innocence. He has practically no actual memory of the facts at all, and the only thing he really does remember is that a long time ago he did attend some theatre with Robinson.

The common doctrine of what is known as "refreshing the memory" in actual practice is notoriously absurd. Witnesses who have made memoranda as to certain facts, or even, in certain cases, of conversations, and who have no independent recollection thereof, are permitted to read them for the purpose of "refreshing" their memories. Having done so, they are then asked if they *now* have, *independently of the paper*, any recollection of them. In ninety-nine cases out of a hundred it would be absolutely impossible for them really to *remember* anything of the sort. They read the entry, know it is probably accurate, and are morally convinced that the fact is as thereon stated. They answer *yes*, that their recollection *has* been refreshed and that they now do remember, and are allowed to testify to the fact as of their own knowledge. In most instances they do not clearly understand the distinction they are called upon to draw between actual independent recollection and a strong belief on their own part that the fact must be as recorded. It is the exceptional witness indeed who makes any such distinction.

There are also many cases where a defendant has been put in jeopardy because some one, remembering that he *intended* to do an act, becomes convinced that he *has* done so, to the extent of being willing to swear thereto. No better illustration of this kind of error could be given than the disappearance of the famous necklace of a prominent resident of Newport during the summer of 1904. There lives hardly a family which has not frequently had such an experience. Some night the husband can't find his pearl shirt-studs. He knows he had them on the evening before. The hue and cry is raised. Maledictions are called down upon Anna or Delia or Nora. But the studs are not in the shirt. Their owner swears he left them there. Then Delia tremblingly suggests that "master dined in his ordinary clothes last evening," and he realizes that it was so late when he got home that at the last minute he decided not to change. Amid great excitement the studs are located in the bureau drawer where they belonged.

The final question to be determined by the juror in regard to the testimony of any witness is how far the latter has succeeded in conveying his actual recollections through the medium of speech and gesture. This necessarily depends upon a variety of considerations. Among these are his familiarity with the English language; inadvertent accentuation of wrong words or of the less important features of his testimony; his physical condition, which in nine cases out of ten is one of extreme nervousness and timidity, if not of actual fear; and a hundred other trifling, but, in the aggregate, material matters.

The most effective testimony is that which is given with what the jury regard as the evidences of candor. It is a familiar fact that the surer a person is of anything, particularly among the laboring classes, the more loudly will he assert its truth. This is so well known to the jury as ordinarily constituted that unless testimony is given with positiveness it might as well not be given at all. Much as it is to be deprecated, an assertive lie is of much more weight with a jury than an anemic statement of the truth. The juror imagines himself telling the story, and feels that if he were doing so and his testimony were true, he would be so convincing that the jury could have no doubt about it at all. Ofttimes a witness leads the jury to suspect that he is a liar simply because he has too strong a sense of the proprieties of his position vehemently to resent a suggestion of untruthfulness. The gentleman who mildly replies "That is not so" to a challenge of his veracity, makes far less impression on the jury than the coal-heaver who leans forward and shakes his fist in the shyster's face, exclaiming: "If ye said that outside, ye little spalpeen, I'd knock yer head off." "Ah," say the jury, "there's a *man* for you." Just as your puritan is at a disadvantage in an alehouse, and your dandy in a mob, so are the hyper-conscientious and the oversensitive and refined before a jury. The most effective witness is he whom the general run of jurors can understand, who speaks their own language, feels about the same emotions, and is not so morbidly conscientious about details that in qualifying testimony he finds himself entangled and rendered helpless in his own refinements. A distinguished lawyer testifying in a recent case was so careful to qualify every statement and refine every bit of his evidence that the jury took the word of a perjured loafer and a street-walker in preference. This kind of thing happens again and again, and the wily witness who thinks himself clever in appearing overdisinterested is "hoist by his own petard." The jury at once distrust him. They feel either that he is making it all up, or is in fact not sure of his evidence, else, they argue, he would be more positive in giving it.

Most witnesses in the general run of criminal cases have no comprehension of the meaning of words of more than three syllables. It is hopeless to make use of even such modest members of our national vocabulary as "preceding," "subsequent," "various," etc. A negro when asked if certain shots were *simultaneous* replied:

"Yas, boss. Dat's it! 'Zactly simultaneous! One *right* after de odder."

The ordinary witness usually says "minutes" when he means "seconds." He will testify without hesitation that the defendant drew his revolver and immediately shot the complainant, illustrating on the stand the rapidity of the movement. When asked how long it took, he will answer: "Oh, about two or three minutes."

A proper medium in which to converse between the lawyer and witness is sometimes difficult to find, and invariably much tact is required in handling witnesses of limited education. The writer remembers one witness who was completely disconcerted by the use of the word "cravat," and at the precise moment the attorney was so confused as not to be able to remember any synonym. The Tenderloin and the Bowery have a vocabulary of their own differing somewhat from that of beggars and professional criminals. The language of the ordinary policeman is a polyglot of all three. Popular writers on the "powers that prey," and dabblers in criminology in general, are apt to become the victims of self-alleged "ex-convicts" and "criminals" who are anxious to sell unreliable information for honest liquor. A large part of the lingo in realistic treatises on prison life and "life among the burglars," originates in the doped imagination of whatever fanciful "reformed" thief happens to be the personal gold mine of that particular author. Thieves, like any distinct class, make use of slang, some of which is peculiar to them alone. But for the most part the "tough" elements in the community make themselves easily understood either in the office or on the witness-stand.

Where the witness speaks a foreign language the task of discovering exactly what he knows, or even what he actually says, is herculean. In the first place interpreters, as a rule, give the substance—as they understand it—of the witness's testimony rather than his exact words. It is also practically impossible to cross-examine through an interpreter, for the whole psychological significance of the answer is destroyed, ample opportunity being given for the witness to collect his wits and carefully to frame his reply. One could cross-examine a deaf-mute by means of the finger alphabet about as effectively as an Italian through a court interpreter, who probably speaks (defectively) seventeen languages.

The reader might perhaps conclude from what has been said that the action of the ordinary jury in most cases must be founded simply upon shrewd guesswork. To a certain degree this cannot be denied, and it is equally true that all the delicate processes of the human mind, and the shadowy presences there of intent, motive, and recollection, can never be demonstrated save by inference. Our machinery is crude indeed. Ofttimes it is like trying to dissect a butterfly with a pair of pincers, and the wonder is that the jury are able to get at the truth as frequently as they do. Hence the necessity for the advocate to assist the jury and remedy their ignorance of the psychology of testimony by his own observation, knowledge, and experience. With the jury keenly alive to all the possibilities of error in the testimony of even the most honest of witnesses, it is for the advocate, the psychologist of the law, to test by his cross-examination and demonstrate in his summing up the precise probative value of the evidence, frequently revealing, below an apparently limpid stream of truth, a turbid bed of conjecture, assumption, belief, hearsay, and inaccuracy of expression, with the rank weeds of perjury growing just beneath the surface.

CHAPTER XIII

THE VERDICT

The judge having delivered his charge, and the jury having gathered up their collection of miscellaneous garments and retired to the jury-room, a court officer claps the prisoner upon the shoulder and leads him away to the prison pen. Once the door of the court-room has closed behind him, he is conducted along a narrow corridor to the head of a flight of iron steps at the foot of which stands a keeper. As he descends the stairs the attendant notifies the keeper that the defendant is on his way down: and once the latter is safely below the keeper shouts "All right!" to the officer above, who returns once more to his duties in the court-room. Since there is little danger of an escape the officers sometimes become a trifle lax in the handling of prisoners awaiting the verdict.

An incident recently occurred which shows how much care is necessary in guarding a defendant who confidently expects a verdict of conviction. At the conclusion of a trial for grand larceny the jury went out and the prisoner was conducted to the head of the stairs leading down to the pen. The court officer notified the keeper when the prisoner was about half-way down, and distinctly heard the latter reply "All right!" He thereupon departed. The keeper, however, had not uttered a syllable and was entirely unaware of the return of the defendant, who, being something of a ventriloquist, had answered for him, and had then calmly reascended the stairs, passed through the corridor to another court-room where he had mingled with the crowd, and later had had no difficulty in making his escape first into the main corridor and thence into the street. When the jury presently returned and the prisoner was sent for, his flight was discovered. The court waited patiently while the pens, corridors and finally the entire building were searched, but without disclosing a trace of the prisoner. Meanwhile the jury, who had found the defendant guilty, wondered why their verdict was not received. According to law, however, all the proceedings incident to a trial for felony up to and including the rendition of the verdict must take place in the presence of the prisoner, and in this case his voluntary absence compelled the court to declare a "mistrial." When it became evident that the defendant was unlikely to return, terrible was the humiliation of the court officers, who, for a few days, lived in terror of losing their official heads, if not of being imprisoned and fined for contempt.

The prisoner's wife, however, had been present throughout the trial in the court-room, although, as his escape was entirely extemporaneous, she was as much surprised as anybody else at his departure. After the discharge of the jury several detectives followed her to her home in Hoboken. Late in the evening she left the house in response to a message and met her husband in a deserted part of the city, where he was recaptured. He was immediately brought back to New York and his case placed once more on trial; but this time he pleaded guilty. From a dramatic point of view it is to be regretted that the jury at the first trial had not found a verdict of "not guilty."

As the first talesman who happens to be selected for the jury in any given case becomes *ipso facto* its foreman, amusing incidents sometimes occur owing to his inexperience. Where an indictment contains but a single count, as, for example, "receiving stolen goods," the foreman's answer to the clerk's interrogation of, "Do you find the prisoner guilty or not guilty," is, of course, simple enough; he answers "guilty" or "not guilty," or "not guilty, with a recommendation to the mercy of the court"; but where the indictment contains either a number of counts set forth separately, or the crime charged is of such a character that the jury may find in a lesser degree, some confusion is apt to result. If, for example, a defendant is being tried for murder in the first degree the court is obliged to submit, under the law, not only murder in its first degree, but the lesser crimes of murder in the second degree, manslaughter in the first degree, manslaughter in the second degree and occasionally assault in one or more degrees. Sometimes the foreman forgets entirely what he was going to say and stands staring, open-mouthed, until the clerk comes to his assistance.

In a case where the court charged the jury that they could find the defendant guilty of murder, manslaughter, or assault, or else acquit him on the ground that he was justified in taking the life of the deceased, the jury retired and deliberated for many hours. As the time dragged on the defendant became convinced that he was to be convicted. Late at night the jury informed the court that they had agreed upon a verdict. They filed back and took their places in the box. The defendant was arraigned, pale with apprehension. The clerk arose.

"Gentlemen of the jury," said he, "have you agreed upon a verdict?"

"We have," replied the foreman.

"The jury will rise," continued the clerk. "The defendant will rise." The jury and prisoner arose.

"Jurymen, look upon the prisoner. Prisoner, look upon the jury," continued the clerk, and turning to the foreman, "How say you? Do you find the defendant guilty or not guilty?"

"Guilty," stammered the foreman.

The defendant uttered a loud groan and collapsed into the arms of the court attendant beside him.

"*Of justifiable homicide,*" hastily added the inexperienced foreman. In spite of the laughter of the rest of the jurymen and the smiles of the court it took some moments to convince the unnerved prisoner that he was not to be electrocuted.

In a recent case the jury returned a verdict of "*Pretty nearly guilty!*"

A very considerable proportion of jury trials in criminal cases result in disagreements. The question of reasonable doubt is always a troublesome one, and even where all the jury believe the defendant guilty, as likely as not half of them will not think that they are convinced beyond what they regard as a reasonable doubt. On this account many jurors are of the opinion that what is known as a Scotch verdict, or a verdict of "Not proven," should be allowed. The writer has been informed on good authority that in one of the recent trials of Nan Patterson eleven of the twelve jurymen believed her guilty, but that only six of them were of the opinion that they were so convinced beyond a reasonable doubt. Had the Scotch verdict been permissible it would probably have been rendered in this case. Inasmuch as the ordinary American petit jury are apt to go outside the evidence and to decide the issue, in some degree at least, on evidence which properly they should not consider at all, no further loopholes of escape from rendering a verdict one way or the other should be afforded them. Had we the Scotch verdict, instead of disagreeing and giving the prosecution the opportunity to try the defendant over again, juries would probably make use of it in all cases where they disliked to render a verdict in accordance with the evidence.

Juries frequently incorporate with the verdict of guilty the words "with a recommendation to mercy." Of course this is no part of the verdict and has no legal effect whatever. It is merely a formal expression of opinion that in the eyes of the jury it would be well for the court to treat the defendant with leniency. The judge usually comments upon this recommendation and intimates that he will give it consideration in imposing sentence. It is not likely, however, that any case which has appealed to the sympathies of the jury the court will not be equally moved. In point of fact, did juries fix the sentence in cases where they found the defendant guilty it is exceedingly probable that they would be much more severe than the bench. Most jurors, however, are under the impression that "a recommendation to mercy" is an integral part of their verdict and it frequently does yeoman's service by inducing a juror or two who have a lingering feeling that perhaps the crime has not been as fully proven as it might have been, or that maybe the defendant is not guilty after all or should be given another chance, to agree with the majority of their fellows. The writer had one panel of jurors in the General Sessions which, having returned a verdict of guilty "with a recommendation to mercy" in the first case tried during the month, affixed the same recommendation to each verdict which they rendered thereafter. It is his impression that they convicted every prisoner who came before them, so that the recommendation must in many cases have seemed to the hapless defendant but a hollow mockery. There is even a traditional case where a jury in a murder trial found the defendant guilty of murder in the first degree, "with a strong recommendation to the mercy of the court."

Verdicts of murder in the first degree are comparatively rare and are, practically, only to be expected when the circumstances surrounding the crime are peculiarly atrocious. It is also a well-known fact that juries rarely find a verdict in a degree of crime higher than the one for which the majority vote upon the first ballot. For example, if on the first ballot the jury stands five for murder in the first degree, six for murder in the second degree and one for manslaughter only a miracle could account for a final verdict of murder in the first degree. In other words, a jury will almost never work *up* their verdict, argument invariably tending to work them *down* to a lesser degree. Most cases of what is technically murder in the first degree result in verdicts of murder in the second degree, and most cases of murder in the second degree result in verdicts of manslaughter.

The jury having rendered a verdict of conviction, say of murder in the first degree, there remains to counsel but one last act which he can perform in his client's behalf, namely, to demand that the jury be polled. This must be done upon the requirement of either the defendant or the People, in which case, "they must be severally asked whether it is their verdict; and if any one answer in the negative, the jury must be sent out for further deliberation." The writer has never heard of a jury which, on being polled, showed a disagreement. It is not unusual, however, as the roll is called to see various members of the jury look apprehensively towards one of their number who has evidently put up in the jury-room a hard fight for a lesser degree and may be "of the same opinion still." A prosecutor always breathes more freely when the ordeal is over, and probably experiences during the process very much the same kind of emotion as that felt by the bride-groom at the altar as he listens apprehensively at the conclusion of the clergyman's announcement that "if any one has any just cause, etc., let him now speak or forever hold his peace."

Defendants who are convicted rarely show any emotion when receiving the verdict. This is of course to be expected, as the defendant, if guilty, has probably been anticipating that he will be so found by the jury, and has steeled himself for the occasion, while an innocent man is practically never convicted. Hundreds of defendants, however, who confidently expect to be convicted, are acquitted through the leniency of the jury. Their exclamations of gratification and joy upon such occasions are frequently most amusing. Such a defendant not seldom thanks the court and the jury for their kindness, and in some cases his thanks are certainly due to those who have violated the letter and spirit of their oaths in acquitting him. The writer recalls one old colored mammy who, on being acquitted of stealing some wash which had been confided to her care, curtsied in all directions and remarked, "Ah t'anks your honor, an' Ah t'anks your Honors, gen'lemen ob de jury, one an' all." An Irishman, who had been but a few weeks in this country, and who had been acquitted on the charge of stealing a truck and horse which had been left in his charge, on learning of his acquittal invited the jury collectively in a loud voice to come across the street and have a drink.

Before the jury is discharged, however, and the prisoner remanded to the Tombs for sentence, he is required to answer certain questions relative to his age, parentage, education, previous convictions, etc. If the spectator is fortunate enough to be able to forget the solemnity of what has taken place, he may well be entertained, not only at the answers given by the defendant, but at the method of conducting the examination by the court officer. The clerk takes the indictment and, with a large rubber die, stamps upon it the statement that the defendant, on being arraigned, made answer to the questions put to him, as follows:

Counsel Assigned ....
Sex ....
Age ....
Nativity ....
Residence ....
Occupation ....
Married or Single ....
Education ....
Religious Instruction ....
Parents Living ....
Temperate or Intemperate ....
Before Convicted ....

Of course, the court officer who repeats the prisoner's answers to the clerk is usually so familiar with the order of the questions as to render any vocal action upon the part of the clerk unnecessary. The officer stands by the prisoner and, leaning over, asks in a low tone how old he is, if his parents are living, if he is addicted to the use of liquor, if he has had any religious instruction, or if he has been previously convicted of crime. It is really the officer to whom the defendant makes his replies, the former repeating them in a loud voice to the clerk. In some courts the clerk does not put the questions at all, but the officer merely gives in their order the answers of the defendant. For example, in Part II, upon the rendition of a verdict one will see Mr. Samuel Wolff, the clerk, stamp the indictment, dip his pen in the ink, turn to the officer of the court and say, "All ready?"

The officer answers, "Yes."

A subdued conversation then takes place between the prisoner and the officer, who raises his voice and answers:

"Twenty-nine;—U.S.—No;—None;—Single—Yes;—No.—" All of which answers are properly recorded opposite the appropriate questions upon the indictment.

All this is a little startling to the juror who has rendered his first verdict. He has no idea at all of what is going on. The officer returns, if possible, a categorical reply to each question, but frequently prisoners make statements which are of course irrelevant in character and are not incorporated in the answer. At times it requires quite a little cross-examining on the part of the officer to determine whether or not the defendant *is* temperate or intemperate, or whether he *has* really ever been convicted of crime theretofore. Any one who could overhear these colloquies would be well repaid for his trouble. The writer knows of one officer of a somewhat waggish disposition who, when he approaches the interrogation directed towards the prisoner's usual habits, first puts the question in its proper form:

"Are you temperate or intemperate?"

The prisoner, who perhaps does not understand these terms, or, at any rate, is a little doubtful himself as to his usual condition, stammers and hesitates. The officer, dropping his voice, remarks, confidentially:

"Say, do you ever take a drink?"

"Sure," says the defendant, without hesitation.

"*Moderate*," shouts the officer to the clerk.

A certain element of humor enters into the situation when a defendant convicted of bigamy is asked if he is married. The answer "Yes" is generally accompanied by an irrepressible grin.

There used to be an old court officer in one of the parts of the General Sessions a few years ago who was a loyal son of Old Erin and a devout member of the Roman Church.

On one occasion, a defendant having been found guilty he was arraigned at the bar for the purpose of having his pedigree taken, old Flaherty officiating. The conversation which ensued may be worth preservation.

Flaherty to Defendant: "Say, me friend, where was ye born?"

Defendant to Flaherty: "*Lowell, Mass.*"

Flaherty to Clerk: "Lowell, Mass."

Flaherty to Defendant: "Where do yez hang out?"

Defendant: "Nowhere."

Flaherty to Clerk: "*Ain't got none.*"

Flaherty to Defendant: "Phat do yez do fer a livin'?"

Defendant: "Nothin'."

Flaherty to Clerk: "*Ain't got none.*"

Flaherty to Defendant: "Are ye married?"

Defendant: "No,—thank God."

Flaherty to Clerk: "*He says 'No, thank God!'*"

Flaherty to Defendant: "Ever receive any previous religious instruction?"

Defendant: "How's that?"

Flaherty to Defendant: "Phat's yer religion?"

Defendant: "Don't believe in nothin'."

Flaherty to Clerk (loudly): "PROTESTANT!"

For a convict to give under oath false answers to the questions thus put to him is, of course, perjury. It is frequently of no small importance for a prisoner to conceal his identity, or at least his record. But if a Bible is thrust into his right hand he is loath to put himself within the statute governing false swearing, for the chances are all in favor of his being found out, in which case his punishment will be severe. The writer recalls a dramatic incident of a man who endeavored to prevent his past offences coming to the knowledge of the judge. He bore, however, all the ear-marks of an ex-convict, and the court became suspicious that all was not right. He had just been convicted of stealing a purse. The jury had remained out until eleven o'clock at night and the court-room was practically deserted. The prisoner was placed before the bar. We will call him James Graham. The clerk put the usual questions and then inquired:

"Have you ever been convicted before?"

"No," answered the prisoner in a low voice.

There was a long pause, and then the judge, looking down intently from the bench, said:

"Graham, is that the truth?"

"Yes, sir," replied the prisoner.

"Are you quite sure?" insisted the court.

"Yes, sir."

"Swear him!" ordered the judge.

The officer started to place the Bible in Graham's hand, but he refused to take it.

"No, no, I can't!" he whispered. "I can't—I—I—it's no use!" he added.

"When were you convicted?"

"I served six months for petty larceny about five years ago."

"Is that all?"

"Yes, sir."

"Are you sure?"

"Yes, sir."

"Quite sure? Think again."

"Yes, sir."

"Swear him!"

Again the book was placed in his hand and again it was declined.

"I served three years in Charlestown for larceny, and was discharged two months ago."

"Is that all?"

"O God! Isn't that enough?" suddenly groaned the prisoner, breaking down completely. "No, sir, it isn't all! It's always been the same old story!

Concord, Joliet, Elmira, Springfield, Sing Sing, Charlestown—Yes, six times. Twelve years!—*I'm a jail bird!*"

Before rendering a verdict the members of almost every jury take the opportunity in the jury-room to stretch their legs and satisfy their craving to smoke. Juries rarely return in less time than it takes to burn a cigar. While this may torture the prisoner it would seem a fairly earned perquisite on the part of his judges. Some jurors are instinctively, and a few are actually lawyers. These rarely add much to the general usefulness of the panel. Jurymen not infrequently seize the opportunity to display their oratorical ability, since their audience cannot get away and must perforce hear them out. The writer recalls one instance where in a well-known extortion case an enthusiastic talesman made a digest of the speeches of counsel for the defence and for the prosecution and then prepared a long harangue of his own which he committed to memory. When the jury were safely locked into their council chamber this self-sacrificing gentleman arose and began, "In this case the defence claims, thus and so." After he had repeated practically in toto the argument of the defence he got his second wind and continued, "On the other hand, the People assert, thus and so." At the end of about an hour he had reached his own humble views of the case, which he expanded at great length, ending with a peroration in which the great American eagle could be heard screaming all the way into the court-room. The jury, probably out of sheer fatigue, took but a single vote and found the defendant guilty. The orator to this day claims that he "did it."

While the deliberations of the jury are theoretically secret, the rooms in which they are confined are often so located with reference to corridors, retiring rooms, etc., that officers on duty, turnkeys, and other persons are occasionally made involuntary eavesdroppers. It is said that in other and more barbarous times interested parties would lurk near by in order to get an idea of how the wind was blowing. There is a story for which the writer assumes no responsibility that ten or fifteen years ago a noted prosecutor was accustomed to follow the jury out, climb upon a ladder, and listen at the transom to their arguments and comments; and there is also a report, which perhaps is but a fable, that there was a knot-hole in the jury-room of the old "Brownstone" building from which the plug was regularly removed to allow of similar surreptitious observations. The rumors which come from the direction of the jury-room are quite as apt to be incorrect as accurate, and neither prosecutor nor prisoner really knows what is the result of the jury's deliberations until the foreman's word ends the suspense.

Many strange and amusing stories are told of how certain historic verdicts in criminal cases were reached. Perhaps the most famous is that of the trial of the first indictment which followed the robbery of the Manhattan Bank. The case was tried before Judge Cowing in the General Sessions, and after a speedy, but conclusive, trial the jury retired. A vote, which was immediately taken, showed that they stood eleven to one for conviction. The twelfth juror was obstinate and no progress whatever was made by the others. The situation remained unchanged during the night and up to twelve o'clock of the next day, which happened to be a Saturday. At that hour Judge Cowing sent word that he was going downtown and would not return until two o'clock. In some way the jury got the idea that the judge intended to lock them up until Monday if they did not agree. They accordingly asked for five minutes more before the judge left the building. This was granted and at the end of that time they announced that they had agreed. Into court they filed.

"Have you agreed upon a verdict?" asked the clerk.

"We have," replied the foreman.

"How say you? Do you find the defendant guilty or not guilty?"

"*Not guilty*," answered the foreman defiantly. The defendant, who was as guilty a man as ever was brought to the bar of justice, almost collapsed from astonishment, and the judge gave the jury a frank piece of his mind in no uncertain language. Rather than suffer any further inconvenience this high-minded jury had simply faced about and voted to acquit.

There are some cases, however, where one strong-minded and able juryman has swung the whole body to his way of thinking after a vote of eleven against him, and this is as true of verdicts of conviction as of acquittal. Few jurors, however, can, as a rule, stand out against the assertions and incriminations of their fellows. Most of them are easy-going and like to be led by a strong hand. A positive stand taken by a fellow talesman will often bring them to his views when they are really inclined to be in doubt. If the flag is raised they will quickly rally to it, but they will never reach the point where they would be willing to elevate it of their own accord. An experienced and highly intelligent juryman once told the writer that the first thing he always did when the jury had retired, whether he was the foreman or not, was to stand up at the end of the table and say:

"Gentlemen, this man is *guilty* [or innocent, as the case might be]! The sooner we say so the better, *but my mind is made up*."

In this way he invariably secured at the outset the support and co-operation of a majority of the jury.

In capital cases where the prisoner's life hangs in the balance there will always be found in the first vote a few blank ballots. These are cast, as the expression is, "to provoke discussion." Shrewd old jurors, realizing that no man can convince another half so well as that other can convince himself, will often vote for "not guilty" in order to get their fellows worked up to a white heat of intellectual frenzy in the effort to bring them over. There is many a wily Odysseus among the variegated personalities of a jury.

"My first jury trial," said one of the judges of the General Sessions recently, "occurred when I was a very young man and had just been admitted to the bar. It was my initial appearance in a court of justice. However, I threw out my chest and tried to make the jury think I was an old hand at the business, by objecting to almost every question and taking exceptions by the score. My client was an old woman who had been illegally ejected, or who claimed to have been illegally ejected, by the agent of a tenement house which belonged to Mr. W.D. Sloane. Of course, I don't suppose Mr. Sloane ever heard of the incident, but I was suing him for damages and put in my case with a great deal of vigor. The lawyer for the defence was a big, good-natured man who did not seem to care very much which way the jury decided the case. The judge charged and the jury retired. They were gone a very long time. At last an officer appeared with a slip of paper. The judge beckoned the lawyer for the other side and myself to the bench and showed us the jury's message.

"'We want a bottle of whiskey and a box of cigars,' it read, and was signed, 'William Smith, Foreman.'

"'Let 'em have them!' remarked the good-natured lawyer. 'I don't blame 'em for being thirsty.'

"'I don't know,' I replied. 'It does not seem to me that whiskey would help them to decide the facts any more clearly!'

"'Of course, if Mr. —— does not agree to it!' exclaimed the lawyer, 'I have nothing to say!' Then he turned away and the judge whispered in my ear:

"'Young man, I should advise you to let these refreshments go into the jury-room. You have not had a great deal of experience and probably do not appreciate the effect which a denial of their request may have upon the jurors. Take a quiet tip from me and let the whiskey go in.'

"'All right, your Honor,' said I. 'I bow to your Honor's long acquaintance with men and your experience at the bar—of justice.'

"Well, the whiskey and cigars went in, and I could see as the officer brought them through the court-room that the whiskey was the very best King William and the cigars were Havana perfectos. I wondered with some misgivings who was paying for them.

"In about an hour the jury filed in flushed and happy and rendered a verdict in favor of Mr. Sloane. Some time afterwards I happened to be in the court-room and learned from the officer that the jury had stood eleven to one in my favor for over three hours. The foreman, the only one against me, had finally remarked that he was thirsty and had offered to treat the rest of the jury. In less than an hour after the refreshments had arrived the other eleven came over and decided that Mr. Sloane was in the right."

Another judge tells of an experience of his when serving upon a jury in Ireland. The case over they retired to the jury-room and found that they stood eleven to one for acquittal, but that one happened to be a very complacent old gentleman in a billy-cock hat who, with his chin resting upon the head of a thick bamboo cane, announced defiantly that he was ready to stay there as long as anybody. The hours dragged slowly by, evening drew on, and still the old gentleman obstinately held out. The jurors disposed their weary bodies as best they could along the floor and the hard benches, and prepared to make a night of it. From time to time the old gentleman would contemplatively suck the head of his bamboo cane. Finally he fell fast asleep and the cane fell heavily to the floor. Then one of the jurors picked it up and found to his surprise *that it was hollow and filled with good old Irish whiskey*. They passed the cane around, relieved it of its contents, and then awoke the owner. Slowly he lifted the cane to his mouth, sucked ineffectually for a moment, looked at his watch and then arose with the announcement:

"B'ys! I'm afther changin' me moind!"

A recent trial, Donohue *vs.* The New York, New Haven and Hartford Railroad, illustrates the vagaries of individuals which may seriously interfere with the course of justice. The judge had been particularly careful to elucidate the point of law which the jury were to apply to the facts as they found them. The jury unanimously agreed that the facts were thus and so, but one of their number refused to follow the law as laid down by the court. At first he insisted that the judge had charged differently, but it soon became obvious that this was not the true cause of his indecision.

"Well," exclaimed the foreman at last, on the verge of distraction, "should we go back into court and the judge should instruct you that what we say *is* the law, would you find a verdict *then*?"

The juryman hesitated and then announced with deliberation:

"No; *not until I had consulted my attorney*."

A frankly unscrupulous member of the criminal bar tells the following story at his own expense. His client was indicted for murder and on the evidence apparently guilty. The lawyer's only chance, as he thought, lay in trying to "work it down" to manslaughter, which would get his client off with twenty years' imprisonment. Accordingly he told his clerk to become friendly with the jurymen, treat them to drinks, and see what he could do. The clerk reported that he had become very thick with the twelfth juror, an old Irishman, who had promised to "hold out for manslaughter." The lawyer told his client, and both ceased to worry about the result, as death no longer stared the prisoner in the face. The jury retired and remained out twenty-three hours. At the end of that time, tired, dishevelled, exasperated, they filed into court and returned a verdict of manslaughter. The lawyer warmly congratulated his client. As the jury were separating the old Irishman leaned over to the lawyer and exultantly whispered:

"Bedad, I had th' divil av a time av it! Elivin o' thim were for *lettin' him go entirely*!"

CHAPTER XIV

THE SENTENCE

"What have you to say why judgment of the court should not be pronounced against you according to law?"

With these words begins the final chapter of the convict's history. He has been arraigned for the last time at the bar of justice, after a jury of his peers has declared him "guilty," and now awaits his sentence.

The judge who presides at the trial of a criminal case does but begin his labors when he receives the jury's verdict. If he be a man of sensibilities the strain of a trial is as nothing compared with the responsibility of determining whether the defendant shall be let go free under a "suspended" sentence or ordered to prison. No one appreciates the horror of prison life or its effect upon the individual better than the judge himself, and he may pass many a sleepless night before sentencing a man whose circumstances and whose years suggest the possibility of reformation.

Where the defendant has been found guilty of murder in any of its degrees the judge is, of course, relieved of the responsibility of determining the sentence, which is fixed by law, and the interrogation of the clerk must seem but a mockery to the prisoner, who knows that, whatever he may say in his own behalf, the judgment of the court will be the same. For this reason counsel rarely address the court upon the sentence in such a case, but sometimes the prisoner himself seeks a last public opportunity to assert his innocence or proclaim his repentance.

On Saturday morning, March 21, 1829, Richard Johnson, convicted of the murder of Ursula Newman, was brought to the bar of the New York Court of Oyer and Terminer, and was asked what he had to say why judgment of death should not be pronounced against him according to law. In the faded ink of the records of the General Sessions is inscribed the following:

> The prisoner replies:
>
> If your Honor please. I am asked what I have to say why judgment of death should not be pronounced against me? To this I reply—To the judgment of the law, nothing. A jury of my country has pronounced me guilty; and there remains no discretion with the court but to pronounce upon me the sentence of the law. But to the judgment of the world I have much to say. I have been convicted of a

crime the bare recital of which causes humanity to shudder. And it is a duty which I owe to myself while living, and to my memory when dead that the circumstances of my offence should be fully explained. Before entering into the detail, I must take this public opportunity in the name of that omniscient and all-merciful Being who will hereafter pronounce his judgment, alike upon my judges & myself, of disclaiming any knowledge of the transactions of that fatal 20th of November. I do not mean to impugn the decision of the jury; the movements of the mind were beyond their power to penetrate; and hard as is my fate I humbly bow to their verdict. I cannot here enter fully into the details of my intimacy with the unfortunate cause of my present awful situation. Duped and betrayed as I have been into sorrow and bitter despair, and lastly involuntary crime I am unwilling while living to indulge in unavailing reproaches. In life the deceased was the object of my tenderest affection. An affection that her own unkind conduct seemed to inflame, and that, baffled in its honorable purpose—expelled reason from her throne, and, in its absence, led to the commission of the offence, for which I am now to satisfy the offended community by my own life. Was I conscious of any moral guilt, at this result I should not repine. Accustomed throughout my life to respect the law, I have not now to learn that the blood of the murderer is alike a propitiating sacrifice to the laws of God and man. Convicted of the legal crime I know my fate. For the moral offence I have to answer to my conscience and my God; and that innate monitor tells me, that I stand before this court and this community a legal but not a moral murderer. To my counsel who have so ably though vainly made my defence, I tender my warmest thanks. Of the court I have but one request to make, that the period allowed me to prepare for my impending fate may be as long as the law will permit.

The sentence of the court was then pronounced.

Compare this solemn and thrilling declaration with what occurred upon the sentence of Dr. Carlyle W. Harris, convicted of the murder of his girl-wife by the administration of morphine capsules which he compounded and furnished to her. He had married her secretly under an assumed name and in all probability had never intended to recognize her as his wife. Events finally rendered it impossible for him to conceal the marriage longer, and, realizing this, he procured for her the medicine which caused her death. Harris was a gentleman,—or rather he was a very debonair, nonchalant, and brazen imitation of one. Throughout his trial he had preserved an absolutely unruffled exterior, chatting affably with counsel and court attendants, and receiving the verdict with undiminished equanimity. On the day set for his sentence he came into court with the easy and gracious manner of a young man paying an afternoon call. He was arraigned at the bar and the Recorder [Smyth] proceeded to rehearse the history of his terrible crime and stigmatize the loathsome character of his act. Harris listened politely, and apparently endeavored to show a considerable interest in his remarks. Then the Recorder made some slight error in giving a date.

"Pardon me, your Honor," interrupted the blithe defendant, "it was the eighteenth and not the nineteenth——" and corrected him.

The Recorder frowned and replied with dignity.

"That is a matter of slight importance!"

"I beg your Honor's pardon," returned Harris flippantly; "you see, I have never been sentenced to death before, and am not as familiar with the procedure as might be."

Unpleasant as is the duty of the prosecutor who is obliged to move that the sentence of death be pronounced, it is less terrible than listening to the few simple but hopeless words that doom a convict to life imprisonment. The murderer must die; but it will soon be over. The ghost of his victim will in a few weeks cease to haunt his dreams. But the "lifer"! Who can picture the horror of a life-time of repentance or of mocking remorselessness? "Civilly dead," he is doomed to drag out his weary years in an earthly tomb, a silent, forgotten creature, numbered like a human specimen, enduring all the tortures of purgatory until the end seems a far distant haven of oblivion. The court-room echoes, like the empty future of the white-faced prisoner, to the dull fall of the words upon his barren soul—"*for the rest of your natural life.*" The listener shudders. "God grant that it be short!" he murmurs, then looks away.

Of course, in the seventeenth century and early in the eighteenth all felonies were punishable, not only in England but in America, by death. When the severity of punishment began to be abated and imprisonment substituted for the extreme penalty, all sentences were for a fixed and definite term, and the only way that the convict could obtain release or secure the modification of his sentence was by pardon from the supreme executive authority of the country.

Sometimes a ray of sunshine illumines the dreary pages of these parchment-bound volumes, the stiff phraseology of the crabbed entries failing to obscure it. For example, on Monday morning, March 29, 1784, "The Court met pursuant to adjournment" and was "opened by proclamation." The grand jury came into court and presented an indictment against one Sylvia, a negro slave, "for stealing monies from Alex^r Johnson."

"The prisoner being set to the bar and arraigned, did plead guilty, and for trial put herself upon God and the country." Her case was immediately moved. One witness, the Alexander Johnson mentioned, testified.

"The jury without going from the Bar say, that they find the prisoner at the bar Guilty of the Felony whereof she stands indicted...."

Just one week later, Sylvia, now a convict, "was called to the Bar, for judgment, and it being demanded of her in the usual manner what she could say for herself why judgment of Death should not now pass against her, according to law, she did produce and plead a pardon of the People of the State of New York, under the Great Seal, bearing test the 31st March, 1784, which was read and allowed, and the Prisoner discharged."

Sylvia was undoubtedly a valuable piece of personal property—valuable enough evidently to make it worth her master's while to urge his claims upon the Governor for clemency.

White offenders did not always fare as well. But for them in the colonial times still occasionally remained that quaint old plea of "benefit of clergy." This lingered on as late as 1784, when the record shows that one John Cullen, having been convicted of forgery,

> "ON MOTION of Mr. Attorney-General ... was sent to the Bar for judgment, and it being demanded of him in the usual form what he could say for himself why judgment of death should not pass against him according to Law, he prayed the Benefit of Clergy, which was granted by the Court.
>
> THEREUPON IT WAS ORDERED that the said John Cullen be branded in the brawn of the left Thumb with the letter T in the presence of the court, and that the sheriff execute the order immediately, which was done accordingly."

Benefit of clergy was the historic privilege accorded in England to all priests of being tried only in the ecclesiastical courts for their crimes. Coke says that "it took its root from a constitution of the Pope that no man should accuse the priests of Holy Church before a secular judge." As all common-law felonies (except petty larceny and mayhem) were *punishable by death* even as late as 1826, and as these felonies included homicide, rape, burglary, arson, robbery and larceny, and *all were clergyable*, it must have been a prerogative of considerable value to any member of the cloth of lively disposition.

Originally the privilege could be claimed *before trial*, and ousted the lay courts of any jurisdiction whatever, the right being strictly limited, however, to those who exhibited all the physical attributes and garb of priesthood, having "*habitum et tonsuram clericalem*," but long before (1350) it was provided that "*all manner of clerks*, as well secular as religious, shall from henceforth freely have and enjoy the privileges of Holy Church." As a priest's trial in the ecclesiastical courts was hardly more than a matter of form, with rarely any result save that of acquittal, he who could plead his "benefit" was practically immune so far as punishment for his crimes was concerned. In course of time the right was accorded only *after* conviction in the secular courts.

In 1487 it was provided that every person convicted of a clergyable felony should be branded in the brawn of his thumb, so that mere inspection would reveal second offenders. The letter M stood for murderer and T for thief or forger, as we have seen in Cullen's case. The statute also provided that no person could plead his clergy a second time unless he were actually in orders. Thus as late as 1487 practically any one who could read or write might commit as many crimes, including murder, as he chose, with no fear of punishment save of having to make his purgation, and after that date could, so to speak, have one murder, arson or larceny and escape with branding, while the priest in orders continued free to violate the law to his heart's content. Perhaps this wholesale extension of the privilege was made in the interest of education and as an incentive to literary accomplishment. It certainly put a premium on learning which a mere "degree" could not offer.

From the beginning of the eighteenth century on (the privilege having been extended by statute to all the inhabitants of England, male or female), *any one*, irrespective of his learning, could plead his clergy once to any crime that remained clergyable, if he could find one, and priests in orders could do so indefinitely. But the crimes which were clergyable were correspondingly reduced in number. In 1779 branding was practically done away with in England. (19 Geo. 3, c. 74 s. 3.)

It is interesting to find the custom still in vogue in America as late as 1784, as shown by the case of Cullen.[41]

In one or two of the Southern States the plea lingered on for nearly another half century.

When the defendant could not avail himself of clergy and no pardon was at hand to save him, the law in the early days took its full and awful course. Thus we read in the first almost illegible volume of the records, the phraseology of the sentence, save for its terms, being practically the same to this day:

Court holden for the tryal of negro
and Indian slaves at the Citty Hall of the
Citty of New-York,
on Tuesday the 15th day of April, Anno
Dom. 1712.

PRESENT:

Caleb Heathsope, } Esquires,

William Smith, } Justices

Edward Blagge }

Court opened—

Dom Regina	{ The defend^t Tom being brought to the Barr & having nothing to say for himself why
vs.	{ judgment of death should not pass ag^t him according to the verdict &c.
Tom the Negro man, slave	{ It is considered by the Court that he be carryed from hence to the place from whence he came and from thence burned with a slow fire that he may continue
of Nicholas Rossvelt J.D.	{ in torment for eight or ten hours and continue burning in said fire untill he be dead and consumed to ashes.

At present, when "benefit of clergy" is but a legal tradition, and pardons are obtained with difficulty, but one legal barrier can be raised to the interposition of sentence upon a convict—proof of his insanity. If, in the opinion of the court, there is reasonable ground for believing him to be mentally unbalanced, the question must be determined as provided in the Code. If he is found to be sane, judgment must then be pronounced, but if found insane he must be committed to the State Lunatic Asylum until he recovers his sanity, and when notice is given of that fact he must be brought before the court for judgment. Of course, he may also allege legal ground why the judgment should be arrested or why a new trial should be granted, but at this time a technical discussion of these motions would be unnecessary.

Defendants are far less likely to feign insanity at the time of their sentence than they are upon the actual trial; for if a man is clever enough to act the part of a lunatic he is shrewd enough to realize that the best time to do so is before he has been convicted of the crime charged against him.

There is a reputed case, the memory of which still lingers around the criminal courts, where it is said that a defendant who was charged with murder in its first degree feigned insanity just before his case was moved for trial. This was many years ago, at a time when such a fact did not, of itself, necessarily excite the same suspicion that it does to-day. The issue of the defendant's sanity was tried before a lay jury, who promptly found that he was incapable of understanding the proceedings against him or of making proper preparation for his defence. He was thereupon committed to the State Asylum for the Insane, where he remained incarcerated for many years. It so happened that there was but a single eye-witness to the shooting, and the circumstances surrounding the affair were such that without the testimony of this witness it would be a practical impossibility to determine whether the deceased had been murdered or had committed suicide. After twenty years, in the course of which the defendant's lawyer had died and the entire family of the prisoner had either died or disappeared, another lawyer, who had found among some old papers a memorandum of the case, went to Matteawan, located the defendant, and discovered, as he had anticipated, that he was entirely sane. A writ of habeas corpus was thereupon procured and the defendant brought back to New York.

In that time the entire aspect of the city had changed. Buildings twenty-five stories in height had replaced those of six; the city had reached far up and entirely covered the island; electric surface cars had taken the place of ramshackle, bobtail horse cars. The defendant, prematurely aged and with clothes long out of date, impressed those in the court-room as a sort of Rip Van Winkle, awakened after a long sleep. There was absolutely no question as to the man's sanity, and he was discharged upon the writ of habeas corpus and remanded to the Tombs to await his trial. The following morning he was brought into court, and the district attorney moved that the indictment against him be dismissed on the ground that there was no longer any evidence upon which the people could proceed to prosecution. Then for the first time *the defendant discovered that the only witness against him had died ten days after he had been committed to the asylum.* Although the writer does not vouch for the authenticity of this story, the incident may well have happened.

In addition to the legal ground of insanity why judgment should not be imposed, a convict or his counsel may properly, on his arraignment, state to the court any general reasons for a mitigation of sentence or for its absolute suspension when such is within the discretion of the court, and few sentences are imposed without a more or less lengthy appeal for clemency from the defendant's lawyer, who usually does not confine himself merely to the contrition of the defendant, his past respectability and his pledges to lead a new and better life, but is prone to discourse volubly upon the reputable connections of the defendant, the hardship which a sentence will impose upon his family, and the fact that the complainant or those who have been interested in the prosecution now have a profound sympathy for the prisoner. The gist of many of these appeals is to the effect that because the defendant, by reason of his education and opportunities, ought to have known better than to commit crime, he should now, since he has discovered his mistake, be excused from paying the penalty. The judge invariably listens with courtesy to these orations, which are not often made with any idea of actually influencing the court's decision. They are grateful to the defendant and his family, and impress the latter with the fact that the lawyer is doing everything in his power to get his client off.

It is now the judge's soul is tried. How far may he temper justice with mercy? How far are the interests of the public and the prisoner irreconcilable? Many youthful offenders, who have not hitherto been convicted, escape with a suspended sentence or a commitment to a reformatory—even when found guilty of crimes as serious as manslaughter or robbery. Little mercy is shown to old offenders. In fact, the law now provides that they may be tried under an indictment charging them with having committed a "second offence," under which, if found guilty, they must be sentenced to the maximum penalty set for a first offence of the same crime.

It should be noticed that originally only one sentence, and that a definite one, could be passed by the judge upon a prisoner for any given offence. At first there were no provisions of law granting to convicts as a matter of right any reduction or commutation of sentence because of good behavior. Then laws were passed which provided for the definite commutation of the sentences of all convicts confined in State's prison. The question as to whether or not the convict had earned his commutation by good behavior was left to a board composed of the State superintendent of prisons and others. A carefully prepared scale or table showed exactly how much commutation it was possible for any prisoner to earn.[42]

In 1889 there was introduced into New York State for the first time what is commonly known as the "indeterminate sentence," that is to say, a sentence consisting of a minimum and a maximum term of imprisonment during which the prisoner may be discharged at the option of a board consisting of various persons, but distinct from that which passes upon the question of whether or not he has earned his "commutation." The introduction of this form of sentence is in conformity with the most recent and most enlightened view of the proper attitude of the State towards its criminals.

Whenever the indeterminate sentence has been introduced into any State it has been invariably attacked as being unconstitutional, but the courts have uniformly upheld it. The principal difference to be noted between "commutation" and "indeterminateness" of sentence is that the latter is vastly broader in effect, since only the prisoner's good behavior while actually undergoing his sentence in State's prison may be considered by the board which passes upon his commutation, while, in the case of the indeterminate sentence, the parole board may consider all the facts surrounding the commission of the crime, the convict's past life, and whatever other facts they see fit, as well as his good behavior during his period of confinement.[43]

After conviction the natural optimism of the human race reasserts itself and the defendant begins to believe that the worst is, after all, over, and to rely upon the assurances of his counsel or his political friends that the judge is going to be easy on him and give him a light sentence. Terrible is the disappointment of such a one who finds that he is going to be sentenced to State's prison when he expected the penitentiary or to the penitentiary when he expected to be set free entirely under a suspended sentence.

The judge usually prefaces the sentence with a few remarks of an admonitory character, commenting upon the severity of the crime which the defendant has committed, and upon the fact that it is within his power to sentence the latter to a long term of imprisonment. He generally adds that, under all the circumstances and considering the fact that the defendant has never been convicted before and has hitherto led a reputable life, he will be merciful and give him only so and so many years in State's prison.

Of course, this occurs only in such cases as deserve leniency. But where the defendant is a hardened criminal, or an ex-convict, or when his crime is one of atrocity, he is apt to learn, in no unmeasured terms, what the judge and the community think of him. The writer has heard a prisoner censured in such language that he blushed for the human race of which the convict could be the offspring. Most defendants receive their sentence with imperturbability, for they are able with approximate accuracy to figure out what punishment they will probably receive. The experiences of their acquaintances in the Tombs are of great assistance in this matter, yet more than one convict falls senseless on the floor when sentence is pronounced upon him, and hundreds lose their nerve and stagger away bewilderedly at the thought of the interminable years before them.

Yet a layman happening to be present on a Friday in the Court of General Sessions would be surprised at the apparent lightness of most of the sentences. The judges of our criminal courts are merciful men and rightly believe that a year or two in State's prison has a better effect upon the defendant than a longer term. A short-term man emerges, at least it is so to be hoped, with some aspirations for the future and with health as yet not undermined. To most judges the infliction of sentence upon a fellow human being ever remains a bitter experience. In the old days, however, there were some judges who, not unlike Jeffries, took a certain grim satisfaction in the performance of this duty. There was, many years ago, one of them who seemed to take a particular delight in so far as possible prolonging the agony of the defendant's uncertainty. When a prisoner had been arraigned for sentence the judge would wait for absolute silence, and would then with the greatest deliberation address a long harangue to the unfortunate man, characterize his crime in the severest manner, excoriate him for having committed it, name the maximum penalty which the law allowed, intimate that he was going to impose it, and then, after a long hiatus, slowly take down his sentence book, ink his pen with annoying deliberation, cough two or three times, look around the court-room and begin carefully inscribing each word upon the record before him, "I—shall—therefore—sentence—you—to—[cough, another glance around the room]—five years in State's prison."

Many pathetic and also amusing incidents occur upon these occasions. There is a true story of an incident which, however, did not occur in the General Sessions of New York County, where a prisoner who had been convicted was arraigned before the judge for sentence. This judge was an aged man with a great reputation for his bitter wit and sarcasm. The convict, who had been convicted of being a common gambler and who was described by the court officers as a "fly guy," appeared in a loudly checked yellow and black suit with a red necktie and a large paste diamond horseshoe pin. The judge from under his beetling eyebrows looked fiercely down upon him from the bench and remarked with intense scorn:

"I sentence you to pay a fine of fifty dollars——'

"That's all right, judge," interrupted the "fly guy" nonchalantly, thrusting his hand into his trousers. "Got it in my pants pocket."

"——And to three years and six months in State's prison," continued his Honor, with a slight twinkle in his eye. "*Have you got THAT in your pants pocket?*"

Recorder Smyth is said to have had a habit of entering the sentences which he proposed to inflict in a book which he kept for that purpose. He also generally made use of a regular set form of expression when imposing them. A miserable little defendant who was gifted with a greater fund of originality than of common-sense, had conceived the extraordinary idea of stealing a ship's anchor belonging to a company which owned a dock in the North River. For this purpose he procured a dray, drawn by six or eight horses, and a derrick, by means of which he hoisted the anchor in question upon the dray in the dead of night and, as might have been expected, succeeded in getting only about half way down the dock with it before he was apprehended by a watchman.

Naturally he had no adequate explanation to offer and promptly pleaded guilty. He was arraigned at the bar in company with several other defendants. Recorder Smyth, his mind still dwelling upon the words with which he had sentenced the latter, thus addressed the trembling miscreant:

"You have pleaded guilty to the crime of stealing a ship's anchor!"—then raising his voice he continued, with perfect solemnity: "The crime of stealing a ship's anchor is *becoming entirely too prevalent*! I sentence you to three years and a half in State's prison."

In contrast with those cheerful days on Manhattan, not much over a century and a half ago, when negroes were burnt to death in chains, and thieves branded in open court and then, tied bareback to the tail of a cart, whipped at every street corner from the City Hall to the Battery and return, the following incident may serve as a pleasant reminder of our progress in civilization:

A young Irishman of excellent address, and employed in a responsible position in an express company, appropriated, at the instigation of evil companions, some of the funds intrusted to his keeping. The larceny was detected, he was arrested and admitted his guilt. Meantime, some one had written to his parents in Ireland who lived in a remote parish in the humblest circumstances. The two old people sold their little cottage, as well as their pig and cow, and took steerage passage from Queenstown to New York. They arrived upon the day set for their son's sentence, entering the court-room as he was arraigned at the bar. A tearful recognition followed, and the prisoner, overwhelmed at this touching proof of his parents' love, begged the judge to listen to their supplication for mercy. Their simple story deeply affected the court, who discharged the defendant in their keeping, under his solemn promise to return with them to Ireland, there to honor and labor for them so long as they should live.

[41] The whipping post and the pillory were in active use until comparatively recent times. Under Dutch rule the former occupied a conspicuous place in front of the Stadt Huys on the strand. As a matter of great leniency the floggings were sometimes conducted in a room to which the public was not admitted. But the disgrace of the performance was regarded as an integral part of the punishment. The offenders were at the same time branded and frequently banished. A New York paper, dated 1712, says that one woman at the whipping post "created much amusement by her resistance." The New York *Gazette* for May 14, 1750, states:

"Tuesday last one David Smith was convicted in the Mayor's Court of Taking or Stealing Goods off a Shop Window in this City, and was sentence to be whipped at the Cart's Tail round this Town and afterwards whipped at the Pillory which sentence was accordingly executed on him." The same paper for October 2, 1752, describes the pillorying of a boy for picking pockets and the whipping of an Irishman for stealing deerskins. In the olden days many a common scold was ducked into quiescence in the North River.

[42] The periods of commutation are shown by the following table:

Sentence	Commutation		Sentence	Commutation	
Years	Years	Months	Years	Years	Months
1	..	2	11	3	11
2	..	4	12	4	4
3	..	8	13	4	9
4	1	..	14	5	2
5	1	5	15	5	7
6	1	10	20	7	8
7	2	3	25	9	9
8	2	8	30	11	10
9	3	1	35	13	11
10	3	6			

[43] Cf. "Some Aspects of the Indeterminate Sentence," by C.D. Warner, 8 Yale Law Journal 219. See also 9 Yale Law Journal 17, as well as "Das Moderne Amerikanische Besserungssystem," Dr. Paul Herr (Berlin, 1907).

CHAPTER XV

WOMEN IN THE COURTS

AS WITNESSES

Women appear in the criminal courts constantly as witnesses, although less frequently as complainants and defendants. As complainants are always witnesses, and as defendants may, and in point of fact generally do become so, whatever generalizations are possible regarding women in courts of law can most easily be drawn from their characteristics as givers of testimony. Roughly speaking, women exhibit about the same idiosyncrasies and limitations in the witness-chair as the opposite sex, and at first thought one would be apt to say that it would be fruitless and absurd to attempt to predicate any general principles in regard to their testimony, but a careful study of female witnesses as a whole will result in the inevitable conclusion that their evidence has virtues and limitations peculiar to itself.

The ancient theory that woman was man's inferior showed itself in the tendency to reject, or at least to regard with suspicion, her evidence in legal matters.

"The following law," says W.M. Best, "is attributed to Moses by Josephus: 'Let the testimony of women not be received on account of the *levity* and *audacity* of their sex'; a law which looks apocryphal, but which, even if genuine, could not have been of universal application.... The law of ancient Rome, though admitting their testimony in general, refused it in certain cases. The civil and canon laws of mediæval Europe seem to have carried the exclusion much further. Mascardus says: '*Feminis plerumque omnino non creditur, et id dumtaxat, quod sunt feminæ, quæ ut plurimum solent esse fraudulentæ, fallaces, et dolosæ*' [Generally speaking, no credence at all is given to women, and for this reason, because they *are* women, who are usually deceitful, untruthful, and treacherous in the very highest degree]. And Lancelottus, in his 'Institutiones Juris Canonici,' lays it down in the most distinct terms, that women cannot in general be witnesses, citing the language of Virgil: '*Varium et mutabile semper femina.*' ...

"Bruneau, although a contemporary of Madame de Sévigné, did not scruple to write, in 1686, that the deposition of three women was only equal to that of two men. At Berne, so late as 1821, in the Canton of Vaud, so late as 1824, the testimony of two women was required to counterbalance that of one man.... A virgin was entitled to greater credit than a widow.... In the 'Canonical Institutions of Devotus,' published at Paris in 1852, it is distinctly stated that, except in a few peculiar instances, women are not competent witnesses in criminal cases. In Scotland also, until the beginning of the eighteenth century, sex was a cause of exclusion from the witness-box in the great majority of instances."

Cockburn in his Memoirs tells of an incident during the trial of Glengarry, in Scotland, for murder in a duel, which is, perhaps, explicable by this extraordinary attitude:—A lady of great beauty was called as a witness and came into court heavily veiled. Before administering the oath, Lord Eskgrove, the judge (to whom this function belongs in Scotland), gave her this exposition of her duty:

"Young woman, you will now consider yourself as in the presence of Almighty God and of this High Court. *Lift up your veil, throw off all your modesty, and look me in the face.*"

Whatever difference does exist in character between the testimony of men and women has its root in the generally recognized diversity in the mental processes of the two sexes. Men, it is commonly declared, rely upon their powers of reason; women upon their intuition. Not that the former is frequently any more accurate than the latter. But our courts of law (at least those in English-speaking countries) are devised and organized, perhaps unfortunately, on the principle that testimony not apparently deduced by the syllogistic method from the observation of relevant fact is valueless, and hence woman at the very outset is placed at a disadvantage and her usefulness as a probative force sadly crippled.

The good old lady who takes the witness-chair and swears that she *knows* the prisoner took her purse has perhaps quite as good a basis for her opinion and her testimony (even though she cannot give a single reason for her belief and becomes hopelessly confused on cross-examination) as the man who reaches the same conclusion ostensibly by virtue of having seen the defendant near by, observed his hand reaching for the purse, and then perceived him take to his heels. She has never been taught to reason and has really never found it necessary, having wandered through life by inference or, more frankly, by guesswork, until she is no longer able to point out the simplest stages of her most ordinary mental processes.

As the reader is already aware, the value of all honestly given testimony depends first upon the witness's original capacity to observe the facts; second upon his ability to remember what he has seen and not to confuse knowledge with *imagination, belief* or *custom,* and lastly, upon his power to express what he has, in fact, seen and remembers.

Women do not differ from men in their original capacity to observe, which is a quality developed by the training and environment of the individual. It is in the second class of the witness's limitations that women as a whole are more likely to trip than men, for they are prone to swear to circumstances as facts, of *their own knowledge*, simply because they confuse what they have really observed with what they believe did occur or should have occurred, or with what they are convinced did happen simply because it was accustomed to happen in the past.

Perhaps the best illustration of the female habit of swearing that facts occurred because they *usually* occurred, was exhibited in the Twitchell murder trial in Philadelphia, cited in Wellman's "Art of Cross-Examination." The defendant had killed his wife with a blackjack, and having dragged her body into the back yard, carefully unbolted the gate leading to the adjacent alley and, retiring to the house, went to bed. His purpose was to create the impression that she had been murdered by some one from outside the premises. To carry out the suggestion, he bent a poker and left it lying near the body smeared with blood. In the morning the servant girl found her mistress and ran shrieking into the street.

At the trial she swore positively that she was first obliged to *unbolt the door* in order to get out. Nothing could shake her testimony, and she thus unconsciously negatived the entire value of the defendant's adroit precautions. He was justly convicted, although upon absolutely erroneous testimony.

The old English lawyers occasionally rejected the evidence of women on the ground that they are "frail." But the exclusion of women as witnesses in the old days was not for psychological reasons, nor did it originate from a critical study of the probative value of their testimony.

Though the conclusions to which women frequently jump may usually be shown by careful interrogation to be founded upon observation of actual fact, their habit of stating inferences often leads them to claim knowledge of the impossible—"wiser in [their] own conceit than seven men that can render a reason."

In a very recent case where a clever thief had been convicted of looting various apartments in New York City of over eighty thousand dollars' worth of jewelry, the female owners were summoned to identify their property. The writer believes that in every instance these ladies were absolutely ingenuous and intended to tell the absolute truth. Each and every one positively identified various of the loose stones found in the possession of the prisoner as her own. This was the case even when the diamonds, emeralds and pearls had no distinguishing marks at all. It was a human impossibility actually to identify any such objects, and yet these eminently respectable and intelligent gentlewomen swore positively that they could recognize their jewels. They drew the inference merely that as the prisoner had stolen similar jewels from them these must be the actual ones which they had lost, an inference very likely correct, but valueless in a tribunal of justice.

Where their inferences are questioned, women, as a rule, are much more ready to "swear their testimony through" than men. They are so accustomed to act upon inference that, finding themselves unable to substantiate their assertion by any sufficient reason, they become irritated, "show fight," and seek refuge in prevarication. Had they not, during their entire lives, been accustomed to mental short-cuts, they would be spared the humiliation of seeing their evidence "stricken from the record."

One of the ladies referred to testified as follows:

"Can you identify that diamond?"

"*I am quite sure that it is mine.*"

"How do you know?"

"*It looks exactly like it.*"

"But may it not be a similar one and not your own?"

"*No; it is mine.*"

"But how? It has no marks."

"*I don't care. I know it is mine. I SWEAR IT IS!*"

The good lady supposed that, unless she swore to the fact, she might lose her jewel, which was, of course, not the case at all, as the sworn testimony founded upon nothing but inference left her in no better position than she was in before.

The writer regrets to say that observation would lead him to believe that women as a rule have somewhat less regard for the spirit of their oaths than men, and that they are more ready, if it be necessary, to commit perjury. This may arise from the fact that women are fully aware that their sex protects them from the same severity of cross-examination to which men would be subjected under similar circumstances. It is to-day fatal to a lawyer's case if he be not invariably gentle and courteous with a female witness, and this is true even if she be a veritable Sapphira.

In spite of these limitations, which, of course, affect the testimony of almost every person, irrespective of sex, women, with the possible exception of children, make the most remarkable witnesses to be found in the courts. They are almost invariably quick and positive in their answers, keenly alive to the dramatic possibilities of the situation, and with an unerring instinct for a trap or compromising admission.

A woman will inevitably couple with a categorical answer to a question, if in truth she can be induced to give one at all, a statement of damaging character to her opponent. For example:

"Do you know the defendant?"

"Yes,—to my cost!"

Or:

"How old are you?"

"Twenty-three,—old enough to have known better than to trust him."

Forced to make an admission which would seem to hurt her position, the explanation, instead of being left for the re-direct examination of her own counsel, is instantly added to her answer then and there.

"Do you admit that you were on Forty-second Street at midnight?"

"Yes. *But it was in response to a message sent by the defendant through his cousin.*"

What is commonly known as "silent cross-examination" is generally the most effective. The jury realize the difficulties of the situation for the lawyer, and are not unlikely to sympathize with him, unless he makes bold to attack the witness, when they quickly change their attitude.

One question, and that as to the witness's means of livelihood, is often sufficient.

"How do you support yourself?"

"I am a lady of leisure!" replies the witness (arrayed in flamboyant colors) snappishly.

"That will do, thank you," remarks the lawyer with a smile. "You may step down."

The writer remembers being nicely hoisted by his own petard on a similar occasion:

"What do you do for a living?" he asked.

The witness, a rather deceptively arrayed woman, turned upon him with a glance of contempt:

"I am a respectable married woman, with seven children," she retorted. "*I do nothing for a living except* cook, wash, scrub, make beds, clean windows, mend my children's clothes, mind the baby, teach the four oldest their lessons, take care of my husband, and try to get enough sleep to be up by five in the morning. I guess if some lawyers worked as hard as I do they would have sense enough not to ask impertinent questions."

An amusing incident is recorded of how a feminine witness turned the laugh upon Mr. Francis L. Wellman, the noted cross-examiner. In his book he takes the opportunity to advise his lawyer readers to "avoid the mistake, so common among the inexperienced, of making much of trifling discrepancies. It has been aptly said," he continues, "that 'juries have no respect for small triumphs over a witness's self-possession or memory!' Allow the loquacious witness to talk on; he will be sure to involve himself in difficulties from which he can never extricate himself. *Some witnesses prove altogether too much; encourage them and lead them by degrees into exaggerations* that will conflict with the common-sense of the jury."

Mr. Wellman is famous for following this precept himself and, with one eye significantly cast upon the jury, is likely to lead his witness a merry dance until the latter is finally "bogged" in a quagmire of absurdities. Not long ago, shortly after the publication of his book, the lawyer had occasion to cross-examine a modest-looking young woman as to the speed of an electric car. The witness seemed conscious that she was about to undergo a severe ordeal, and Mr. Wellman, feeling himself complete master of the situation, began in his most winsome and deprecating manner:

"And how fast, Miss ——, would you say the car was going?"

"I really could not tell exactly, Mr. Wellman."

"Would you say that it was going at ten miles an hour?"

"Oh, fully that!"

"Twenty miles an hour?"

"Yes, I should say it was going twenty miles an hour."

"Will you say it was going thirty miles an hour?" inquired Wellman with a glance at the jury.

"Why, yes, I will say that it was."

"Will you say it was going forty?"

"Yes."

"Fifty?"

"Yes, I will say so."

"Seventy?"

"Yes."

"Eighty?"

"Yes," responded the young lady with a countenance absolutely devoid of expression.

"A hundred?" inquired the lawyer with a thrill of eager triumph in his voice.

There was a significant hush in the court-room. Then the witness, with a patient smile and a slight lifting of her pretty eyebrows, remarked quietly:

"Mr. Wellman, *don't you think we have carried our little joke far enough?*"

There is no witness in the world more difficult to cope with than a shrewd old woman who apes stupidity, only to reiterate the gist of her testimony in such incisive fashion as to leave it indelibly imprinted on the minds of the jury. The lawyer is bound by every law of decency, policy and manners to treat the aged dame with the utmost consideration. He must allow her to ramble on discursively in defiance of every rule of law and evidence in answer to the simplest question; must receive imperturbably the opinions and speculations upon every subject of both herself and (through her) of her neighbors; only to find when he thinks she must be exhausted by her own volubility, that she is ready, at the slightest opportunity, to break away again into a tangle of guesswork and hearsay, interwoven with conclusions and ejaculation. Woe be unto him if he has not sense enough to waive her off the stand! He might as well try to harness a Valkyrie as to restrain a pugnacious old Irishwoman who is intent on getting the whole business before the jury in her own way.

In the recent case of Gustav Dinser, convicted of murder, a vigorous old lady took the stand and testified forcibly against the accused. She was as "smart as paint," as the saying goes, and resolutely refused to answer any questions put to her by counsel for the defence. Instead, she would raise her voice and make a savage onslaught upon the prisoner, rehearsing his brutal treatment of the deceased on previous occasions, and getting in the most damaging testimony.

"Do you say, Mrs. ——," the lawyer would inquire deferentially, "that you heard the sound of *three* blows?"

"Oh, thim blows!" the old lady would cry—"thim turrible blows! I could hear the villain as he laid thim on! I could hear the poor, pitiful groans av her, and she so sufferin'! 'Twas awful! Howly Saints, 'twould make yer blood run cowld!"

"Stop! stop!" exclaimed the lawyer.

"Ah, stop is it? Ye can't stop me till Oi've had me say to tell the whole truth. I says to me daughter Ellen, says I: 'Th' horrid baste is afther murtherin' the poor thing,' says I; 'run out an' git an officer!'"

"I object to all this!" shouts the lawyer.

"Ah, ye objec', do ye?" retorts the old lady. "Shure an' ye'd have been after objectin' if ye'd heard thim turrible blows that kilt her—the poor, sufferin', swate crayter! I hope he gits all that's comin' to him—bad cess to him for a blood-thirsty divil!"

The lawyer ignominiously abandoned the attack.

The writer recalls a somewhat similar instance, but one even better exhibiting the cleverness of an old woman, which occurred in the year 1901. A man named Orlando J. Hackett, of prepossessing appearance and manners, was on trial, charged with converting to his own use money which had been intrusted to him for investment in realty. The complainant was a shrewd old lady, who, together with her daughter, had had a long series of transactions with Hackett which would have entirely confused the issue could the defence have brought them before the jury. The whole contention of the prosecution was that Hackett had received the money for one purpose and used it for another. During preparation for the trial the writer had had both ladies in his office and remembers making the remark:

"Now, Mrs. ——, don't forget that the charge here is that you gave Mr. Hackett the money to put into real estate. Nothing else is comparatively of much importance."

"Be sure and remember that, mother," the daughter had admonished her.

In the course of a month the case came on for trial before Recorder Goff, in Part II of the General Sessions. Mrs. —— gave her testimony with great positiveness. Mr. Lewis Stuyvesant Chanler, now Lieutenant-Governor of the State, arose to cross-examine her.

"Madam," he began courteously, "you say you gave the defendant money?"

"I told him to put it into real estate, *and he said he would!*" replied Mrs. —— firmly.

"I did not ask you that, Mrs. ——," politely interjected Mr. Chanler. "How *much* did you give him?"

"*I told him to put it into real estate*, and he said he would!" repeated the old lady wearily.

"But, madam, you do not answer my question!" exclaimed Chanler. "How *much* did you give him?"

"I told him to put it into real——" began the old lady again.

"Yes, yes!" cried the lawyer; "we know that! Answer the question."

"——estate, *and he said he would!*" finished the old woman innocently.

"If your Honor please, I will excuse the witness. And I move that her answers be stricken out!" cried Chanler savagely.

The old lady was assisted from the stand, but as she made her way with difficulty towards the door of the court-room she could be heard repeating stubbornly:

"I told him to put it *into real estate,—and he said he would!*"

Almost needless to say, Hackett was convicted and sentenced to seven years in State's prison.

To recapitulate, the quickness and positiveness of women make them ordinarily better witnesses than men; they are vastly more difficult to cross-examine; their sex protects them from many of the most effective weapons of the lawyer, with the result that they are the more ready to yield to prevarication; and, even where the possibility of complete and unrestricted cross-examination is afforded, their tendency to inaccurately inferential reasoning, and their elusiveness in dodging from one conclusion to another, render the opportunity of little value.

In general, however, women's testimony differs little in quality from that of men, all testimony being subject to the same three great limitations irrespective of the sex of the witness, and the conclusions set forth above are merely the result of an effort on the part of the writer to comment somewhat upon those small differences which, under close scrutiny, may fairly be said to exist. These differences are quite as noticeable at the breakfast-table as in the court-room; and are no more patent to the advocate than to the ordinary male animal whose forehead habitually reddens when he hears the unanswerable reason which, in default of all others, explains and glorifies the mental action of his wife, sister or mother: "Just because!"

AS COMPLAINANTS AND DEFENDANTS

The ratio of women to men indicted and tried for crime is, roughly, about one to ten. Could adequate statistics be procured, the proportion of female to male complainants in criminal cases would very likely prove to be about the same. In a very substantial proportion, therefore, of all prosecutions for crime a woman is one of the chief actors. The law of the land compels the female prisoner to submit the question of her guilt or innocence to twelve individuals of the opposite sex; and permits the female complainant to rehearse the story of her wrongs before the same collection of colossal intellects and adamantine hearts.

The first thing the ordinary woman hastens to do if she be summoned to appear in a court of justice is not, as might be expected, to think over her testimony or try to recall facts obliterated or confused by time, but to buy a new hat; and precisely the same thing is true of the female defendant called to the bar of justice, whether it be for stealing a pair of gloves or poisoning her lover.

Yet how far does the element of sex defeat the ends of justice? To answer this question it is necessary to determine how far juries are liable to favor the testimony of a woman plaintiff merely because she is a woman, and how far sympathy for a woman arraigned as a prisoner is likely to warp their judgment.

As to the first, it is fairly safe to say that a woman is much more likely to win a verdict in a civil court or to persuade the jury that the prisoner is guilty in a criminal case than a man would be in precisely similar circumstances. In most criminal prosecutions for the ordinary run of felonies little injustice is likely to result from this. There is one exception, however, where juries should reach conclusions with extreme caution, namely, where certain charges are brought by women against members of the opposite sex. Here the jury is apt to leap to a conclusion, rendered easy by the attractiveness of the witness and the feeling that the defendant is a "cur anyway," and ought to be "sent up."

The difficulty of determining, even in one's office, the true character of a plausible woman is enhanced tenfold in the court-room, where the lawyer is generally compelled to proceed upon the assumption that the witness is a person of irreproachable life and antecedents. Almost any young woman may create a favorable impression, provided her taste in dress be not too crude, and, even when it is so, the jury are not apt to distinguish carefully between that which cries to Heaven and that which is merely "elegant."

When the complaining witness is a woman who has merely lost money through the acts of the defendant, the jury are not so readily moved to accept her story *in toto* as when the crime charged is of a different character. They realize that the complainant, feeling that she has been injured, may be inclined to color her testimony, perhaps unconsciously, until the wrong becomes a crime.

An ordinary example of this variety of prosecution is where the witness is a young woman from the East Side, usually a Polish or Russian Jewess, who charges the defendant, a youth of about her own age, with stealing her money by means of false pretences. They have been engaged to be married, and she has turned over her small savings to him to purchase the diamond ring and perhaps set him up in a modest business of his own. He has then fallen in love with some other girl, has broken the engagement, and the ring now adorns the fourth finger of her rival. Her money is gone. She is without a *dot*. She hurries with her parents and loudly vociferating friends to the Essex Market Police Court, and secures a warrant for the defendant on the theory that he defrauded her by "trick and device" or "false representations." Usually the only "representation" has been a *promise* to marry her. Her real motive is revenge upon her faithless *fiancé*. In nine cases out of ten the fellow is a cad, who has deliberately deserted her after getting her money, but it is doubtful whether any real crime is involved.

If the judge lets the case go to the jury it is a pure gamble as to what the result will be, and it may largely turn on the girl's physical attractiveness. If she be pretty and demure a mixture of emotions is aroused in the jury. "He probably did love her," say the twelve, "because any one would be likely to do so. If he did love her, of course he didn't falsely pretend to do so; but if he deserted a woman like that he ought to be in jail anyway." Thus the argument that ought to *acquit* in fact may *convict* the defendant. If the rival also is pretty, hopeless confusion results; while if the complainant be a homely girl the jury feels that he must have intended to swindle her anyway, as he could never have honestly intended to marry her. Thus in any case the Lothario is apt to pay a severe penalty for his faithlessness.

The man prosecuted by a woman, provided she cannot be persuaded to withdraw the charge against him, is likely to get but cold consideration for his side of the story and short shrift in the jury-room. Turn about, if he can get a young and attractive woman to swear to his alibi or good reputation, the honest masculine citizen whom he has defrauded may very likely have to whistle for his revenge. Many a scamp has gone free by producing some sweetly demure maiden who faithfully swears that she knows him to be an honest man. A blush at the psychological moment and a wink from the lawyer is quite enough to lead the jury to believe that, if they acquit the defendant, they will "make the young lady happy," whereas if he is convicted she will remain for aye a heart-broken spinster. Like enough she may be only the merest acquaintance.

The writer is not likely to forget a distinguished lawyer's instructions to his client—who happened also to be a childhood acquaintance—as she was about to go into court as the plaintiff in a suit for damages:

"I would fold my hands in my lap, Gwendolyn—yes, like that—and be calm, very calm. And, Gwendolyn, above all things, be *demure*, Gwendolyn! Be *demure*!"

Gwendolyn was the demurest of the demure, letting her eyes fall beneath their pendant black lashes at the conclusion of each answer, and won her case without the slightest difficulty.

The unconscious or conscious influence of women upon the intellects of jurymen has given rise to a very prevalent impression that it is difficult if not impossible successfully to prosecute a woman for crime. This feeling expresses itself in general statements to the effect that as things stand to-day a woman may commit murder with impunity. Experience, supplemented by the official records, demonstrates, however, that, curious as it must seem, the same sentiment aroused by a woman supposed to have been *wronged* is not inspired in a jury by a woman *accused* of crime. It is, indeed, true that juries are apt to be more lenient with women than with men, but this leniency shows itself not in acquitting them of the crimes charged against them, but of finding them guilty in lower degrees.

Of course flagrant miscarriages of justice frequently occur, which, by reason of their widespread publicity in the press, would seem to justify the almost universal opinion that women are immune from the penalties for homicide. It is also true that such miscarriages of justice are more likely when the defendant is a woman than if he be a man.

One of these hysterical acquittals which give color to popular impression, but which the writer believes to be an exception, was the case of a young mother tried and acquitted for murder in the first degree, December 22, 1904. This young woman, whose history was pathetic in the extreme, was shown clearly by the evidence to have deliberately taken the life of her child by giving it carbolic acid. The story was a shocking one, yet the jury apparently never considered at all the possibility of convicting her, but on retiring to the jury-room spent their time in discussing how much money they should present her on her acquittal.

No better actor ever played a part upon the court-room stage than old "Bill" Howe. His every move and gesture was considered with reference to its effect upon the jury, and the climax of his summing-up was always accompanied by some dramatic exhibition calculated to arouse sympathy for his client. Himself an adept at shedding tears at will, he seemed able to induce them when needed in the lachrymal glands of the most hardened culprit whom he happened to be defending.

Mr. Wellman tells the story of how he was once prosecuting a woman for the murder of her lover, whom she had shot rather than allow him to desert her. She was a parson's daughter who had gone wrong and there seemed little to be said in her behalf. She sat at the bar the picture of injured innocence, with a look of spirituality which she must have conjured up from the storehouse of her memories of her father. Howe was rather an exquisite so far as his personal habits were concerned, and allowed his finger-nails to grow to an extraordinary length. He had arranged that at the climax of his address to the jury he would turn and, tearing away the slender hands of his client from her tear-stained face, challenge the jury to find guilt written there. Wellman was totally unprepared for this and a shiver ran down his spine when he saw Howe, his face apparently surcharged with emotion, turn suddenly towards his client and roughly thrust away her hands. As he did so he embedded his finger-nails in her cheeks, and the girl uttered an involuntary scream of nervous terror and pain that made the jury turn cold.

"Look, gentlemen! Look in this poor creature's face! Does she look like a guilty woman? No! A thousand times no! Those are the tears of innocence and shame! Send her back to her aged father to comfort his old age! Let him clasp her in his arms and press his trembling lips to her hollow eyes! Let him wipe away her tears and bid her sin no more!"

The jury acquitted, and Wellman, aghast, followed them downstairs to inquire how such a thing were possible. The jurors said that they had agreed to disclose nothing of their deliberations.

"But," explained Wellman, "you see, in a way I am your attorney, and I want to know how to do better next time. She had offered to plead guilty if she could get off with twenty years!"

The abashed jury slunk downstairs in silence and the secret of their deliberations remains as yet untold.

In spite of such cases, where guilty women have been acquitted through maudlin sentiment or in response to popular clamor, nothing could be more erroneous than the idea that few women who are brought to the bar of justice are made to suffer for their offences. Thus, although no woman has suffered the death penalty in New York County in twenty years, *the average number of convictions for crime is practically the same for women as for men in proportion to the number indicted.* The last unreversed conviction of a woman for murder in the first degree was that of Chiara Cignarale, in May, 1887. Her sentence was commuted to life imprisonment. Since then thirty women have been actually tried before juries for homicide with the following results:

Convicted of murder in first degree	0
" " murder in second degree	3
" " manslaughter in first degree	10
" " manslaughter in second degree	10
Acquitted	7

Total   30

The percentage of convictions to acquittals is as follows:

	Convictions	Acquittals	Convictions Per Cent	Acquittals Per Cent
1887-1907	23	7	77	23

It is distinctly interesting to compare this with the table showing the results of all the homicide trials for the past eight years irrespective of the sex of the defendants:

	Convictions	Acquittals	Convictions Per Cent	Acquittals Per Cent
1900	5	12	29	71
1901	17	17	50	50
1902	15	11	58	42
1903	24	8	75	25
1904	19	14	58	42
1905	18	13	58	42
1906	21	22	49	51
1907	16	10	62	38
Total	135	107	Aver.55	Aver.45

The reader will observe that the percentage of convictions to acquittals of women defendants averages twenty-two per cent greater than the percentage for both sexes. A more elaborate table would show that where the defendants are men there are a greater proportionate number of *acquittals*, but more verdicts in higher degrees. A verdict of manslaughter in the second degree in the case of a man charged with murder is infrequent, but convictions of murder in the second degree are exceedingly common.

The reason for the higher percentage of convictions of women is that fewer women who commit crime are prosecuted than men, and that they are rarely indicted unless they are clearly guilty of the degree of crime charged against them; while practically every man who is charged with homicide and who, it seems, may be found guilty is indicted for murder in the first degree.

The trial of women for crime invariably arouses keen public interest, and the dethronement of a Czar, or the assassination of an Emperor, pales to insignificance before the prosecution of a woman for murder. Some of this interest is fictitious and stimulated merely by the yellow press, but a great deal of it is genuine. The writer remembers attending a dinner of gray-headed judges and counsellors during the trial of Ann Eliza, alias "Nan," Patterson, where one would have supposed that the lightest subject of conversation would be not less weighty than the constitutionality of an income tax, and finding to his astonishment that the only topic for which they showed any zest was whether "Nan" would be found guilty.

One of the earliest, if not the earliest, record of a woman being held for murder is that of Agnes Archer, indicted by twelve men on April 4, 1435, sworn before the mayor and coroner to inquire as to the death of Alice Colynbourgh. The quaint old report begins in Latin, but "the pleadings" are set forth in the language of the day, as follows:

"Agnes Archer, is that thy name? which answered, yes.... Thou art endyted that thou ... feloney moderiste her with a knyff fyve tymes in the throte stekyng, throwe the wheche stekyng the saide Alys is deed.... I am not guilty of thoo dedys, ne noon of hem, God help me so.... How wylte thou acquite the?... By God and by my neighbours of this town."

The subsequent history of Agnes is lost in obscurity, but since she had to procure but thirty-six compurgators who were prepared to swear that they believed her innocent, and as she was at liberty to choose these herself from her native village of Winchelsea, it is probable that she escaped.[44]

Fortunately the sight of a woman, save of the very lowest class, at the bar of justice is rare. The number of cases where women of good environment appear as defendants in the criminal courts in the course of a year may be numbered upon the fingers of a single hand, and, although the number of female defendants may equal ten per cent of the total number of males, not one-tenth of the women brought to the bar of justice have had the benefit of an honest bringing up and good surroundings.

FOOTNOTES:

[44] Cf. Thayer, as cited, *supra*.

CHAPTER XVI

TRICKS OF THE TRADE

"Tricks and treachery," said Benjamin Franklin, "are the practice of fools that have not wit enough to be honest." Had the kindly philosopher been familiar with all the exigencies of the criminal law he might have added a qualification to this somewhat general, if indisputably moral, maxim. Though it doubtless remains true as a guiding principle of life that "Honesty is the best policy," it would be an unwarrantable aspersion upon the intellectual qualities of the members of the criminal bar to say that the tricks by virtue of which they often get their clients off are "*the practice of fools.*" On the contrary, observation would seem to indicate that in many instances the wiser, or at least the more successful, the practitioner of criminal law becomes, the more numerous and ingenious become the "tricks" which are his stock in trade. This must not be taken to mean that there are not high-minded and conscientious practitioners of criminal law, many of them financially successful, some filled with a noble humanitarian purpose, and some drawn to their calling by a sincere enthusiasm for the vocation of the advocate which, in these days of "business" law and commercial methods, reaches perhaps its highest form in the criminal courts.

There are no more "tricks" practised in these tribunals than in the civil, but they are more ingenious in conception, more lawless in character, bolder in execution and less shamefaced in detection.

Let us not be too hard upon our brethren of the criminal branch. Truly, their business is to "get their clients off." It is unquestionably a generally accepted principle that it is better that ninety-nine guilty men should escape than that one innocent man should be convicted. However much persons of argumentative or philosophic disposition may care to quarrel with this doctrine, they must at least admit that it would doubtless appear to them of vital truth were they defending some trembling client concerning whose guilt or innocence they were themselves somewhat in doubt. "Charity believeth all things," and the prisoner is entitled to every reasonable doubt, even from his own lawyer. It is the lawyer's business to create such a doubt if he can, and we must not be too censorious if, in his eagerness to raise this in the minds of the jury, he sometimes oversteps the bounds of propriety, appeals to popular prejudices and emotions, makes illogical deductions from the evidence, and impugns the motives of the prosecution. The district attorney should be able to take care of himself, handle the evidence in logical fashion, and tear away the flimsy curtain of sentimentality hoisted by the defence. These are hardly "tricks" at all, but sometimes under the name of advocacy a trick is "turned" which deserves a much harsher name.

Not long ago a celebrated case of murder was moved for trial after the defendant's lawyer had urged him in vain to offer a plea of murder in the second degree. A jury was summoned and, as is the usual custom in such cases, examined separately on the "*voir dire*" as to their fitness to serve. The defendant was a German, and the prosecutor succeeded in keeping all Germans off the jury until the eleventh seat was to be filled, when he found his peremptory challenges exhausted. Then the lawyer for the prisoner managed to slip in a stout old Teuton, who replied, in answer to a question as to his place of nativity, "Schleswig-Holstein." The lawyer made a note of it, and, the box filled, the trial proceeded with unwonted expedition.

The defendant was charged with having murdered a woman with whom he had been intimate, and his guilt of murder in the first degree was demonstrated upon the evidence beyond peradventure. At the conclusion of the case, the defendant not having dared to take the stand, the lawyer arose to address the jury in behalf of what appeared a hopeless cause. Even the old German in the back row seemed plunged in soporific inattention. After a few introductory remarks the lawyer raised his voice and in heart-rending tones began:

"In the beautiful county of *Schleswig-Holstein* sits a woman old and gray, waiting the message of your verdict from beyond the seas." (Number 11 opened his eyes and looked at the lawyer as if not quite sure of what he had heard.) "There she sits" (continued the attorney), "in *Schleswig-Holstein*, by her cottage window, waiting, waiting to learn whether her boy is to be returned to her outstretched arms." (Number 11 sat up and rubbed his forehead.) "Had the woman, who so unhappily met her death at the hands of my unfortunate client, been *like those women of Schleswig-Holstein*—noble, sweet, pure, lovely women of *Schleswig-Holstein*—I should have naught to say to you in his behalf." (Number 11 leaned forward and gazed searchingly into the lawyer's face.) "But alas, no! *Schleswig-Holstein* produces a virtue, a loveliness, a nobility of its own." (Number 11 sat up and proudly expanded his chest.)

When, after about an hour or more of *Schleswig-Holstein* the defendant's counsel surrendered the floor to the district attorney, the latter found it quite impossible to secure the slightest attention from the eleventh juror, who seemed to be spending his time in casting compassionate glances in the direction of the prisoner. In due course the jury retired, but had no sooner reached their room and closed the door than the old Teuton cried,

"Dot man iss *not guilty!*" The other eleven wrestled with him in vain. He remained impervious to argument for seventeen hours, declining to discuss the evidence, and muttering at intervals, "Dot man iss *not guilty!*" The other eleven stood unanimously for murder in the first degree, which was the only logical verdict that could possibly have been returned upon the evidence.

At last, worn out with their efforts, they finally induced the old Teuton to compromise with them on a verdict of manslaughter. Wearily they straggled in, the old native of Schleswig-Holstein bringing up the rear, bursting with exultation and with victory in his eye.

"Gentlemen of the jury, have you agreed upon a verdict?" inquired the clerk.

"We have," replied the foreman.

"How say you, do you find the defendant guilty or not guilty?"

"Guilty—of manslaughter," returned the foreman feebly.

The district attorney was aghast at such a miscarriage of justice, and the judge showed plainly by his demeanor his opinion of such a verdict. But the old inhabitant of Schleswig-Holstein cared for this not a whit. The old mother in Schleswig-Holstein might still clasp her son in her arms before she died! The defendant was arraigned at the bar. Then for the first time, and to the surprise and disgust of No. 11, he admitted in answer to the questions of the clerk that his parents were *both dead* and that he was born in *Hamburg,* a town for whose inhabitants the old juryman had, like others of his compatriots, a constitutional antipathy.

The "tricks" of the trade as practised by the astute and unscrupulous criminal lawyer vary with the stage of the case and the character of the crime charged. They are also adapted with careful attention to the disposition, experience and capacity of the particular district attorney who happens to be trying the case against the defendant. An illustration of one of these occurred during the prosecution of a bartender for selling "spirituous liquors" without a proper license. He was defended by an old war-horse of the criminal bar famous for his astuteness and ability to laugh a case out of court. The assistant district attorney who appeared against him was a young man recently appointed to office, and who was almost overcome at the idea of trying a case against so well known a practitioner. He had personally conducted but very few cases, had an excessive conception of his own dignity, and dreaded nothing so much as to appear ridiculous. Everything, except the evidence, favored the defendant, who, however, was, beyond every doubt, guilty of the offence charged.

The young assistant put in his case, calling his witnesses one by one, and examining them with the most feverish anxiety lest he should forget something. The lawyer for the defence made no cross-examination and contented himself with smiling blandly as each witness left the stand. The youthful prosecutor became more and more nervous. He was sure that something was wrong, but he couldn't just make out what. At the conclusion of the People's case the lawyer inquired, with a broad grin, "if that was all."

The young assistant replied that it was, and that, in his opinion, it was "quite enough."

"Let that be noted by the stenographer," remarked the lawyer. "Now, if your Honors please," he continued, addressing the three judges of the Special Sessions, "you all know how interested I am to see these young lawyers growing up. I like to help 'em along—give 'em a chance—teach 'em a thing or two. I trust it may not be out of place for me to say that I like my young friend here and think he tried his case very well. But he has a great deal to learn. I'm always glad, as I said, to give the boys a chance—to give 'em a little experience. I shall not put my client upon the stand. It is not necessary. *The fact is*," turning suddenly to the unfortunate assistant district attorney—"my client *has* a license." He drew from his pocket a folded paper and handed it to the paralyzed young attorney with the harsh demand: "What do you say to that?"

The assistant took the paper in trembling fingers and perused it as well as he could in his unnerved condition.

"Mr. District Attorney," remarked the presiding justice dryly (which did not lessen the confusion of the young lawyer), "is this a fact? Has the defendant a license?"

"Yes, your Honors," replied the assistant; "this paper seems to be a license."

"Defendant discharged!" remarked the court briefly.

The prisoner stepped from the bar and rapidly disappeared through the door of the court-room. After enough time had elapsed to give him a good start and while another case was being called, the old lawyer leaned over to the assistant and remarked with a chuckle:

"I am always glad to give the boys a chance—help 'em along—teach 'em a little. That license was a *beer* license!"

BEFORE TRIAL

To begin at the beginning, whenever a person has been arrested, charged with crime, and has secured a criminal lawyer to defend him, the first move of the latter is naturally to try and nip the case in the bud by inducing the complaining witness to abandon the prosecution. In a vast number of cases he is successful. He appeals to the charity of the injured party, quotes a little of the Scriptures and the "Golden Rule," pictures the destitute condition of the defendant's family should he be cast into prison, and the dragging of an honored name in the gutter if he should be convicted. Few complainants have ever before appeared in a police court, and are filled with repugnance at the rough treatment of prisoners and the suffering which they observe upon every side. After they have seen the prisoner emerge from the cells, pale, hollow-eyed, bedraggled, and have beheld the tears of his wife and children as they crowd around the husband and father, they begin to realize the horrible consequences of a criminal prosecution and to regret that they ever took the steps which have brought the wrong-doer where he is. The district attorney has not yet taken up the case; the prosecution up to this point is of a private character; there are loud promises of "restitution" and future good behavior from the defendant, and the occasion is ripe for the lawyer to urge the complainant to "temper justice with mercy" and withdraw "before it be too late and the poor man be ruined forever."

If the complainant is, however, bent on bringing the defendant to justice and remains adamantine to the arguments of the lawyer and the tears of the defendant's family connections, it remains for the prisoner's attorney to endeavor to get the case adjourned "until matters can be adjusted"—to wit, restitution made if money has been stolen, or doctors' bills paid if a head has been cracked, with perhaps another chance of "pulling off" the complainant and his witnesses. Failing in an attempt to secure an adjournment, two courses remain open: first, to persuade the court that the matter is a trivial one arising out of petty spite, is all a mistake, or that at best it is a case of "disorderly conduct" (and thus induce the judge to "turn the case out" or inflict some trifling punishment in the shape of a fine); or, second, if it be clear that a real crime has been committed, to clamor for an immediate hearing in order, if it be secured, to subject the prosecution's witnesses to a most exhaustive cross-examination, and thus get a clear idea of just what evidence there is against the accused.

At the conclusion of the complainant's case, if it appear reasonably certain that the magistrate will "hold" the prisoner for the action of a superior court, the lawyer will then "waive further examination," or, in other words, put in no defence, preferring the certainty of having to face a jury trial to affording the prosecution an opportunity to discover exactly what defence will be put in and to secure evidence in advance of the trial to rebut it. Thus it rarely happens in criminal cases of importance that the district attorney knows what the defence is to be until the defendant himself takes the stand, and, by "waiving further examination" in the police court, the astute criminal attorney may select at his leisure the defence best suited to fit in with and render nugatory the prosecution's evidence.

The writer has frequently been told by the attorney for a defendant *on trial* for crime that "the defence has not yet been decided upon." In fact, such statements are exceedingly common. In many courts the attitude of all parties concerned seems to be that the defendant will put up a perjured defence (so far as his own testimony is concerned, at any rate) as a matter of course, and that this is hardly to be taken against him.

On the other hand, if a guilty defendant has been so badly advised as to give his own version of the case before the magistrate in the first instance, it requires but slight assiduity on the part of the district attorney to secure, in the interval between the hearing and the jury trial, ample evidence to rebut it.

As illustrating merely the fertility and resourcefulness of some defendants (or perhaps their counsel), the writer recalls a case which he tried in the year 1902 where the defendant, a druggist, was charged with manslaughter in having caused the death of an infant by filling a doctor's prescription for calomel with morphine. It so happened that two jars containing standard pills had been standing side by side upon an adjacent shelf, and, a prescription for morphine having come in at the same time as that for the calomel, the druggist had carelessly filled the morphine prescription with calomel, and the calomel prescription with morphine. The adult for whom the morphine had been prescribed recovered immediately under the beneficent influence of the calomel, but the baby for whom the calomel had been ordered died from the effects of the first morphine pill administered. All this had occurred in 1897—five years before. The remainder of the pills had disappeared.

Upon the trial (no inconsistent contention having been entered in the police court) the prisoner's counsel introduced six separate defences, to wit: That the prescription had been *properly* filled with calomel and that the child had died from natural causes, the following being suggested:

1. Acute gastritis.

2. Acute nephritis.

3. Cerebro-spinal meningitis.

4. Fulminating meningitis.

5. That the child had died of *apomorphine*, a totally distinct poison.

6. That it had received and taken calomel, but that, having eaten a small piece of pickle shortly before, the conjunction of the vegetable acid with the calomel had formed, in the child's stomach, a precipitate of corrosive sublimate, from which it had died.

These were all argued with great learning. During the trial the box containing the balance of the pills, which the defence contended were calomel, unexpectedly turned up. It has always been one of the greatest regrets of the writer's life that he did not then and there challenge the defendant *to eat one of the pills* and thus prove the good faith of his defence.

This was one of the very rare cases where a chemical analysis has been conducted in open court. The chemist first tested a standard trade morphine pill with sulphuric acid, so that the jury could personally observe the various color reactions for themselves. He then took one of the contested pills and subjected it to the same test. The first pill had at once turned to a brilliant rose, but the contested pill, being antiquated, "hung fire," as it were, for some seconds. As nothing occurred, dismay made itself evident on the face of the prosecutor, and for a moment he felt that all was lost. Then the five-year-old pill slowly turned to a faint brown, changed to a yellowish red, and finally broke into an ardent rose. The jury settled back into their seats with an audible "Ah!" and the defendant was convicted.

Let us return, however, to that point in the proceedings where the defendant has been "held for trial" by the magistrate. The prisoner's counsel now endeavors to convince the district attorney that "there is nothing in the case," and continues unremittingly to work upon the feelings of the complainant. If he finds that his labors are likely to be fruitless in both directions, he may now seek an opportunity to secure permission for his client to appear before the grand jury and explain away, if possible, the charge against him.

We will assume, however, that, in spite of the assiduity of his lawyer, the prisoner has at last been indicted and is awaiting trial. What can be done about it? Of course, if the case could be indefinitely adjourned, the complainant or his chief witness might die or move away to some other jurisdiction, and if the indictment could be "pigeon-holed" the case might die a natural death of itself. Indictments, however, in New York County, whatever may be the case elsewhere, are no longer "pigeon-holed," and they cannot be adequately "lost," since certified copies are made of each. The next step, therefore, is to secure as long a time as possible before trial.

Usually a prisoner has nothing to lose and everything to gain by delay, and the excuses offered for adjournment are often ingenious in the extreme.

The writer knows one criminal attorney who, if driven to the wall in the matter of excuses, will always serenely announce the death of a near relative and the obligation devolving upon him to attend the funeral. Another, as a last resort, regularly is attacked in open court by severe cramps in the stomach. If the court insists on the trial proceeding, he invariably recovers. Of course, there are many legitimate reasons for adjourning cases which the prosecution is powerless to combat.

The most effective method invoked to secure delay, and one which it is practically useless for the district attorney to oppose, is an application "to take testimony" upon commission in some distant place. Here again it must be borne in mind that such applications are often legitimate and proper and should be granted in simple justice to the defendant. Although this right to take the testimony of absent witnesses is confined in New York State to the defendant and does not extend to the prosecution, and is undoubtedly often the subject of much abuse, it not infrequently is the cause of saving an innocent man.

An example of this was the case of William H. Ellis, recently brought into the public eye through his connection with the treaty between the United States Government and King Menelik of Abyssinia. Ellis was accused in 1901 by a young woman of apparently excellent antecedents and character of a serious crime. Prior to his indictment a colored man employed in his office (the alleged scene of the crime) disappeared. When the case was moved for trial, Ellis, through his attorneys, moved for a commission to take the testimony of this absent, but clearly material, witness in one of the remote States of Mexico—a proceeding which would require a journey of some two weeks on muleback, beyond the railway terminus. The district attorney, in view of the peculiarly opportune disappearance of this person from the jurisdiction, strenuously opposed the application and hinted at collusion between Ellis and the witness. The application, however, was granted, and a delay of over a month ensued. During that time evidence was procured by the counsel of the prisoner showing conclusively that the complaining witness *was mentally unsound and had made similar and groundless charges against others*. The indictment was at once dismissed.

But such delays are not always so righteously employed. There is a story told of a case where a notorious character was charged with the unusual crime of "mayhem"—biting off another man's finger. The defendant's counsel secured adjournment after adjournment—no one knew why. At last the case was moved for trial and the prosecution put in its evidence, clearly showing the guilt of the prisoner. At the conclusion of the People's testimony, the lawyer for the defendant arose and harshly stigmatized the story of the complainant as a "pack of lies."

"I will prove to you in a moment, gentlemen," exclaimed he to the jury, "how absurd is this charge against my innocent client. Take the stand!"

The prisoner arose and walked to the witness-chair.

"Open your mouth!" shouted the lawyer.

The defendant did so. He had not a tooth in his head. The delay had been advantageously employed.

The importance of mere delay to a guilty defendant cannot well be overestimated. "You never can tell what may happen to knock a case on the head." For this reason a sufficiently paid and properly equipped counsel will run the whole gamut of criminal procedure, and—

1. Demur to the indictment.

2. Move for an inspection of the minutes of the proceedings before the grand jury.

3. Move to dismiss the indictment for lack of sufficient evidence before that body.

4. Move for a commission to take testimony.

5. Move for a change of venue.

6. Secure, where possible, a writ of habeas corpus and a stay of proceedings from some federal judge on the ground that his client is confined without due process of law.

All these steps he will take *seriatim*, and some cases have been delayed for as much as two years by merely invoking "legitimate" legal processes. In point of fact it is quite possible for any defendant absolutely to prevent an immediate trial provided he has the services of vigilant counsel, for these are not the only proceedings of which he can avail himself.

A totally distinct method is for the defendant to secure bail, and, after securing as many adjournments as possible, simply flee the jurisdiction. He will then remain away until the case is hopelessly stale, or he no longer fears prosecution.

In default of all else he may go "insane" just before the case is moved for trial. This habit of the criminal rich when brought to book for their misdeeds is too well known to require comment. All that is necessary is for a sufficient number of "expert" alienists to declare it to be their opinion that the defendant is mentally incapable of understanding the proceedings against him or of preparing his defence, and he is shifted off to a "sanitarium" until some new sensation occupies the public mind and his offences are partially forgotten.

In this way justice is often thwarted and the law cheated of its victim, but unless fortune favors him, sooner or later the indicted man must return for trial and submit the charge against him to a jury. But if this happens, even if he be guilty, all hope need not be lost. There are still "tricks of the trade" which may save him from the clutches of the law.

AT THE TRIAL

What can be done when at last the prisoner who has fought persistently for adjournment has been forced to face the witnesses against him and submit the evidence to a jury of peers? Let us assume further that he has been "out on bail," with plenty of opportunity to prepare his defence and lay his plans for escape.

When the case is finally called and the defendant takes his seat at the bar after a lapse of anywhere from six months to a year or more after his arrest, the first question for the district attorney to investigate is whether or no the person presenting himself for trial be in point of fact the individual mentioned in the indictment. This is often a difficult matter to determine. "Ringers"—particularly in the magistrates' courts—are by no means unknown. Sometimes they appear even in the higher courts. If the defendant be an ex-convict or a well-known crook, his photograph and measurements will speedily remove all doubt upon the subject, but if he be a foreigner (particularly a Pole, Italian or a Chinaman), or even merely one of the homogeneous inhabitants of the densely-populated East Side of New York, it is sometimes a puzzling problem. "Mock Duck," the celebrated Highbinder of Chinatown, who was set free after two lengthy trials for murder, was charged not long ago with a second assassination. He was pointed out to the police by various Chinamen, arrested and brought into the Criminal Courts building for identification, but for a long time it was a matter of uncertainty whether friends of his (masquerading as enemies) had not surrendered a substitute. Luckily the assistant district attorney who had prosecuted this wily and dangerous Celestial in the first instance was able to identify him.

Many years ago, during the days of Fernando Wood, a connection of his was reputed to be the power behind the "policy" business in New York City—the predecessor of the notorious Al Adams. A "runner" belonging to the system having been arrested and policy slips having been found in his possession, the reigning Policy King retained a lawyer of eminent respectability to see what could be done about it. The defendant was a particularly valuable man in the business and one for whom his employer desired to do everything in his power. The lawyer advised the defendant to plead guilty, provided the judge could be induced to let him off with a fine, which the Policy King agreed to pay. Accordingly, the lawyer visited the judge in his chambers and the latter practically promised to inflict only a fine in case the defendant, whom we will call, out of consideration for his memory, "Johnny Dough," should plead guilty. Unfortunately for this very satisfactory arrangement, the judge, now long since deceased, was afflicted with a serious mental trouble which occasionally manifested itself in peculiar losses of memory. When "Johnny Dough," the Policy King's favorite, was arraigned at the bar and, in answer to the clerk's interrogation, stated that he withdrew his plea of "not guilty" and now stood ready to plead "guilty," the judge, to the surprise and consternation of the lawyer, the defendant, and the latter's assembled friends, turned upon him and exclaimed:

"Ha! So you plead guilty, do you? Well, I sentence you to the penitentiary for one year, you miserable scoundrel!"

Utterly overwhelmed, "Johnny Dough" was led away, while his lawyer and relatives retired to the corridor to express their opinion of the court. About three months later the lawyer, who had heard nothing further concerning the case, happened to be in the office of the district attorney, when the latter looked up with a smile and inquired:

"Well, how's your client—Mr. Dough?"

"Safe on the Island, I suppose," replied the lawyer.

"Not a bit of it," returned the district attorney. "He never went there."

"What do you mean?" inquired the lawyer. "I heard him sentenced to a year myself!"

"I can't help that," said the district attorney. "The other day a workingman went down to the Island to see his old friend 'Johnny Dough.' There was only one 'Johnny Dough' on the lists, but when he was produced the visitor exclaimed: '*That* Johnny Dough! That ain't him *at all*, at all!' The visitor departed in disgust. We instituted an investigation and found that the man at the Island was a 'ringer.'"

"You don't say!" cried the lawyer.

"Yes," continued the district attorney. "But that is not the best part of it. You see, the 'ringer' says he was to get two hundred dollars per month for each month of Dough's sentence which he served. The prison authorities have refused to keep him any longer, and *now he is suing them for damages*, and is trying to get a writ of mandamus to compel them to take him back and let him serve out the rest of the sentence!"

Probably the most successful instance on record of making use of a dummy occurred in the early stages of the now famous Morse-Dodge divorce tangle. Dodge had been the first husband of Mrs. Morse, and from him she had secured a divorce. A proceeding to effect the annulment of her second marriage had been begun on the ground that Dodge had never been legally served with the papers in the original divorce case—in other words, to establish the fact that she was still, in spite of her marriage to Morse, the wife of Dodge. Dodge appeared in New York and swore that he had never been served with any papers. A well-known and reputable lawyer, on the other hand, Mr. Sweetser, was prepared to swear that he had served them personally upon Dodge himself. The matter was sent by the court to a referee. At the hour set for the hearing in the referee's office, Messrs. Hummel and Steinhardt arrived early, in company with a third person, and took their seats with their backs to a window on one side of the table, at the head of which sat the referee, and opposite ex-Judge Fursman, attorney for Mrs. Morse. Mr. Sweetser was late. Presently he appeared, entered the office hurriedly, bowed to the referee, apologized for being tardy, greeted Messrs. Steinhardt and Hummel, and then, turning to their companion, exclaimed: "How do you do, Mr. Dodge?" It was not Dodge at all, but an acquaintance of one of Howe & Hummel's office force who had been asked to accommodate them. Nothing had been said, no representations had been made, and Sweetser had voluntarily walked into a trap.

The attempt to induce witnesses to identify "dummies" is frequently made by both sides in criminal cases, and under certain circumstances is generally regarded as professional. Of course, in such instances no false suggestions are made, the witness himself being relied upon to "drop the fall." In case he does identify the wrong person, he has, of course, invalidated his entire testimony.

Not in one case out of five hundred, however, is any attempt made to substitute a "dummy" for the real defendant, the reason being, presumably, the prejudice innocent people have against going to prison even for a large reward. The question resolves itself, therefore, into how to get the client off when he is actually on trial. First, how can the sympathies of the jury be enlisted at the very start? Weeping wives and wailing infants are a drug on the market. It is a friendless man indeed, even if he be a bachelor, who cannot procure for the purposes of his trial the services of a temporary wife and miscellaneous collection of children. Not that he need swear that they are his! They are merely lined up along a bench well to the front of the court-room—the imagination of the juryman does the rest.

A defendant's counsel always endeavors to impress the jury with the idea that all he wants is a fair, open trial—and that he has nothing in the world to conceal. This usually takes the form of a loud announcement that *he* is willing "to take the first twelve men who enter the box." Inasmuch as the defence needs only to secure the vote of one juryman to procure a disagreement, this offer is a comparatively safe one for the defendant to make, since the prosecutor, who must secure unanimity on the part of the jury (at least in New York State), can afford to take no chances of letting an incompetent or otherwise unfit talesman slip into the box. Caution requires him to *examine* the jury in every important case, and frequently this ruse on the part of the defendant makes it appear as if the State had less confidence in its case than the defence. This trick was invariably used by the late William F. Howe in all homicide cases where he appeared for the defence.

The next step is to slip some juryman into the box who is likely for any one of a thousand reasons to lean towards the defence—as, for example, one who is of the same religion, nationality or even name as the defendant. The writer once tried a case where the defendant was a Hebrew named Bauman, charged with perjury. Mr. Abraham Levy was the counsel for the defendant. Having left an associate to select the jury the writer returned to the court-room to find that his friend had chosen for foreman a Hebrew named *Abraham Levy*. Needless to say, a disagreement of the jury was the almost inevitable result. The same lawyer not many years ago defended a *client* named Abraham Levy. In like manner he managed to get an Abraham Levy on the jury, and on that occasion succeeded in getting his client off scot-free.

No method is too far-fetched to be made use of on the chance of "catching" some stray talesman. In a case defended by Ambrose Hal. Purdy, where the deceased had been wantonly stabbed to death by a blood-thirsty Italian shortly after the assassination of President McKinley, the defence was interposed that a quarrel had arisen between the two men owing to the fact that the deceased had loudly proclaimed anarchistic doctrines and openly gloried in the death of the President, that the defendant had expostulated with him, whereupon the deceased had violently attacked the prisoner, who had killed him in self-defence.

The whole thing was so thin as to deceive nobody, but Mr. Purdy, as each talesman took the witness-chair to be examined on the *voir dire*, solemnly asked each one:

"Pardon me for asking such a question at this time—it is only my duty to my unfortunate client that impels me to it—but have you *any sympathy with anarchy* or with *assassination?*"

The talesman, of course, inevitably replied in the negative.

"Thank you, sir," Purdy would continue. "In *that event* you are *entirely acceptable!*"

Not long ago two shrewd Irish attorneys were engaged in defending a client charged with an atrocious murder. The defendant had the most Hebraic cast of countenance imaginable, and a beard that reached to his waist. Practically the only question which these lawyers put to the different talesmen during the selection of the jury was, "Have you any prejudice against the defendant *on account of his race?*" In due course they succeeded in getting several Hebrews upon the jury who managed in the jury-room to argue the verdict down from murder to manslaughter in the second degree. As the defendant was being taken across the bridge to the Tombs he fell on his knees and offered up a heartfelt prayer such as could only have emanated from the lips of a devout Roman Catholic.

Lawyers frequently secure the good-will of jurors (which may last throughout the trial and show itself in the verdict) by some happy remark during the early stages of the case. During the Clancy murder trial each side exhausted its thirty peremptory challenges and also the entire panel of jurors in filling the box. At this stage of the case the foreman became ill and had to be excused. No jurors were left except one who had been excused by mutual consent for some trifling reason, and who out of curiosity had remained in court. He rejoiced in the name of Stone. Both sides then agreed to accept him as foreman provided he was still willing to serve, and this proving to be the case he triumphantly made his way towards the box. As he did so, the defendant's counsel remarked: "The Stone which the builders refused is become the head Stone of the corner." The good-will generated by this meagre jest stood him later in excellent stead.

In default of any other defence, some criminal attorneys have been known to seek to excite sympathy for their helpless clients by appearing in court so intoxicated as to be manifestly unable to take care of the defendant's interests, and prisoners have frequently been acquitted simply by virtue of their lawyer's obvious incapacity. The attitude of the jury in such cases seems to be that the defendant has not had a "fair show" and so should be acquitted anyway. Of course, this appeals to the juryman's sympathies and he overlooks the fact that by his action the prosecution is given no "show" at all.

Generally speaking, the advice credited to Mr. Lincoln, as being given by him to a young attorney who was about to defend a presumably guilty client, is religiously followed by all criminal practitioners:

"Well, my boy, if you've got a good case, stick to the evidence; if you've got a weak one, go for the People's witnesses; but—if you've got no case at all, *hammer the district attorney!*"

As a rule, however, criminal lawyers are not in a position to "hammer" the prosecuting officer, but endeavor instead to suggest by innuendo or even open declaration his bias and unfairness.

"Be *fair*, Mr. ——!" is the continual cry. "Try to be *fair!*"

The defendant, whether he be an ex-convict or thirty-year-old professional thief, is always "this poor boy," and, as he is not compelled by law to testify, and as his failure to do so must not be weighed against him by the jury, he frequently walks out of court a free man, because the jury believe from the lawyer's remarks that he is in fact a mere youthful offender of hitherto good reputation and deserves another chance.

By all odds the greatest abuse in criminal trials lies in the open disregard of professional ethics on the part of lawyers who deliberately supply of themselves, in their opening and closing addresses to the jury, what incompetent bits of evidence, true or false, they have not been able to establish by their witnesses. There is no complete cure for this, for even if the judge rebukes the lawyer and directs the jury to disregard what he has said as "not being in the evidence," the damage has been done, the statement still lingering in the jury's mind without any opportunity on the part of the prosecutor to disprove it. There is no antidote for such jury-poison. A shyster lawyer need but to keep his client off the stand and he can saturate the jury's mind with any facts concerning the defendant's respectability and history which his imagination is powerful enough to supply. On such occasions an ex-convict with no relatives may become a "noble fellow, who, rather than have his family name tainted by being connected with a criminal trial, is willing to risk even conviction"—"a veteran of the glorious war which knocked the shackles from the slave"—"the father of nine children"—"a man hounded by the police." The district attorney may shout himself hoarse, the judge may pound his gavel in righteous indignation, the lawyer may apologize because in the zeal with which he feels inspired for his client's cause he perhaps (which only makes matters worse) has *overstepped the mark*—but some juryman may suppose that, after all, the prisoner *is* a hero or nine times a father.

There is one notorious attorney who poses as a philanthropist and who invariably promises the jury that if they acquit his client he will personally give him employment. If he has kept half of his promises he must by this time have several hundred clerks, gardeners, coachmen, choremen and valets.

In like manner attorneys of this feather will deliberately state to the jury that *if* the defendant had taken the stand he *would have* testified thus and so; or that if certain witnesses who have not appeared (and who perhaps in reality do not exist at all) *had* testified they would have established various facts. Such lawyers should be locked up or disbarred; courts are powerless to negative entirely their dishonesty in individual cases.

Clever counsel, of course, habitually make use of all sorts of appeals to sympathy and prejudice. In one case in New York in which James W. Osborne appeared as prosecutor the defendant wore a G.A.R. button. His lawyer managed to get a veteran on the jury. Mr. Osborne is a native of North Carolina. The defendant's counsel, to use his own words, "worked the war for all it was worth," and the defendant lived, bled and died for his country over and over again. In summing up the case, the attorney addressed himself particularly to the veteran on the back row, and, after referring to numerous imaginary engagements, exclaimed: "Why, gentlemen, my client was pouring out his life blood upon the field of battle when the ancestors of Mr. Osborne were raising their hands against the flag!" For once Mr. Osborne had no adequate words to reply.

By far the most effective and dangerous "trick" employed by guilty defendants is the deliberate shouldering of the entire blame by one of two persons who are indicted together for a single offence. A common example of this is where two men are caught at the same time bearing away between them the spoil of their crime and are jointly indicted for "criminally receiving stolen property." Both, probably, are "side partners," equally guilty, and have burglarized some house or store in each other's company. They may be old pals and often have served time together. They agree to demand separate trials, and that whoever is convicted first shall assume the entire responsibility. Accordingly, A. is tried and, in spite of his asseveration that he is innocent and that the "stuff" was given him by a strange man, who paid him a dollar to transport it to a certain place, is properly convicted.[45] The bargain holds. B.'s case is moved for trial and he claims never to have seen A. in his life before the night in question, and that he volunteered to help the latter carry a bundle which seemed to be too heavy for him. He calls A., who testifies that this is so—that B., whom he did not know from Adam, tendered his services and that he availed himself of the offer. The jury are usually prone to acquit, as the weight of evidence is clearly with the defendant.

Many changes are rung upon this device. There is said to have been a case in which the defendant was convicted of murder in the first degree and sentenced to be executed. It was one of circumstantial evidence and the verdict was the result of hours of deliberation on the part of the jury. The prisoner had stoutly denied knowing anything of the homicide. Shortly before the date set for the execution, another man turned up who admitted that he had committed the crime and made the fullest sort of a confession. A new trial was thereupon granted by the Appellate Court, and the convict, on the application of the prosecuting attorney, was discharged and quickly made himself scarce. It then developed that apart from the prisoner's own confession there was practically nothing to connect him with the crime.

Under a statute making such evidence obligatory in order to render a confession sufficient for a conviction, the prisoner had to be discharged.

In the case of Mabel Parker, a young woman of twenty, charged with the forgery of a large number of checks, many of them for substantial amounts, her husband made an almost successful attempt to procure her acquittal by means of a new variation of the old game. Mrs. Parker, after her husband had been arrested for *passing* one of the bogus checks, had been duped by a detective into believing that the latter was a fellow criminal who was interested in securing Parker's release. In due course she took this supposed friend into her confidence, made a complete confession, and illustrated her skill by impromptu copies of her forgeries from memory upon a sheet of pad paper. This the detective secured and then arrested her. She was indicted for forging the name *Alice Kauser* to a check upon the Lincoln National Bank. On her trial she denied having done so, and claimed that the detective had found the sheet containing her supposed handwriting in her husband's desk, and that she had written none of the alleged copies upon it. The door of the court-room then opened, and James Parker was led to the bar and *pleaded guilty* to the forgery of the check in question. (For the benefit of the layman it should be explained that as a rule indictments for forgery also contain a count for "uttering.") He then took the stand, admitted that he had not only uttered but had also written the check, and swore that it was *his handwriting* which appeared on the pad.

The prosecutor was nonplussed. If he should ask the witness to prove his capacity to forge such a check from memory on the witness-stand, the latter, as he had had ample time to practise the signature while in prison, would probably succeed in doing so. If, on the other hand, he should not ask him to write the name, the defendant's counsel would argue to the jury that he was *afraid* to do so. The district attorney therefore took the bull by the horns and challenged Parker to make from memory a copy of the signature, and, much as he had suspected, the witness produced a very good one. An acquittal seemed certain, and the prosecutor was at his wit's end to devise a means to meet this practical demonstration that the husband was in fact the forger. At last it was suggested to him that it would be comparatively easy to memorize such a signature, and acting on this hint he found that after half an hour's practice he was able to make almost as good a forgery as Parker. When therefore it came time for him to address the jury he pointed out the fact that Parker's performance on the witness-stand really established nothing at all—that any one could forge such a signature from memory after but a few minutes' practice.

"To prove to you how easily this can be done," said he, "I will volunteer to write a better Kauser signature than Parker did."

He thereupon seized a pen and began to demonstrate his ability to do so. Mrs. Parker, seeing the force of this ocular demonstration, grasped her counsel's arm and cried out: "For God's sake, don't let him do it!" The lawyer objected, the objection was sustained, but the case was saved. Why, the jury argued, should the lawyer object unless the making of such a forgery were in fact an easy matter?

In desperate cases, desperate men will take desperate chances. The traditional instance where the lawyer, defending a client charged with causing the death of another by administering poisoned cake, met the evidence of the prosecution's experts with the remark: "*This is my answer to their testimony!*" and calmly ate the balance of the cake, is too familiar to warrant detailed repetition. The jury retired to the jury-room and the lawyer to his office, where a stomach pump quickly put him out of danger. The jury is supposed to have acquitted.

Such are some of the tricks of the legal trade as practised in its criminal branch. Most of them are unsuccessful and serve only to relieve the gray monotony of the courts. When they achieve their object they add to the interest of the profession and teach the prosecutor a lesson by which, perhaps, he may profit in the future.

FOOTNOTES:

[45] The defence that the accused innocently received the stolen property into his possession was a familiar one even in 1697, as appears by the following record taken from the Minutes of the Sessions. It would seem that it was even then received with some incredulity.

CITY & COUNTY OF NEW YORK: ss:

Att a Meeting of the Justices of the Peace for the said City & County att the City Hall of the said City on Thursday the 10th day of June Anno Dom 1697.

PRESENT

| William Morrott | } Esquires |
| James Graham | } quorum |

Jacobus Cortlandt	} Esquires
Grandt Schuylor	} Justices
Leonard Lowie	} of the Peace

Jacobus Cortlandt, Esq., one of his Majestys Justices of the peace for ye said City and County Informed the Kings Justices that a peace of Linnen Ticking was taken out of his Shop this Morning. That he was informed a Negro Slave Named Joe was seen to take the same whereupon the said Jacobus Van Cortlandt Pursued the said Joe and apprehended him and found the said piece of ticking in his custody and had the said Negro Joe penned in the cage, upon which the said Negro man being brought before the said Justices said he did not take the said ticking out of the Shop window but that a Boy gave itt to him, but upon Examination of Sundry other Evidence itt Manifestly Appeareth to the said Justices that the said Negro man Named Joe, did steal the said piece of linnen ticking out of the Shop Window of the said Jacobus Van Cortlandt and thereupon doe order the punishment of the said Negro as follows vigt. That the said Negro man Slave Named Joe shall be forthwith by the Common whipper of the City or some of the Sheriffs officers att the Cage be stripped Naked from the Middle upwards and then and there shall be tyed to the tayle of a Cart and being soe stripped and tyed shall be Drove Round the City and Receive upon his naked body att the Corner of each Street nine lashes until he return to the place from whence he sett out and that he afterwards Stand Committed to the Sheriffs custody till he pay his fees. #/

CHAPTER XVII

WHAT FOSTERS CRIME

To lack of regard for law is mainly due the existence of crime, for a perfect respect for law would involve entire obedience to it. Yet crime continues and from time to time breaks forth to such an extent as to give ground for a popular impression that it is increasing out of proportion to our growth as a nation. Now, while it may be fairly questioned whether there is any actual increase of crime in the United States, and while, on the contrary, observation would seem to show an actual decrease, not only in crimes of violence, but in all major crimes, there nevertheless exists to-day a widespread contempt for the criminal law which, if it has not already stimulated a general increase of criminal activity, is likely to do so in the future. This contempt for the law is founded not only upon actual conditions, but also upon belief in conditions erroneously supposed to exist, which is fostered by current literature and by the sensational press.

Thus, as has already been pointed out, while it is popularly believed that women are almost never convicted of crime, and particularly of homicide, the fact is, at least in New York County, that a much greater proportion of women charged with murder are convicted than of men charged with the same offence. To read the newspapers one would suppose that the mere fact that the defendant was a female instantly paralyzed the minds of the jury and reduced them to a state of imbecility. The inevitable result of this must be to encourage lawlessness among the lower orders of women and to lead them to look upon arrest as a mere formality without ultimate significance. The writer recalls trying for murder a negress who had shot her lover not long after the discharge of a notorious female defendant in a recent spectacular trial in New York. When asked why she had killed him she replied:

"Oh, Nan Patterson did it and got off."

This is not offered as a reflection upon the failure of the jury to reach a verdict in the Patterson case, but as an illuminating illustration of the concrete and immediate effect of all actual or supposed failures of justice.

A belief that the course of criminal justice is slow and uncertain, that the chances are all in favor of the defendant, and that he has but to resort to technicalities to secure not only indefinite delay but generally ultimate freedom, breeds an indifference amounting almost to arrogance among law-breakers, powerful and otherwise, and a painful yet hopeless conviction among honest men that nothing can prevent the wicked from flourishing. Honesty seems no longer even a good policy, and the young business man resorts to sharp practices to get ahead of his unscrupulous competitor. In some localities the uncertainty and delay attendant upon the execution of the law is the alleged, and maybe the actual, cause of the community crime of lynching. Even where the administration of justice is seen at its best many people who have been wronged believe that there is so little likelihood that the offender will after all be punished that the cheapest and easiest course is to let the matter drop. All this gives aid and comfort to the powers of darkness.

The widespread impression as to the uncertainty of the law is not entirely a misapprehension. "We have long since passed the period when it is possible to punish an innocent man. We are now struggling with the problem whether it is any longer possible to punish the guilty." It is a melancholy fact that at the present time "penal statutes and procedure tend more to defeat and retard the ends of justice than to protect the rights of the accused."

The subject of criminal-law reform is too extensive to be discussed here even superficially, but historically the explanation of existing conditions is simple enough. The present overgrown state of the criminal law is the direct result of our exaggerated regard for personal liberty, coupled with a wholesale adoption of the technicalities of English law invented when only such technicalities could stand between the minor offender and the barbarous punishments of a bygone age. We forget that the community is composed of individuals, and we tend to disregard its interests for those of any particular individual who happens to be a prisoner at the bar. We revolted from England and incidentally from her system of administering the criminal law, by which the defendant could have no voice at his own trial, where practically every crime was punishable with death, and where only the Crown could produce and examine witnesses. Every one will have to agree that the English system was very harsh and very unfair indeed. To-day it is better than ours, simply because its errors have been systematically and wisely corrected, without diminution in the national respect for law. When we devised our own system we adopted those humane expedients for evading the law which were only justified by the existing penalties attached to convictions for crime,—and then discarded the penalties. We were through with tyrants once and for all. The Crown had always been opposed to the defendant and the Crown was a tyrant. We naturally turned with sympathy towards the prisoner.

We gave him the right of appeal on all matters of law through all the courts of our States, and even into the courts of the United States, while we allowed the People no right of appeal at all. If the prisoner was convicted he could go on and test the case all along the line,—if he was acquitted the People had to rest satisfied. We stopped the mouth of the judge and made it illegal for him to "sum up" the case or discuss the facts to any extent. We clipped the wings of the prosecutor and allowed him less latitude of expression than an English judge. Then we gazed on the work of our intellects and said it was good. If an ignorant jury acquitted a murderer under the eyes of a gagged and helpless judge, we said that it was all right and that it was better that ninety-nine guilty men should escape than that one innocent man should be convicted. Yes,—better for whom? If another murderer, about whose guilt the highest court in one of the States said there was no possible doubt, secured three new trials and was finally acquitted on the fourth, it merely demonstrated how perfectly we safeguarded the rights of the individual.

The result is that we have unnecessarily fettered ourselves, have furnished a multitude of technical avenues of escape to wrong-doers, and have created a popular contempt for courts of justice, which shows itself in the sentimental and careless verdicts of juries, in a lack of public spirit, and in an indisposition to prosecute wrong-doers. In addition, the impression sought to be conveyed by the yellow press that our judiciary is corrupt and that money can buy anything—even justice—leads the jury in many cases to feel that their presence is merely a formal concession to an archaic procedure and that their oaths have no real significance.

The community, the "People," have a sufficiently hard task to secure justice at any criminal trial. On the one hand is the abstract proposition that the law has been violated, on the other sits a human being, ofttimes contrite, always an object of pity. He is presumed innocent, he is to be given the benefit of every reasonable doubt. He has the right to make his own powerful appeal to the jury and to have the services of the best lawyer he can secure to sway their emotions and their sympathies. If the prosecutor resorts to eloquence he is stigmatized as "over-zealous" and as a "persecutor." If a plainly guilty defendant be acquitted, not the trampled ideal of justice, but the vision of a liberated prisoner rejoicing in his freedom hovers in the talesman's dreams.

So far so good; we can afford to stand by a system which in the long run has served us fairly well. But an occasional evil, an evil which when it occurs is productive of great harm and serves to give color to the popular opinion of criminal law, begins only when the lawyers have had their opportunity for elocution. At the conclusion of the charge the defendant's attorney proceeds to put the judge through what is familiarly known as "a course of sprouts." He makes twenty or thirty "requests to charge the jury" on the most abstract propositions of law which his fertile mind can devise,—relevant or irrelevant, applicable or inapplicable to the facts,—and the judge is compelled to decide from the bench, without opportunity for reflection, questions which the attorney has labored upon, perchance, for weeks. If he guesses wrong, the lawyer "excepts" and the case may be reversed on appeal. This is not a test of the defendant's guilt or innocence, but a test of the abstract learning and quickness of the presiding judge.

It is generally believed that appellate courts are prone to reverse criminal cases on purely technical grounds. Whether this belief be well founded or ill, its wide acceptance as fact is fertile in bringing the law into disrepute.[46] Justice to be effective must be not only sure but swift. An "iron hand" cannot always compensate for a "leaden heel."

It is probably true that in some of the States such a tendency exists and may result in making the administration of justice a laughing stock, but it is far from being so in States of the character of New York and Massachusetts. The Appellate Division, First Department, and Court of Appeals in New York are distinctly opposed to reversing criminal cases on technical grounds and are prone to disregard trivial error where the guilt of the defendant is clear. The writer can recall no recent criminal case where the district attorney's office has felt aggrieved at the action of the higher courts, and on the contrary believes that their action is generally based on broad principles of public policy and common-sense.

During the year 1905 the district attorney of New York County defended forty-seven appeals from convictions in criminal cases in the Appellate Division. Of these convictions only *three* were reversed. He defended eighteen in the Court of Appeals, of which only *two* were reversed. One of the writer's associates computed that he had secured, during a four years' term of office, twenty-nine convictions in which appeals had been taken. Of these but two were reversed, one of them immediately resulting in the defendant's re-conviction for the same crime. The other is still pending and the defendant awaiting his trial. Certainly there is little in the actual figures to give color to the impression that the criminal profits by mere technicalities on appeal,—at least in New York State.

In nine cases out of ten the reversal of a conviction in a criminal case is due to the carelessness or inefficiency of the prosecuting officer or trial judge and not to any inadequacy in our methods of procedure. Yet the tenth case, the case where the criminal does beat the law by a technicality, does more harm than can easily be estimated. That is the one case everybody knows about,—the one the papers descant upon, the one that cheers the heart of the grafter and every criminal who can afford to pay a lawyer.

Yet the evil influence of the reversal of a conviction on appeal, however much it is to be deprecated, is as nothing compared with a deliberate acquittal of a guilty defendant by a reckless, sentimental, or lawless jury.

Few can appreciate as does a prosecutor the actual, practical and immediate effect of such a spectacle upon those who witness it.

Two men were seen to enter an empty dwelling-house in the dead of night. The alarm was given by a watchman near by, and a young police officer, who had been but seven months on the force, bravely entered the black and deserted building, searched it from roof to cellar, and found the marauders locked in one of the rooms. He called upon them to open, received no reply, yet without hesitation and without knowing what the consequences to himself might be, smashed in the door and apprehended the two men. One was found with a large bundle of skeleton keys in his pocket and several candles, while a partially consumed candle lay upon the floor. In the police court they *pleaded guilty* to a charge of burglary, and were promptly indicted by the grand jury.

At the trial they claimed to have gone into the house *to sleep*, said they had found the bunch of keys on the stairs, *denied* having the candles at all or that they were in a room on the top story, and asserted that they were in the entrance hall when arrested.

The story told by the defendants was so utterly ridiculous that one of the two could not control a grin while giving his version of it on the witness-stand. The writer, who prosecuted the case, regarded the trial as a mere formality and hardly felt that it was necessary to sum up the evidence at all.

Imagine his surprise when an intelligent-looking jury *acquitted* both the defendants after practically no deliberation. Both had offered to plead guilty to a slightly lower degree of crime before the case was moved for trial.

These two defendants, who were neither insane nor degenerates, consorted with others in Bowery hotels and saloons,—incubators of crime. What effect could such a performance have upon them and their friends save to inculcate a belief that they were licensed to commit as many burglaries as they chose? They had a practical demonstration that the law was "no good" and the system a failure. If they could beat a case in which they had already pleaded *guilty*, what could they not do where the evidence was less obvious? They were henceforth immune. Who shall say how many embryonic law-breakers took courage at the story and started upon an experimental attempt at crime?

The news of such an acquittal must instantly have been carried to the Tombs, where every other guilty prisoner took heart and prepared anew his defence. Those about to plead guilty and throw themselves upon the mercy of the court, abandoned their honest purpose and devised some perjury instead. Criminals almost persuaded that honesty was the best policy changed their minds. The barometer of crime swung its needle from "stormy" to "fair."

But, apart from the law-breakers, consider the effect of such a miscarriage of justice upon a young, honest and zealous officer. First, all his good work, his bravery, his conscientious effort at safeguarding the sleeping public had been disregarded, tossed aside with a sneer, and had gone for naught. The jury had stamped his story as a lie and stigmatized him, by their action, as a perjurer. They had chosen two professional criminals as better men. His whole conduct of the case instead of being commended as meritorious had resulted in a solemn public declaration that he was not worthy of credence and that he had attempted wilfully to railroad to State's prison two innocent men. In other words, that he ought to be there himself. What was the use of trying to do good work any longer? He might just as well loiter in an area on a barrel and smoke a furtive cigar when he ought to be "on post." Perhaps he might better "stand in" with those who would inevitably be preferred to him by a jury of their peers.

What must have been the effect on the court officers, the witnesses, the defendants out on bail, the complainants, the spectators? That the whole business was nonsense and rot! That the jury system was ridiculous. That the jurymen were either crooks or fools. That the only people who were not insulted and sneered at were the law-breakers themselves. That if two such rogues were to be set free all the other jailbirds might as well be let go. That an honest man could whistle for his justice and might better straightway put on his hat and go home. That the only way to punish a criminal was to punish him yourself—kill him if you got the chance or get the crowd to lynch him. That if a thief stole from you the shrewdest thing to do was to induce him as a set-off to give you the proceeds of his next thieving. That it was humiliating to live in a town where a self-confessed rascal could snap his fingers at the law and go unwhipped of justice.

The jury's action must have been due either to a wilful disregard of their oath or an entire misconception of it. Assuming that the jury deliberately declined to obey the law, the whole twelve elected to become, and thereby did become, law-breakers. They disqualified themselves forever as talesmen. No prosecutor in his senses would move a case before a jury which numbered any one of them. They had arraigned themselves upon the side, and under the standard, of crime. They became accessories after the fact. If on the other hand they misconceived the purpose for which they were there the performance was a shocking example of what is possible under present conditions.

Just as there are three general classes of wrongs, so there are three general and varyingly effective forms of restraint against their perpetration. First there is the moral control exerted by what is ordinarily called conscience, secondly there is the restraint which arises out of the apprehension that the commission of a tort will be followed by a judgment for damages in a civil court, and lastly there is the restraint imposed by the criminal law. All these play their part, separately or in conjunction. For some men conscience is a sufficient barrier to crime or to those acts which, while equally reprehensible, are not technically criminal; for others the possibility of pecuniary loss is enough to keep them in the straight and narrow way; but for a large proportion of the community the fear of criminal prosecution, with implied disgrace and ignominy, forfeiture of citizenship, and confinement in a common jail is about the only conclusive reason for doing unto others as they would the others should do unto them. Were the criminal law done away with in our present state of civilization, religion, ethics and civil procedure would be absolutely inefficacious to prevent anarchy. It is as imperative to the ordinary citizen to know that if he steals he will be locked up as it is for the child to know that if he puts his hand into the fire it will be burned. The acquittal of every thief breeds another, and the unpunished murder is an incentive for a dozen similar homicides.

Crimes are either deliberate or the result of accident or impulse. The last class may rise to a high degree of enormity,—such as manslaughter, but these crimes are rarely possible of restraint. The perpetrator does not stop to consider, even if he be sober enough to think at all, whether his act be moral, whether it will entail any civil liability, or what will be its consequences, if it be a crime. So far as such acts are concerned those who commit them are hardly criminals in the ordinary sense, and no influence in the world is able to prevent them.

The question is how far these different kinds of restraint operate upon the community as a whole in the prevention of *deliberate* crime. Clearly the fear of pecuniary loss through actions brought to judgment in the civil courts is practically *nil*. Most persons who set out to commit crime have no bank account, the absence of one being generally what leads them into a criminal career.

The writer has no intention of attempting to discuss or estimate the efficacy of religion or ethics as restraining influences. A certain limited proportion of the community would not commit crime under any circumstances. It is enough for them that the act is forbidden by the State even if it be not really wrong from their own personal point of view. Side by side with these very good people are a very large number who wear just as fashionable clothing, have the same friends, attend the same churches, but who would commit almost any crime so long as they were sure of not being caught. If we had no criminal law we should soon discover who were the hypocrites.

But for an overwhelming majority of the community something more practical than either religion, ethics, or philosophy is necessary to keep them in order. They must be convinced that the transgressor will surely be punished,—not some time, not next year or the year after, but *now*. Not, moreover, that his way will be merely hard, but that he will be put in stripes and made to break stones.

Hence the necessity for a vigorous and adequate criminal law and procedure which shall command the respect and loyalty of the community, administered by a fearless judiciary who will hold jurors to a rigid and conscientious obedience to their oath.

There is nothing sacred about an archaic criminal procedure which in some respects is less devised for the protection of the community than for the exculpation of the guilty. The portals of liberty would not fall down or the framers of the constitution turn in their graves if the peremptory challenges allowed to both sides in the selection of a jury were reduced to a reasonable number, or if persons found guilty of crime after due process of law were compelled to stay in jail until their appeals were decided, instead of walking the streets free as air under a certificate of "reasonable doubt" issued by some judge who personally knew nothing of the actual trial of the case. As things stand to-day, a thief caught in the very act of picking a pocket in the night-time may challenge arbitrarily the twenty most intelligent talesmen called to sit as jurors in his case. Does such a practice make for justice? It is even possible that the sacred bird of liberty would not scream if eleven jurors, instead of twelve, were permitted to convict a defendant or set him free, while the question of how far the right of appeal in criminal cases might properly be limited or, in default of such limitation, how far under certain conditions it might be correspondingly extended to the community, is by no means purely academic.[47] It is also conceivable that some means might be found to do away with the interminable technicalities which can now be interposed on behalf of the accused to prevent trials or the infliction of sentence after conviction.

Yet these considerations are of slight moment in contrast to that most crying of all present abuses,—the domination of the court-room by the press.[48] It is no fiction to say that in many cases the actual trial is conducted in the columns of yellow journals and the defendant acquitted or convicted purely in accordance with an "editorial policy." Judges, jurors, and attorneys are caricatured and flouted. There is no evidence, however incompetent, improper, or prejudicial to either side, excluded by the judge in a court of criminal justice, that is not deliberately thrust under the noses of the jury in flaring letters of red or purple the moment they leave the court-room. The judge may charge one way in accordance with the law of the land, while the editor charges the same jury in double-leaded paragraphs with what "unwritten" law may best suit the owner of his conscience and his pen. "Contempt of court" in its original significance is something known to-day only to the reader of text books.[49]

Each State has its own particular problem to face, but ultimately the question is a national one. Lack of respect for law is characteristic of the American people as a whole. Until we acquire a vastly increased sense of civic duty we should not complain that crime is increasing or the law ineffective. It would be a most excellent thing for an association of our leading citizens to interest itself in criminal-law reform and demand and secure the passage of new and effective legislation, but it would accomplish little if its individual members continued to evade jury service and left their most important duty to those least qualified by education or experience to perform it.[50] It would serve some of this class of reformers right, if one day, when after a life-time of evasion, they perchance came to be tried by a jury of their peers, they should find that among their twelve judges there was not one who could read or write the English language with accuracy and that all were ready to convict anybody because he lived in a brown-stone front.

Merchants, who in return for a larger possible restitution habitually compound felonies by tacitly agreeing not to prosecute those who have defrauded them, have no right to complain because juries acquit the offenders whom they finally decide it to be worth their while to pursue. The voter who has not the courage to insist that hypocritical laws should be wiped from the statute books should express no surprise when juries refuse to convict those who violate them. The man who perjures himself to escape his taxes has no right to expect that his fellow citizens are going to place a higher value upon an oath than he.

FOOTNOTES:

[46] Cf. "Criminal Law Reform," G.W. Alger, "The Outlook," June, 1907. Also article having same title in "Moral Overstrain," by same author. See also, by Hon. C.F. Amidon, "The Quest for Error and the doing of Justice," 40 American Law Rev. 681, and article on same subject in "The Outlook" for June, 1906.

[47] "Limitation of the Right of Appeal in Criminal Cases," by Nathan A. Smythe, 17 Harvard Law Rev. 317 (1905).

[48] Cf. "Sensational Journalism and the Law," in "Moral Overstrain," by G.W. Alger.

[49] By the New York Penal Code § 143, an editor is only guilty of contempt of court (a misdemeanor) if he publishes "a false or grossly inaccurate report" of its proceedings. The most insidious, dangerous,

offensive and prejudicial matter spread broadcast by the daily press does not relate to actual trials at all, but to matters entirely outside the record, such as what certain witnesses of either side could establish were they available, the "real" past and character of the defendant, etc. The New York Courts, under the present statute, are powerless to prevent this abuse. In Massachusetts half a dozen of our principal editors and "special writers" would have been locked up long ago to the betterment of the community and to the increase of respect for our courts of justice.

[50] "The Citizen and the Jury," in "Moral Overstrain," by G.W. Alger.

CHAPTER XVIII

INSANITY AND THE LAW

Harry Kendall Thaw shot and killed Stanford White on the 25th day of June, 1905. Although most of the Coroner's jury which first sat upon the case considered him irrational, he was committed to the Tombs and, having been indicted for murder, remained there over six months pending his trial. During that time it was a matter of common knowledge that his defence was to be that he was insane at the time of the shooting, but as under the New York law it is not necessary specifically to enter a plea of insanity to the indictment in order to take advantage of that defence (which may be proven under the general plea of "not guilty"), there was nothing officially on record to indicate this purpose. Neither was it possible for the District Attorney to secure any evidence of Thaw's mental condition, since he positively refused either to talk to the prosecutor's medical representatives or to allow himself to be examined by them. Mr. Jerome therefore was compelled to enter upon an elaborate and expensive preparation of the case, not only upon its merits, but upon the possible question of the criminal irresponsibility of the defendant.

The case was moved in January, 1906, and the defence thereupon proceeded to introduce a limited amount of testimony tending to show that Thaw was insane when he did the shooting. While much of this evidence commended itself but little to either the prosecutor or the jury, it was sufficient to raise grave doubt as to whether the accused was a fit subject for trial. The District Attorney's experts united in the opinion that, while he knew that he was doing wrong when he shot White, he was, nevertheless, the victim of a hopeless progressive form of insanity called *dementia præcox*. In the midst of the trial, therefore, Mr. Jerome moved for a commission to examine into the question of how far Thaw was capable of understanding the nature of the proceedings against him and consulting with counsel, and frankly expressed his personal opinion in open court that Thaw was no more a proper subject for trial than a baby. A commission was appointed which reported the prisoner sane enough to be tried, and the case then proceeded at great length with the surprising result that, in spite of the District Attorney's earlier declaration that he believed Thaw to be insane, the jury disagreed as to his criminal responsibility, a substantial number voting for conviction. Of course, logically, they would have been obliged either to acquit entirely on the ground of insanity or convict of murder in the first degree, but several voted for murder in the second degree.

A year now elapsed, during which equally elaborate preparations were made for a second trial. The State had already spent some $25,000, and yet its experts had never had the slightest opportunity to examine or interrogate the defendant, for the latter had not taken the stand at the first trial. The District Attorney still remained on record as having declared Thaw to be insane, and his own experts were committed to the same proposition, yet his official duty compelled him to prosecute the defendant a second time. The first prosecution had occupied months and delayed the trial of hundreds of other prisoners, and the next bid fair to do the same. But at this second trial the defence introduced enough testimony within two days to satisfy the public at large of the unbalanced mental condition of the defendant from boyhood.

After a comparatively short period of deliberation the jury acquitted the prisoner "on the ground of insanity," which may have meant either one of two things: (*a*) that they had a reasonable doubt in their own minds that Thaw knew that he was doing wrong when he committed the murder— something hard for the layman to believe, or (*b*) that, realizing that he was undoubtedly the victim of mental disease, they refused to follow the strict legal test.

Nearly two years had elapsed since the homicide; over a hundred thousand dollars had been spent upon the case; every corner of the community had been deluged with detailed accounts of unspeakable filth and depravity; the moral tone of society had been depressed; and the only element which had profited by this whole lamentable and unnecessary proceeding had been the sensational press. Yet the sole reason for it all was that the law of the land in respect to insane persons accused of crime was hopelessly out of date.

The question of how far persons who are victims of diseased mind shall be held criminally responsible for their acts has vexed judges, jurors, doctors, and lawyers for the last hundred years. During that time, in spite of the fact that the law has lagged far behind science in the march of progress, we have blundered along expecting our juries to reach substantial justice by dealing with each individual accused as most appeals to their enlightened common sense.

And the fact that they have obeyed their common sense rather than the law is the only reason why our present antiquated and unsatisfactory test of who shall be and who shall not be held "responsible" in the eye of the law remains untouched upon the statute-books. Because its inadequacy is so apparent, and because no experienced person seriously expects juries to apply it consistently, it fairly deserves first place in any discussion of present problems.

Thanks to human sympathy, the law governing insanity has had comparatively few victims, but the fact remains that more than one irresponsible insane man has swung miserably from the scaffold. But "hard cases" do more than "make bad law," they make lawlessness. A statute systematically violated is worse than no statute at all, and exactly in so far as we secure a sort of justice by evading the law as it stands, we make a laughing-stock of our procedure.

The law is, simply, that any person is to be held criminally responsible for a deed unless he was at the time laboring under such a defect of reason as not to know the nature and quality of his act and that it was wrong.

This doctrine first took concrete form in 1843, when, after a person named McNaughten, who had shot and killed a certain Mr. Drummond under an insane delusion that the latter was Sir Robert Peel, had been acquitted, there was such popular uneasiness over the question of what constituted criminal responsibility that the House of Lords submitted four questions to the fifteen judges of England asking for an opinion on the law governing responsibility for offences committed by persons afflicted with *certain forms* of insanity. It is unnecessary to set forth at length these questions, but it is enough to say that the judges formulated the fore-going rule as containing the issue which should be submitted to the jury in such cases.[51]

Now, with that commendable reverence for judicial utterance which is so characteristic of the English nation, and is so conspicuously absent in our own country, it was assumed until recently that this solemn pronunciamento was the last word on the question of criminal responsibility and settled the matter once and forever. Barristers and legislators did not trouble themselves particularly over the fact that in 1843 the study of mental disease was in its infancy, and judges, including those of England, probably knew even less about the subject than they do now. In 1843 it was supposed that insanity, save of the sort that was obviously maniacal, necessitated "delusions," and unless a man had these delusions no one regarded him as insane. In the words of a certain well-known judge:

> "The true criterion, the true test of the absence or presence of insanity, I take to be the absence or presence of what, used in a certain sense of it, is comprisable in a single term, namely, delusion.... In short, I look on delusion ... and insanity to be almost, if not altogether, convertible terms."[52]

This in a certain broad sense, probably not intended by the judge who made the statement, is nearly true, but, unfortunately, is not entirely so.

The dense ignorance surrounding mental disease and the barbarous treatment of the insane within a century are facts familiar to everybody. Lunatics were supposed to be afflicted with demons or devils which took possession of them as retribution for their sins, and in addition to the hopelessly or maniacally insane, medical science recognized only a so-called "partial" or delusionary insanity. To-day it would be regarded about as comprehensive to relate all mental diseases to the old-fashioned "delusion" as to regard as insane only those who frothed at the mouth.

But the particular individual out of whose case in 1843 arose the rule that is in 1908 applied to all defendants indiscriminately was the victim of a clearly defined insane delusion, and the four questions answered by the judges of England relate only to persons who are "*afflicted with insane delusions in respect to one or more particular subjects or persons.*" Nothing is said about insane persons *without* delusions, or about persons with *general* delusions, and the judges limit their answers even further by making them apply "to those persons who labor under such partial delusion only *and are not in other respects insane*"—a medical impossibility.

Modern authorities agree that a man cannot have insane delusions and not be in other respects insane, for it is mental derangement which is the cause of the delusion.

In the first place, therefore, a fundamental conception of the judges in answering the questions was probably fallacious, and in the second, although the test they offered was distinctly limited to persons "*afflicted with insane delusions,*" it has ever since been applied to all insane persons irrespective of their symptoms.

Finally, whether the judges knew anything about insanity or not, and whether in their answers they weighed their words very carefully or not, the test *as they laid it down* is by no means clear from a medical or even legal point of view.

Was the accused laboring under such a defect of reason as not to *know* the nature and quality of the act he was doing, or not to *know* that it was wrong? What did these judges mean by *know*? What does the reader mean by *know*? What does the ordinary juryman mean by it?

We are left in doubt as to whether the word should be given, as Justice Stephens contended it should be, a very broad and liberal interpretation such as "able to judge calmly and reasonably of the moral or legal character of a proposed action,"[53] or a limited and qualified one. There are all grades and degrees of "knowledge," and it is more than probable that there is a state of mind which I have heard an astute expert call upon the witness stand "an insane knowledge," and equally obvious that there may be "imperfect" or "incomplete knowledge," where the victim sees "through a glass darkly." Certainly it seems far from fair to interpret the test of responsibility to cover a condition where the accused may have had a hazy or dream-like realization that his act was technically contrary to the law, and even more dangerous to make it exclude one who was simply unable to "judge calmly and reasonably" of his proposed action, a doctrine which could almost be invoked by any one who committed homicide in a state of anger.

Ordinarily the word is not defined at all and the befuddled juryman is left to his own devices in determining what significance he shall attach not only to this word but to the test as a whole.

An equally ambiguous term is the word "wrong." The judges made no attempt to define it in 1843, and it has been variously interpreted ever since. Now it may mean "contrary to the dictates of conscience" *or*, as it is usually construed, "contrary to the law of the land"—and exactly *what* it means may make a great difference to the accused on trial. If the defendant thinks that God has directed him to kill a wicked man, he may know that such an act will not only be contrary to law, but also in opposition to the moral sense of the community as a whole, and yet he may believe that it is his conscientious duty to take life. In the case of Hadfield, who deliberately fired at George III in order to be hung, the defendant believed himself to be the Lord Jesus Christ, and that only by so doing could the world be saved. Applying the legal test and translating the word "wrong" as contrary to the common morality of the community wherein he resided or contrary to law, Hadfield ought to have achieved his object and been given death upon the scaffold instead of being clapped, as he was, into a lunatic asylum.

On the other hand, if the word "wrong" is judicially interpreted to mean "contrary to the dictates of conscience," it would seem to be given an elasticity which would invite inevitable confusion as well as abuse.

Moreover, the test in question takes no cognizance of persons who have no power of control. The law of New York and most of the states does not recognize "irresistible impulses," but it should admit the medical fact that there are persons who, through no fault of their own, are born practically without any inhibitory capacity whatever, and that there are others whose control has been so weakened, through accident or disease, as to render them morally irresponsible,—the so-called psychopathic inferiors.

Most of us are only too familiar with the state of a person just falling under the influence of an anesthetic, when all the senses seem supernaturally acute, the reasoning powers are active and unimpaired, and the patient is convinced that he can do as he wills, whereas, in reality, he says and does things which later on seem impossible in their absurdity. Such a condition is equally possible to the victim of mental disease, where the knowledge of right and wrong has no real relevancy.

The test of irresponsibility as defined by law is hopelessly inadequate, judged by present medical knowledge. There is no longer any pretence that a perception of the nature and quality of an act or that it is wrong or right is conclusive of the actual insanity of a particular accused. In a recent murder case a distinguished alienist, testifying for the prosecution, admitted that over seventy per cent. of the patients under his treatment, all of whom he regarded as insane and irresponsible, knew what they were doing and could distinguish right from wrong.

Countless attempts have been made to reconcile this obvious anachronism with justice and modern knowledge, but always without success, and courts have wriggled hard in their efforts to make the test adequate to the particular cases which they have been trying, but only with the result of hopelessly confounding the decisions.

But, however it is construed, the test as laid down in 1843 is insufficient in 1908. Medical science has marched on with giant strides, while the law, so far as this subject is concerned, has never progressed at all. It is no longer possible to determine mental responsibility by any such artificial rule as that given by the judges to the Lords in McNaughten's case, and which juries are supposed to apply in the courts of to-day. I say "supposed," for juries do not apply it, and the reason is simple enough—you cannot expect a juryman of intelligence to follow a doctrine of law which he instinctively feels to be crude and which he knows is arbitrarily applied.

No juryman believes himself capable of successfully analyzing a prisoner's past mental condition, and he is apt to suspect that, however sincere the experts on either side may appear, their opinions may be even less definite than the terms in which they are expressed. The spectacle of an equal number of intellectual-looking gentlemen, all using good English and all wearing clean linen, reaching diametrically opposite conclusions on precisely the same facts, is calculated to fill the well-intentioned juror with distrust. Painful as it is to record the fact, juries are sometimes almost as sceptical in regard to doctors as they always are in regard to lawyers.

The usual effect of the expert testimony on one side is to neutralize that on the other, for there is no practical way for the jury to distinguish between experts, since the foolish ones generally look as learned as the wise ones. The result is hopeless confusion on the part of the juryman, an inclination to "throw it all out," and a resort to other testimony to help him out of his difficulty. Of course he has no individual way of telling whether the defendant "*knew* right from *wrong*," whatever that may mean, and so the ultimate test that he applies is apt to be whether or not the defendant is really "queer," "nutty" or "bughouse," or some other equally intelligible equivalent for "medically insane."

The unfortunate consequence is that there is so general and growing a scepticism about the plea of insanity, entirely apart from its actual merits, that it is difficult in ordinary cases, whatever the jurors may think or say in regard to the matter, to secure twelve men who will give the defence fair consideration at the outset.

This is manifest in frequent expressions from talesmen such as: "I think the defence of insanity is played out," or "I believe everybody is a little insane, anyhow" (very popular and regarded by jurymen as witty), or "Well, I have an idea that when a fellow can't cook up any other defence he claims to be insane."

The result is a rather paradoxical situation: The attitude of the ordinary jury in a homicide case, where the defence of insanity is interposed, is usually at the outset one of distrust, and their impulse is to brush the claim aside. This tendency is strengthened by the legal presumption, which the prosecutor invariably calls to their attention, that the defendant is sane. Every expert who has testified for the defence in the ordinary "knock down and drag out" homicide case must have felt with the prisoner's attorneys, that it was "up to them" not so much to create a *doubt* of the defendant's sanity as to *prove* that he was insane, if they expected consideration from the jury.

Now let us assume that the defence is meritorious and that the prisoner's experts have created a favorable impression. Let us go even further and assume that they have generated a reasonable doubt in the mind of the jury as to the defendant's responsibility at the time he committed the offence. What generally occurs? Not, as one would suppose, an *acquittal*, but, in nine cases out of ten, a *conviction* in a lower degree.

The only usual result of an honest claim of irresponsibility on the ground of insanity is to lead the jury to reduce the grade of the offence from murder in the first, entailing the death penalty, to murder in the second degree. The jury have no intention of "taking the chance" involved in turning the man loose on the community and their minds are filled with the predominating fact that a human being has been killed. They have an idea that it is as easy to get "sworn out" of a lunatic asylum as they suppose it is to get "sworn into" one, and they know that if the prisoner is found to be insane when sent to State's prison he will be transferred elsewhere. They, therefore, as a rule, waste little time upon the question of how far the defendant was irresponsible within the legal definition when he committed the deed, but convict him "on general principles," trusting the prison officials to remedy any possible injustice. The jury in such cases ignore the law and decline either to acquit *or* to convict in accordance with the test. Their action becomes rather that of a lay commission condemning the prisoner to hard labor for life on the ground that he is medically insane.

Assuming that the jury take the defence seriously, there is only one class of cases where, in the writer's opinion, they follow the legal test as laid down by the court—that is to say, in cases of extreme brutality. Here they hold the prisoner to the letter of the law, and the more abhorrent the crime (even where its nature might indicate to a physician that the accused was the victim of some sort of mania) the less likely they are to acquit. The writer has prosecuted perhaps a dozen homicide and other cases where the defence was insanity. In his own experience he has known of no acquittal. In several instances the defendants were undoubtedly insane, but, strictly speaking, probably vaguely knew the nature and quality of their acts and that they were wrong. In a few of these the juries convicted of murder in the first degree because the circumstances surrounding the homicides were so brutal that the harshness of the technical doctrine they were required to apply was overshadowed in their minds by their horror of the act itself. In other cases, where either the accused appeared obviously abnormal as he sat at the bar of justice, or the details of the crime were less abhorrent, they convicted of murder in the second degree in accordance with the reasoning set forth in the fore-going paragraph. The writer seriously advances the suggestion that the more the brutality of a homicide indicates mental derangement the less chance the defendant has to secure an acquittal upon the plea of insanity.

And this leads us to that increasingly large body of cases where the usual scepticism of the jury in regard to such defences is counterbalanced by some real or imaginary element of sympathy. In cities like New York, where the jury system is seen at its very best, where the statistics show seventy per cent. of convictions by verdict for the year 1907, and where the sentiment of the community is against the invocation of any law supposedly higher than that of the State, our talesmen are unwilling to condone homicide or to act as self-constituted pardoning bodies, for they know that an obviously lawless verdict will bring down upon them the censure of the public and the press. This is perhaps demonstrated by the fact that in New York County a higher percentage of women are convicted of homicide than of men.

But the plea of insanity, with its vague test of responsibility, whose terms the juryman may construe for himself (or which his fellow-jurors may construe for him) offers an unlimited and fertile field for the "reasonable" doubt and an easy excuse for the conscientious talesman who wants to acquit if he can. Juries take little stock in irresistible impulses and emotional or temporary insanity save as a cloak to cover an unrighteous acquittal.

In no other class of cases does "luck" play so large a part in the final disposition of the prisoner. A jury is quite as likely to send an insane man to the electric chair as to acquit a defendant who is fully responsible for his crime.

To recapitulate from the writer's experience:

(1) The ordinary juror tends to be sceptical as to the good faith of the defence of insanity.

(2) When once this distrust is removed by honest evidence on the part of the defence, he usually declines to follow the legal test as laid down by the court on the general theory that any one but an idiot or a maniac has some knowledge of what he is doing and whether it is right or wrong.

(3) He applies the strict legal test only in cases of extreme brutality.

(4) In all other cases he follows the medical rather than the legal test, but instead of acquitting the accused on account of his medical irresponsibility, merely convicts in a lower degree.

The following deductions may also fairly be made from observation:

(1) That the present legal test for criminal responsibility is admittedly vague and inadequate, affording great opportunity for divergent expert testimony and a readily availed of excuse for the arbitrary and sentimental actions of juries, to which is largely due the distrust prevailing of the claim of insanity when interposed as a defence to crime.

(2) That expert medical testimony in such cases is largely discounted by the layman.

(3) That in no class of cases are the verdicts of jurors so apt to be influenced solely by emotion and prejudice, or to be guided less by the law as laid down by the court.

(4) That a new definition of criminal responsibility is necessary, based upon present knowledge of mental disease and its causes.

(5) Lastly, that, as whatever definition may be adopted will inevitably be difficult of application by an untutored lay jury, our procedure should be so amended that they may be relieved wherever possible of a task sufficiently difficult for even the most experienced and expert alienists.

A classification of the different forms of insanity, based upon its causes to which the case of any particular accused might be relegated, such as has recently been urged by a distinguished young neurologist, would not, with a few exceptions, assist us in determining his responsibility. It would be easy to say then, as now, that lunatics or maniacs should not be held responsible for their acts, but we should be left where we are at present in regard to all those shadowy cases where the accused had insane, incomplete or imperfect knowledge of what he was doing. It would be ridiculous, for example, to lay down a general rule that no person suffering from hysterical insanity should be punished for his acts. Yet, even so, such a classification would instantly remedy that anachronism in our present law which refuses to recognize as irresponsible those born without power to control their emotions—the psychopathic inferiors of science, and the real victims of *dementia præcox*.

Of course, if the insanity under which the defendant labors bears no relation to or connection with the deed for which he is on trial, there would logically be no reason why his insanity on other subjects should be any defence to his crime. For example, there is the well-known case of the Harvard professor who was apparently sane on all other matters, yet believed himself to be possessed of glass legs. Had this man in wanton anger struck and killed another, his "glass leg" delusion could not logically have availed him. If, however, he had struck and killed one who he believed was going to shatter his legs it might have been important. The illustration is clear enough, but its application probably involves a mistaken premise. If he thought he had glass legs his mind was undoubtedly deranged—whether enough or not enough to constitute him irresponsible or beyond the effect of penal discipline might be a difficult question. The generally accepted doctrine is, that if a man has a delusion concerning something, which if *actually existing* as he believed it to be would be *no excuse* for his committing the criminal act, he is responsible and liable to punishment; but, as Bishop well says:

> "This branch of the doctrine should be cautiously received; for delusion of any kind is strongly indicative of a generally diseased mind."

The new test to determine responsibility will recognize, as does the law of Germany, that there can be no criminal act where the free determination of the will is excluded by disease, and that the capacity to distinguish between right and wrong is inconclusive. It may perhaps have to take a general form, leaving it to a lay, expert, or a mixed lay-and-expert jury to say merely whether the accused had a disease of the mind of a type recognized by science, and whether the alleged criminal act was of such a character as would naturally flow from that type of insanity, in which case it would seem obviously just to regard the defendant as partially irresponsible, and perhaps entirely so. Possibly the practical needs of the moment might be met by permitting such a jury to determine whether the defendant had *such* a knowledge of the wrongful nature and consequences of his act and such a control over his will as to be a proper subject of punishment.[54] This would require the jury to find that the defendant had some knowledge of right and wrong and the power to choose between them. In any event, to render the accused entirely irresponsible, his act should arise out of and be caused solely by the diseased condition of his mind. The law, while asserting the responsibility of many insane people, should recognize "partial" responsibility as well.

The reader may feel that little after all would be gained, but he will observe that at any rate such a test, however imperfect, would permit juries to do lawfully that which they now do by violating their oaths. The writer believes that the best concrete test yet formulated and applied by any court is that laid down in Parsons *vs.* The State of Alabama (81 Ala., 577):

> "1. Was the defendant at the time of the commission of the alleged crime, as matter of fact, afflicted with a disease of the mind, so as to be either idiotic, or otherwise insane?
>
> "2. If such be the case, did he know right from wrong as applied to the particular act in question? If he did not have such knowledge, he is not legally responsible.
>
> "3. If he did have such knowledge, he may nevertheless not be legally responsible if the two following conditions concur:
>
> "(1) If, by reason of the duress of such mental disease, he had so far lost the power to choose between the right and wrong, and to avoid doing the act in question, as that his free agency was at the time destroyed.
>
> "(2) And if, at the same time, the alleged crime was so connected with such mental disease, in the relation of cause and effect, as to have been the product of it solely."

But whatever modification in the present test of criminal responsibility is adopted, there must come an equally, if not even more important, reform in the procedure in insanity cases, which to-day is as cumbersome and out of date as the law itself. As things stand now in New York and most other jurisdictions there are no adequate means open to the State to find out the actual present or past mental condition of the defendant until the trial itself, and ofttimes not even then.

In New York, in cases like Thaw's, the accused, while fully intending to interpose the defense of insanity (which he is now permitted to do simply under the general plea of "not guilty") may not only conceal the fact until the trial, but may likewise successfully block every effort of the authorities to examine him and find out his present mental condition. He may thus keep it out of the power of the District Attorney to secure the facts upon which to move for a commission to determine whether or not he ought to be in an insane asylum or is a fit subject for trial, and at the same time prevent the prosecutor from obtaining any evidence through direct medical observation by which to meet the claim, which may be "sprung" suddenly upon him later at the trial, that the defendant was irresponsible.

In order that this may be clearly understood by the reader he should fully appreciate the distinction between (1) the claim on the part of an accused that he is at present insane, and for that reason should not be either tried or punished for his alleged offence, and (2) the defence that he was (irrespective of his *present* mental condition) insane within the legal definition of irresponsibility at the time he committed it. No person who is incapable of understanding the nature of the proceedings against him or of consulting with counsel and preparing his defence can be placed on trial at all, or, if already on trial, can continue to be tried, and if a defendant "appears to the court to be insane," the judge may appoint a commission to examine him and report as to his present condition. This may be done upon the application either of the State or of the accused through his counsel.

It was such a commission to determine the accused's present mental condition that District Attorney Jerome, upon the basis of the evidence introduced by the defence, applied for and secured during the first trial of Harry K. Thaw. The commission reported that Thaw was sane enough to be tried and the court then proceeded with the original case for the purpose of allowing the jury to say whether he knew the nature and quality of his act and that it was wrong when he shot and killed White.

This was a totally distinct proceeding from the interposition of the DEFENCE that the accused was irresponsible *when he committed the crime* charged against him and was not inconsistent with it.

Now supposing that the Commission had reported that Thaw *was* insane at the time of examination and not a fit subject for trial, but, on the contrary, ought to be confined in an insane asylum, the District Attorney would have spent some twenty odd thousand dollars and a year's time of one or more of his assistants in fruitless preparation. Yet, as the law stands on the books to-day in New York, there is no adequate way for the prosecution to find out whether this enormous expenditure of time or money is necessary or not, for it cannot compel the defendant to submit either to a physical or mental examination. To do so has been held to be a violation of his constitutional rights and equivalent to compelling him to give evidence against himself.

Thus when Thaw came to the bar at his first trial the State had never had any opportunity, through an examination by its physicians, to learn what his present condition was or past mental condition had been. The accused, on the other hand, had had over six months to prepare his defence and had fully availed himself of the time to submit to the most exhaustive examinations on the part of his own experts. The defendant's physicians came to court brimming with facts to which they could testify; while the State's experts had only the barren opportunity for determining the defendant's condition afforded by observing him daily in the court room and hearing what Thaw's own doctors claimed that they had discovered. There was no chance to rebut anything which the latter alleged that they had observed, and their testimony, save in so far as it was inconsistent or contradictory in itself, remained irrefutable.

There is probably no procedure which would be held constitutional whereby a compulsory examination of the accused could be had upon the mere application of the prosecuting authorities; but as a commission may generally be appointed at any time after an accused has been indicted if he "appears" to the court to be "insane," and as it is usually within the power of the District Attorney where such is the case to bring sufficient evidence of it to the attention of the court before the prisoner is brought to trial, little time is actually lost and justice is rarely defeated except in those cases (such as Thaw's) where an attempt is to be made to prove the accused insane *at the time of the alleged crime* although *sane* at the time of trial. Even here it would be the simplest thing in the world to remedy the difficulty and the proper legal steps in all jurisdictions should be taken immediately.

The two chief objects of such reforms should be, first, to relieve the ordinary jury in as many cases as possible from the necessity of passing upon the delicate issue of a defendant's mental condition at a previous time, and second, where this may not be avoided, to make their task as easy as possible by providing (*a*) a more scientific and definite test of legal responsibility and (*b*) an opportunity for adequate examination of defendants availing themselves of this defence.

This last and most practical reform can be easily secured by a slight alteration in the New York Code of Criminal Procedure, which already provides both for the entering of the specific plea of insanity and for the introduction of the defence and the proof of insanity under the general plea of "not guilty." At present the defendant has his choice of openly announcing or of concealing until the trial his intention of claiming that he was insane and so irresponsible for his crime. This is an advantage the results of which were probably not fully contemplated by the Legislature, and one to which an accused has no fair claim.

Fortunately, in the same section of the Code (658), which provides that the court may appoint a Commission to inquire into the sanity of a defendant at the time of his trial, there exists another provision, hitherto little noticed, that

"When a defendant PLEADS INSANITY, as prescribed in Section 336, the court in which the indictment is pending, instead of proceeding with the trial of the indictment, may appoint a commission of not more than three disinterested persons to examine him and report to the court as to his insanity *at the time of the commission of the crime.*"

If a defendant intends to prove himself irresponsible for his offence, why should he not be compelled to enter a specific plea to that effect? Once he has entered that plea, the law as it stands just quoted will do the rest. No reason has been brought to the attention of the writer why the admission of any evidence upon the defendant's trial tending to show that he was mentally irresponsible at the time of committing the crime should not be made contingent upon the defence of insanity having been *specifically pleaded* either at the time of his arraignment or later by substitution for or in conjunction with the plea of "not guilty." This would deprive him of no constitutional right whatever. There is no legal necessity of permitting an accused to prove insanity under a general answer of "not guilty." Then upon his own plea *that he had been insane* he could instantly be committed to some place of observation where a permanent medical board of inquiry could be given full opportunity to examine him and study his case with a view to determining his present and past mental condition. He would still have in prospect his regular jury trial, but if this board found him at the present time insane, the court could immediately commit him to an asylum pending recovery, precisely as under the present procedure, while if they found him sane at the present time, but reported that, in their opinion (whatever test, "medical" or "legal," they might have applied), he was *irresponsible at the time he committed the crime*, it is unlikely that any prosecutor would bring him to trial. If, however, they reported *that he was not only sane, but had been sane* at the time of his crime, it is probable that any proposed defence of insanity would be abandoned, while if it was still urged by the accused, the opinion of such a board would carry far greater weight at the ultimate trial of the case than the individual opinions of experts retained and paid by either side for that particular occasion only, and having had only a comparatively limited opportunity for examination. At any rate, if the court called in the services of such a board of medical judges to assist as *amici curiæ* in determining the defendant's condition, while their opinion would not be conclusive upon the jury, it would at least do away with the present lamentable necessity of learned men answering "yes" or "no" to a hypothetical question fifty thousand words long, when the most superficial personal examination of the accused would settle the matter definitely in their minds. Such a procedure is in general use in Germany and other continental countries, and is likewise substantially followed in Massachusetts, Maine, Vermont, and New Hampshire.[55]

There is good reason to hope that we may soon see in all the states adequate provision for preliminary examination upon the plea of insanity, and a new test of criminal responsibility consistent with humanity and modern medical knowledge. Even then, although murderers who indulge in popular crime will probably be acquitted on the ground of insanity, we shall at least be spared the melancholy spectacle of juries arbitrarily committing feeble-minded persons charged with homicide to imprisonment at hard labor for life, and in a large measure do away with the present unedifying exhibition of two groups of hostile experts, each interpreting an archaic and inadequate test of criminal responsibility in his own particular way, and each conscientiously able to reach a diametrically opposite conclusion upon precisely the same facts.

FOOTNOTES:

[51] The questions propounded to the judges and their answers are here given:

Question 1.—"What is the law respecting alleged crimes committed by persons *afflicted with insane delusion in respect of one or more particular subjects or persons*, as, for instance, where, at the time of the commission of the alleged crime, the accused knew he was acting contrary to law, but did the act complained of with a view, under the influence of insane delusion, of redressing or revenging some supposed grievance or injury, or of producing some supposed public benefit?

Answer 1.—"Assuming that your lordships' inquiries are confined to those persons who labor *under such partial delusions only, and are not in other respects insane*, we are of opinion that, notwithstanding the accused did the act complained of with a view, under the influence of insane delusion, of redressing or revenging some supposed grievance or injury, or of producing some public benefit, he is, nevertheless, punishable, according to the nature of the crime committed, if he knew at the time of committing such crime that he was acting contrary to law, by which expression we understand your lordships to mean the law of the land.

Question 4.—"If a person under an insane delusion as to existing facts commits an offence in consequence thereof, is he thereby excused?

Answer 4.—"The answer must of course depend on the nature of the delusion; but, making the same assumption as we did before, namely, that he labors under such partial delusion only, and is not in other respects insane, we think he must be considered in the same situation as to responsibility as if the facts with respect to which the delusions exist were real. For example, if under the influence of his delusion he supposes another man to be in the act of attempting to take away his life, and kills the man, as he supposes in self-defence, he would be exempt from punishment. If his delusion was that the deceased had inflicted a serious injury to his character and fortune, and he killed him in revenge for such supposed injury, he would be liable to punishment.

Question 2.—"What are the proper questions to be submitted to the jury when a person, afflicted with insane delusions respecting one or more particular subjects or persons, is charged with the commission of a crime (murder, for instance), and insanity is set up as a defence?

Question 3.—"In what terms ought the question to be left to the jury as to the prisoner's state of mind when the act was committed?

Answers 2 and 3.—"As these two questions appear to us to be more conveniently answered together, we submit our opinion to be that the jurors ought to be told, in all cases, that every man is presumed to be sane, and to possess a sufficient degree of reason to be responsible for his crimes, until the contrary be proved to their satisfaction; and that, to establish a defence on the ground of insanity it must be clearly proved that at the time of committing the act the accused was laboring under such a defect of reason, from disease of the mind, as not to know the nature and quality of the act he was doing, or, if he did know it, that he did not know he was doing what was wrong." (The remainder of the answer goes on to discuss the usual way the question is put to the jury.)

[52] Dew *vs.* Clark.

[53] "General View of the Criminal Law," p. 80.

[54] See State *vs.* Richards, 1873, Conn.

[55] Another equally efficacious means of dealing with the matter would be to substitute, upon a defendant's plea of insanity, a full jury of experts—like any "special" jury—for the ordinary petit jury.

Milton Keynes UK
Ingram Content Group UK Ltd.
UKHW030718041024
449263UK00004B/400